Regulating Artificial Intelli

Exploring potential scenarios of artificial intelligence regulation which prevent automated reality harming individual human rights or social values, this book reviews current debates surrounding AI regulation in the context of the emerging risks and accountabilities. Considering varying regulatory methodologies, it focuses mostly on EU's regulation in light of the comprehensive policy making process taking place at the supranational level.

Taking an ethics and humancentric approach towards artificial intelligence as the bedrock of future laws in this field, it analyses the relations between fundamental rights impacted by the development of artificial intelligence and ethical standards governing it. It contains a detailed and critical analysis of the EU's Ethic Guidelines for Trustworthy AI, pointing at its practical applicability by the interested parties. Attempting to identify the most transparent and efficient regulatory tools that can assure social trust towards AI technologies, the book provides an overview of horizontal and sectoral regulatory approaches, as well as legally binding measures stemming from industries' self-regulations and internal policies.

Dominika Ewa Harasimiuk, PhD, an assistant professor of EU law at Lazarski University, Warsaw. From 2018 deputy dean for research and international co-operation at the same University. Research interests comprise the fields of EU citizenship, EU constitutional law, Internal market law, in particular free movement of goods and services, as well as regulatory and ethical challenges of algorithmic society.

Tomasz Braun, PhD, a Deputy Rector and Assistant Professor at Łazarski University and Lecturer of Financial, Corporate and Economic Law at numerous other Universities. He connects private legal practice with his research interests which combine normative studies on law, ethics, culture and politics.

Routledge Research in the Law of Emerging Technologies

Regulating Artificial Intelligence

Binary Ethics and the Law

Dominika Ewa Harasimiuk
and Tomasz Braun

Routledge
Taylor & Francis Group

LONDON AND NEW YORK

First published 2021
by Routledge
2 Park Square, Milton Park, Abingdon, Oxon OX14 4RN

and by Routledge
52 Vanderbilt Avenue, New York, NY 10017

Routledge is an imprint of the Taylor & Francis Group, an informa business

British Library Cataloguing-in-Publication Data
A catalogue record for this book is available from the British Library

Library of Congress Cataloging-in-Publication Data
A catalog record has been requested for this book

ISBN: 978-0-367-46881-1 (hbk)
ISBN: 978-0-367-68213-2 (pbk)
ISBN: 978-1-003-13472-5 (ebk)

Typeset in Galliard
by MPS Limited, Dehradun

Contents

8   Conclusions   155

1 Instead of Introduction – Algorithmic Society, Artificial Intelligence and Ethics

1.1 Topic's relevance

The development of digital technologies, which entails fast and more efficient growth of capacity of Artificial Intelligence, brings significant changes to all aspects of everyday lives of individuals and societies. Whatever the world is experiencing right now is compared to the times when electricity transformed the economy, culture and politics.[1] Digital technologies based on algorithms are widespread and present in the surrounding reality of an average person who uses mobile phones, personal computers, home appliances, TV sets, cars, and many other electronic devices. AI-based technologies may have hugely beneficial impact on human lives. Technology enables the improvement of diagnoses and development therapies for diseases by reducing energy consumption and lessening the need for pesticides, contributing to a cleaner environment, optimising resources, anticipating disasters by improving weather prediction, establishing faster and safer transportation by increasing general road safety. It also drives economic productivity growth and contributes to sustainability, improving financial risk management and detecting fraud and cybersecurity threats. Aside from those listed, it also enables law enforcement and helps prevent crime more efficiently.[2] Benefits are counterbalanced by serious concerns, which relate to growing automation leading to possible increase in unemployment rates, biased decision-making, excessive access to privacy by authorities, overcomplicated technological solutions increasing the imbalance in

---

1 More on Industrial, through Digital, towards AI Revolution, see Spyros Makridakis, 'The Forthcoming Artificial Intelligence Revolution' (2017) 1 Neapolis University of Paphos (NUP), Working Papers Series https://www.researchgate.net/publication/312471523_The_Forthcoming_Artificial_Intelligence_AI_Revolution_Its_Impact_on_Society_and_Firms accessed 20 July 2020.
2 The High Level Strategy Group on Industrial Technologies has recommended including AI as one of the key enabling technologies due to its cross cutting enabling potential crucial for European industry, see High Level Group on industrial technologies, Report on 'Re-Defining Industry. Defining Innovation' (Publication Office of the EU Luxembourg 2018). See also, Commission, 'Artificial Intelligence for Europe' (Communication) COM(2018) 237 final, 1. See also, Paula Boddington, *Towards a Code of Ethics for Artificial Intelligence, Artificial Intelligence: Foundations, Theory, and Algorithms* (Springer Int. Publishing 2017) 2.

the access to knowledge and extraordinary power concentration over in the hands of few corporations of the worldwide reach, like Google, Facebook or Amazon. Finally, development of AI industry causes fierce competition between major global actors, namely USA, China and EU.[3]

AI technologies are not only impacting industries and economy, but also political structures and democratic mechanisms. It is well established that the market for AI includes both business-to-consumer (B2C) and business-to-business (B2B) markets and platforms. What goes beyond these traditional spheres are public-to-citizens services (P2C), with new tools of civic participation, e-democracy and e-government.[4] In all these areas there is a need for a comprehensive regulatory approach towards AI, embedded in ethics and trust. These are two paradigms around which all the legislative and regulatory measures are being adopted nowadays at the European level. The European approach towards AI technologies, which is the topic of this book, consists in putting various European values at the heart of policymaking processes. The European Union perceives itself nowadays as a major global stakeholder in the field of AI regulation. Such a position is part of the broader European Digital Single Market policy, in which AI is becoming a strategic area for European economic development. The EU's approach towards AI regulation intends to cover socio-economic, legal and ethical issues. In longer term, such a holistic vision is about creating the European Single Market for Trustworthy AI, where the EU could benefit from the value of AI, while minimising and preventing its risks.[5]

The relevance of the research topic stems from its up-to-date character and its future impact. The regulatory approach towards AI adopted at present, will shape our reality in the following years and decades. The thorough analysis of current EU policies, regulatory and legislative processes and proposals touching upon AI technologies, will give us the possible insight on how the development of our economies and societies will look like in the long-term perspective. It could also bring some reflections on the most appropriate approach towards discussed topic.

1.2 Goal of the book

As stated above, digital technology breakthrough and artificial intelligence in particular can help to address many of the world's biggest challenges. The pace of technological progress that is now being developed across the world is

3 Commission, 'Coordinated Plan on AI' (Communication) COM(2018) 795 final, 1; See also, Paul Nemitz, 'Constitutional Democracy and Technology in the Age of Artificial Intelligence' (2018) 376 Philosophical Transactions A, The Royal Society, 3 https://ssrn.com/abstract=3234336 accessed 20 July 2020.
4 See, Deloitte Insights, 'How Artificial Intelligence Could Transform Government' (2017) https://www2.deloitte.com/insights/us/en/focus/artificial-intelligence-in-government.html accessed 20 July 2020.
5 High-Level Expert Group on AI (HLEG AI), 'Policy and Investment Recommendations for Trustworthy AI' (Brussels 2019) 6–7.

incredibly rapid. At the same time AI itself brings new challenges and raises serious legal and ethical questions.[6] This phenomenon is not new. Usually, legal concepts and norms had to adjust to the novelty challenges posed by the progress in the sphere of science, culture, politics, economy. It is not different with the current technological changes.[7]

This phenomenon is being seen from various angles. Eventually it is about locating the phenomenon of algorithmic changes within the societies in the governance and regulatory environment. The regulation can be seen as polycentric social system with six elements, creating its dynamics: goals and values, knowledge and understanding, tools and techniques, behaviours of individuals, behaviours of organisations and trust and legitimacy.[8] Regulatory environment could be defined as organised attempts to manage risks or behaviour to achieve a publicly stated objective or set of objectives.[9] According to this theory there are two main forms of regulation: command and control regulation and design-based regulation. The first form of regulation refers to the use of legal or regulatory rules that dictate behaviour. They come with punishment and incentive mechanism. In reaction to them, on the side of the addressee of these norms is an arbitrage to comply for the reward or to ignore and risk punitive consequences.[10] The second form of regulation, which is design-based, is to create regulatory standards adjusted to the design of the entire regulated system. In other words, it is based on constructing an architecture adapted to human behaviour that matches the preferred behaviours.[11]

According to this concept much of the present algorithmic governance and regulatory framework constitutes a design-based sort of regulation.[12] In line with this theory, a design-based regulation and algorithmic decision support system is a type of nudging. Nudging is a regulatory philosophy that has its origins in

6 Commission, 'Building Trust in Human-Centric Artificial Intelligence' (Communication) COM(2019)168 final, 1.
7 Expert Group on Liability and New Technologies, 'Liability for Artificial Intelligence and Other Emerging Digital Technologies', (Report from New Technologies Formation) (Publication Office of the EU Luxembourg 2019) 11.
8 Julia Black, Andrew D. Murray, 'Regulating AI and Machine Learning: Setting the Regulatory Agenda' (2019) 10 European Journal of Law and Technology http://eprints.lse.ac.uk/102953/ accessed 22 July 2020.
9 Julia Black, 'Learning from Regulatory Disasters', (2014) 24 LSE Law, Society and Economy Working Papers, 3 http://dx.doi.org/10.2139/ssrn.2519934 accessed 22 July 2020.
10 Julia Black, 'Decentring Regulation: Understanding the Role of Regulations and Self-Regulation in a <Post-Regulatory> World' (2001) 54 Current Legal Problems, 105–106.
11 Robert van den Hoven van Genderen, 'Legal Personhood in the Age of Artificially Intelligent Robots' in Woodraw Barfield, Ugo Pagallo (eds.), *Research Handbook on the Law of Artificial Intelligence* (Edward Elgar 2018) 224 ff.
12 Karen Yeung, 'Hypernudge: Big Data as a Mode of Regulation by Design' (2016) 1,19 TLI Think! Paper Information, Communication and Society, 4; John Danaher, 'Algocracy as Hypernudging: A New Way to Understand the Threat of Algocracy' (2017) https://ieet.org/index.php/IEET2/more/Danaher20170117?fbclid=IwAR3gm6lIWN8Twb8bE6lTI dtintwhYSWF2FTDkRGzMs1xa8XTD4bGgoQJiXw accessed 22 July 2020.

behavioural economics based on the assumption deriving from cognitive psychology claiming that people are less rational than universally believed. They display biases and psychologically preferred stereotypes.[13] That sometimes deviates them from the expectations of rational choices theory and causes damages to their own long-term well-being. The best example of this is shown in the general tendency to over prioritise the short-term future. People discount the value of future events too much that is instead of doing it according to an exponential according to a hyperbolic curve. They favour sooner rewards even though they are smaller rather than larger ones if they ought to come later.[14]

The same concept can also apply to regulatory domains. Legislators and regulators may create a kind of decision-making situation building so called choice architectures that benefits from the nature of human psychology and nudge them into preferred behavioural patterns.[15] This approach has gained a lot of popularity only recently. The public authorities have started to set up behavioural analysis units to implement nudge-based policy settings in multiple areas.[16]

Therefore, nudging is a type of design-based regulation because it is not about enforcing the created rules and regulations but about handwriting policy preferences into behavioural architectures. The algorithmic governance systems work like nudges especially within decision-support systems. These are forms of algorithmic governance which use data-mining techniques to present choice options. People typically do not question the defaults provided by our algorithmic systems they use on a daily basis. This same mechanism might be used as a support regulatory framework where algorithmic decision support systems are used in many policy domains.[17]

Against this theoretical background, we would like to draw the goal of our book, which is to outline the general regulatory approach of the EU towards algorithmic reality. Ethics is the central notion around which all regulatory steps are revolving. And regulation of what is supposed to be an ethical AI takes various forms. It is both commands based, and design based. It combines proper centralised legislative measures with decentred regulation resting in hands of interested stakeholders. Thus, there is a complex network of top-down measures and bottom-up initiatives, binding and non-binding rules, hard and soft laws, horizontal and sectoral rules, supranational, international, national and industry-based regulations. Such a complex, intertwined regulatory environment makes it extremely difficult to navigate through, to follow which are mutual relations between different levels and kinds of regulations. Even if the debate on AI

---

13 Jonathan Beever, Rudy McDaniel, Nancy A. Stamlick, *Understanding Digital Ethics. Cases and Contexts* (Routledge 2020) 82.
14 Danaher, 'Algocracy as Hypernudging' (n 12).
15 Antje von Ungern-Sternberg, *Autonomous Driving: Regulatory Challenges Raised by Artificial Decision-Making and Tragic Choices* in Woodrow Barfield, Ugo Pagallo (eds.), *Research Handbook on the Law of Artificial Intelligence* (Edward Elgar 2018) 257.
16 Yeung (n 12) 4–6.
17 Ibid.

governance through law, ethics and technology is a global one,[18] our goal is to present the current state of the art in the field of regulatory environment of ethical AI in the EU. We are aware that many of the rules are still to be adopted, that there are ongoing policy making processes within the EU institutions taking place right now. Yet, we would like to systematise the actual body of laws, rules and regulations and indicate possible challenges and directions for upcoming measures. Since regulating AI seems like a never ending story, we believe that our goal is not premature and can be of value to those who would like to learn about the position of the EU towards Artificial Intelligence, which due to its omni-presence is the most discussed phenomena of the contemporary times.

1.3 Research design and methodology

The research carried out in this book aimed to provide an overall perspective on ethical regulation and trustworthy artificial intelligence in the EU. Aware of the wide range of legal, ethical and regulatory issues, but also of the fact that the process of integrating artificial intelligence into a single legal and ethical framework is not yet complete, and in fact is only at the beginning of the road, we have attempted to put the most important issues in order and place them in the context of the activities of the EU institutions. The research method adopted, based on a dogmatic analysis of the source texts and a general qualitative approach, has allowed us to point out 'from the bird's eye view' the current challenges, but also the legislative and regulatory work already being carried out more specifically in the artificial intelligence sector. The analysis of source texts, the majority of which are the European Commission's communications and policy documents prepared by the High Level Expert Groups, is complemented by doctrinal analysis in the field of new technology law, ethics and human rights. The layout of our deliberations is based on six substantive chapters. The second chapter is aimed at explaining basic concepts from the area of science and information technology, concerning the concept of artificial intelligence, machine learning. The next chapter points to extensive legislative, regulatory and policy-making activities that take place at the level of EU institutions, and the European Commission in particular. Chapter 4 is devoted to analysing the ethical framework for artificial intelligence in the EU – we take the Ethic Guidelines on Trustworthy AI as a starting point for more detailed consideration, analysing the foundations of the ethical approach to artificial intelligence, the challenges of its implementation and a possible assessment of its effectiveness. Chapter 5 examines regulatory instruments to ensure that ethical and legal principles in the area of Artificial Intelligence are effectively applied as far as possible. Chapter 6 is devoted to the characteristics of horizontal solutions – i.e. those that apply to all economic and social activities that also include artificial intelligence applications. Chapter 7, in turn, indicates the sectoral approach in selected, most important socio-economic areas.

---

18 Corinne Cath, 'Governing Artificial Intelligence: Ethical, Legal and Technical Opportunities and Challenges' (2018) 376 Philosophical Transactions A, The Royal Society, 3.

2 Re-defining of Artificial Intelligence

2.1 Artificial intelligence – review of definitions

The notion of artificial intelligence (AI) is very vague and contains an explicit reference to the concept of intelligence which itself is unclear and disputable yet is strongly connected with human capacities. There have been numerous attempts to propose a definition of artificial intelligence (AI), many of which being useful, sometimes expressing strong convictions of their authors. Russel and Norvig[19] systemise various scholar definitions and conclude that the attempts to define AI may be approached from two different angles. The first one is human-centred, in which the systems are defined through their fidelity to human behaviour and performance (systems thinking or acting humanly). The second group of definitions avoids links to humanity and stress rationality, where the systems are assessed through their ideal performance (thinking rationally and acting rationally).[20] The notion of rationality has been studied by psychologists, biologists, neuroscientists, and AI researchers. This refers to the ability to choose the best action to achieve a certain goal with the use of given criteria to be optimised, and the available resources. Rationality is not the sole or even a dominant element in the concept of intelligence, however it constitutes a significant part of it. The system shall think and act rationally. The former means that the system has goals and reasons related to these goals, the latter means that AI system performs in a goal-directed way.[21] An AI system could achieve rationality by perceiving the environment in which the system is immersed through sensors, collecting, processing and interpreting data, reasoning on what is perceived, deciding what the best action is, and then acting accordingly, through some actuators, thus possibly modifying the environment.[22] The goal-directed

---

19 Stuart Russel, Peter Norvig, *Artificial Intelligence. A Modern Approach* (3rd edn, Prentice Hall 2010) 1–5.
20 Ibid; See also, van den Hoven van Genderen, 'Legal Personhood in the Age of Artificially Intelligent Robots' (n 11) 235.
21 Russel, Norvig (n 19) 1–5.
22 Jean-Sebastien Borghetti, 'How can Artificial Intelligence be Defective?' in Sebastian Lohsse, Reiner Schulze, Dirk Staudenmayer (eds.), *Liability for Artificial Intelligence and*

AI systems are capable of achieving a goal in the result of a receipt of the specification received from a human. The systems themselves do not define their own goals, however they might be capable of deciding which path to take to achieve the given goal—this is usually based on certain machine learning techniques deployed within those systems.[23]

In the legal context, there are opinions that there is no need for a single, all-encompassing definition of AI, in particular for legal and regulatory purposes, since the notion's meaning may change depending on the industry and proper applications of AI-based technologies.[24] However, as Turner points, the necessity to define the concept of AI is dictated by the attempts to regulate it. If the law is to be complied with, the addressees of legal norms need to know their scope and possible application areas.[25]

As the ontological analysis of what AI might be is not the focal point this book, it is still proposed to be used as a starting point, as it is a simple and functional definition drafted by the European Commission's Communication on AI. According to this document, 'Artificial Intelligence (AI) refers to systems that display intelligent behaviour by analysing their environment and taking actions—with some degree of autonomy—to achieve specific goals. AI-based systems can be purely software-based, acting in the virtual world (e.g. voice assistants, image analysis software, search engines, speech and face recognition systems) or AI can be embedded in hardware devices (e.g. advanced robots, autonomous cars, drones or Internet of Things applications)'.[26] The research presented in this book expands this definition by clarifying specific elements of AI in particular as a technology, but also as the socio-economic phenomenon from the point of view of regulatory and governance frameworks led during the discussions at EU level. In any case, artificial intelligence being a product of human intelligence remains with it in a meta relationship. Therefore, all the consequences of this are visible in particular in the field of ethically-anchored decision-making processes powered by AI applications.

There are two major typologies around the definitions of AI: general and narrow.[27] One of them defines a general AI system as an information technology which exhibits human-level intelligence and can perform most activities that humans are able to do.[28] Whereas narrow AI systems are the most specific ones that can

the *Internet of Things. Muenster Colloquia on EU Law and the Digital Economy IV* (Hart Publishing, Nomos 2019) 68.

23 HLEG AI, 'A Definition of AI: Main Capabilities and Disciplines' (Brussels 2019) 5.

24 Agnieszka Jabłonowska et al., 'Consumer Law and Artificial Intelligence. Challenges to the EU Consumer Law and Policy Stemming from the Business' Use of Artificial Intelligence', Final Report of the ARTSY Project EUI Working Papers Law 2018/11, 4.

25 Jacob Turner, *Robot Rules. Regulating Artificial Intelligence* (Palgrave Macmillan 2019) 8–9.

26 Commission, COM(2018)237 final, 1 (n 2).

27 Turner (n 25) 6–7.

28 Ragnar Fjelland, 'Why General Artificial Intelligence Will Not be Realized' (2020) 7 Humanities and Social Sciences Communications, 2.

perform one or a few selected tasks.[29] All currently deployed AI systems are examples of narrow AI. There are still too many unresolved ethical, scientific and technological challenges to overcome, to approach to general AI in practice. The common-sense reasoning, self-awareness and the ability of the machine to define its own purpose are just a few of them. Some researchers use the terminology of weak and strong AI which more or less correspond to narrow and strong AI.[30]

The limitations of currently available AI systems are multiple. One of them relates to data issues. For the systems to perform properly it is crucial to understand how data could be influencing the behaviour of an AI system. For example, if the data is biased (it is not balanced or inclusive) the AI system trained on such data would not be able to generalise and risks to make unfair decisions that can favour some groups over others. The challenge for AI developers and deployers has been to agree on methods to detect and mitigate bias in training datasets and also in other parts of an AI system. This problem is one of the most fundamental ethical concerns, which is addressed by the policy making processes.[31] The question of bias and discrimination will be further discussed in the following chapters of our book. Another important issue impacting operations of AI systems and also bringing serious governance challenges is transparency. Several machine learning techniques have not been very transparent about the outcomes of their decision-making processes.[32] The notion of black-box AI defines situations where it is not possible to trace back to the reason for certain decisions. Explainability is a reversed property of those AI systems that allows to provide an explanation for their actions. Again, how to achieve the demanded level of explainability is an almost unresolved question, yet crucial for trust-building processes of ethical AI.[33]

In conclusion, we would like to recall the definitions of AI which are currently used for policy making purposes at EU level. The first, proposed by the High Level Expert Group on AI, defines AI systems as the ones which are 'software (and possibly also hardware) systems designed by humans that, given a complex goal, act in the physical or digital dimension by perceiving their environment through data acquisition, interpreting the collected structured or unstructured data, reasoning on the knowledge, or processing the information, derived from

---

29 Ibid.
30 See, Fjelland (n 28) 2. Author makes a distinction between General AI (AI) and strong AI. General AI is the one which is human-like AI, but at the same time may be regarded as the weak; Rex Martinez, 'Artificial Intelligence: Distinguishing Between Types & Definitions' (2019) 19 Nevada Law Journal, 1027–1028.
31 Nizan Geslevich Packin, Yafit Lev-Aretz, 'Learning Algorithms and Discrimination' in Woodrow Barfield and Ugo Pagallo (eds.), *Research Handbook on the Law of Artificial Intelligence* (Edward Elgar 2018) 97.
32 Herbert Zech, 'Liability for Autonomous Systems: Tackling Specific Risks of Modern IT' in Sebastian Lohsse, Reiner Schulze, Dirk Staudenmayer (eds.), *Liability for Artificial Intelligence and the Internet of Things. Muenster Colloquia on EU Law and the Digital Economy IV* (Hart Publishing, Nomos 2019) 192.
33 HLEG AI, 'A Definition of AI' (n 23) 5.

this data and deciding the best action(s) to take to achieve the given goal. AI systems can either use symbolic rules or learn a numeric model, and they can also adapt their behaviour by analysing how the environment is affected by their previous actions. As a scientific discipline, AI includes several approaches and techniques, such as machine learning (of which deep learning and reinforcement learning are specific examples), machine reasoning (which includes planning, scheduling, knowledge representation and reasoning, search, and optimisation), and robotics (which includes control, perception, sensors and actuators, as well as the integration of all other techniques into cyber-physical systems)'.[34] The HLEG's AI definition is a very broad one, covering robotics, software-based systems, encompassing all sorts of techniques presently used in the AI industry. For the purpose of our book, we will also be using term AI in its broadest scope.

A more detailed definition, in terms of distinction made, is the one proposed by the European Parliament in its motion for a new EU regulation on ethical aspects of artificial intelligence.[35] The proposed legal definitions separate three notions—artificial intelligence, robotics and related technologies.[36] Artificial intelligence shall be understood as 'software systems that, inter alia, collect, process and interpret structured or unstructured data, identify patterns and establish models to reach conclusions or take actions in the physical or virtual dimension based on such conclusions'. Robotics are 'technologies that enable machines to perform tasks traditionally performed by human beings including by way of AI or related technologies'. Finally, related technologies are the ones which enable the software to control with a partial or full degree of autonomy a physical or virtual process, technologies capable of detecting the identity of persons or specific features of persons by way of their biometric data and technologies that copy or otherwise make use of human traits'.[37]

2.2 Legal and ethical challenges of artificial intelligence deployment

2.2.1 Machine learning

The true legal and ethical challenges start when AI is considered to be deployed. Before that, it in a way remains an interesting intellectual concept. Before AI becomes what it is, however, it needs to be able to learn. Ability to learn is considered as one of the indispensable elements of any intelligence. What

---

34 Ibid.

35 European Parliament, 'Draft Report with Recommendations to the Commission on a Framework of Ethical Aspects of AI, Robotics and Related Technologies', 2020/ 2012(INL) https://www.europarl.europa.eu/doceo/document/JURI-PR-650508_EN. pdf accessed 22 July 2020.

36 van den Hoven van Genderen, 'Legal Personhood in the Age of Artificially Intelligent Robots' (n 11) 229.

37 European Parliament, 2020/2012 (INL) (n 35) art. 4 (a-c) of the proposed regulation.

is learning itself then? One of the attempts of the descriptive definition refers to the techniques, or more precisely a group of techniques which several features and abilities design to enable for the information technology systems to recognise and self-orientate upon the information absorbed. In other words, it refers to perception and the processing of the information perceived.[38] That definition enumerates namely these techniques that include machine learning, neural networks, deep learning, decision trees, and 'many other learning techniques'. The obvious weakness of this definition stems from the *idem per idem* mistake, that neither logically, nor cognitively or semantically explains little to none. Although it is said, that these techniques allow an AI system to learn how to resolve given problems, it is not determined what actually the learning is.[39] These problems even though appear to be easy for humans are not so for non-human systems. The reason why they are not easy for AI systems originates in the fact that human learning depends on human perception abilities and relies on common sense reasoning. However, the common sense, in this case, exceeds the commonality itself and cannot be easily replicated by, for example, the widening of the number of cases uploaded to a system. It continues to be particularly difficult when a system is supposed to interpret data that remains unstructured. Much of progress in approaching to the human-like learning has been achieved within the machine learning techniques.[40] Some of these techniques, like language understanding, debatably, fall outside of the learning scope and refer more to one of the processing techniques which is interpreting.

Three most common machine learning techniques are supervised learning, unsupervised learning, and reinforcement learning.[41] In supervised machine learning the system is fed with examples of input-output behaviours. Developers use labelled data sets to teach the system, which is processing the given data to determine how items with the same features are similar. In supervised learning, the system is generalising given examples to be able to behave accordingly, based on the shown situations, but also the ones which were not shown, but which could actually happen in the future. One of the problems of supervised machine learning is linked to perception difficulty. It is due to the fact that usually the system is given a number of

---

38 Luciano Floridi, *The 4th Revolution. How Infosphere is Reshaping Human Reality* (Oxford University Press 2016) 37.

39 The definition refers however to the complexity of problems by the fact that they either cannot be upfront specified, or their solution methods cannot be described by symbolic reasoning rules. Indicated problems to perception capabilities cover speech and language understanding, as well as computer vision or behaviour prediction.

40 Machine learning techniques are hoped to be used also for tasks outside of perception only. They are designed upon the mathematical numeric formula that are used to compute the decision from the analysed data.

41 Within supervised machine learning, the behavioural rules normally uploaded to the system are replaced by examples of input-output behavioural processes. The system is designed to generalise from these given examples. The historic behavioural patterns are expected to suffice to for extrapolating them into the future situations which are not reflected in the uploaded examples.

examples, e.g. pictures or voice samples and is programmed to interpret them. If the system is given enough differing examples corresponding to a variety of situations, the learning algorithms are expected to generalise and propose an interpretation that is rightly classifying pictures or voices that have not been seen by this system before.[42] The weakness of this technique is that the number of data (in this case pictures or voices) will always be limited to the known examples only. Some techniques of machine learning refer to the concept of neural networks, constructed similarly to the human neural system which connects a number of small interconnected processing units.[43] In fact, the neural system is a characteristic that refers to the structure of the system and by itself does not solve the more fundamental problem of the efficiency and accuracy of the learning outcomes. Therefore, what is meant by machine learning refers to those agents that are the intelligent agents derived from the sets of data on which the algorithms are run to complete a prescribed goal.[44]

Given the fact that in all machine learning techniques there is always a certain percentage of error, an essential characteristic of any problem-solving system is the accuracy. This is a criterion upon which the system efficiency can be measured based on the percentage of correct answers. Among several approaches to machine learning problems, there are not only neural networks but also several others like random forests and boosted trees, clustering methods, matrix factorisation, etc. One of the most successful is deep learning. This method refers to the feature that any neural network has usually multiple layers between the input and the output that allow learning the general input-output relation within following consecutive steps. This assures more accuracy and requires less human direction, check and correction.

Reinforcement learning is another type of machine learning, or more precisely a teaching methodology designed for machines to enable their learning features. In the reinforcement learning, a system is expected to make its decisions and at each decision, the system is rewarded, by the means of an appropriate signal that tells it whenever the decision was good. The aim of this methodology is to improve the accuracy by maximising the positive rewards the system receives. This learning–teaching methodology is widely used in marketing and in all sorts of sales engines that recommend buyers the products or services they might like to purchase.[45]

---

42 Beever, McDaniel, Stamlick (n 13) 89.

43 An input of a neural network is the data coming from the sensors and an output is the interpretation of the data. The analysis of the examples allows the connections to adjust to match what the available examples say. After the training and the testing phase the neural network is expected to be as much accurate as technologically available in interpreting the data.

44 Allan Schuller, 'At the Crossroads of Control: The Intersection of Artificial Intelligence in Autonomous Weapon Systems with International Humanitarian Law' (2017) 8 Harvard National Security Journal, 404.

45 Frank Pasquale, *The Black Box Society. The Secret Algorithms That Control Money and Information* (Harvard University Press 2015) 61.

Machine learning techniques are useful in all sorts of perception tasks, like texts, pictures or sound (voice) recognitions. But they are also useful in all those tasks that and cannot be comprehensively defined or described with the use of symbolic behavioural rules.

Machine learning through sensors refers to quasi perception capabilities. In practice, the system's sensors could be any input devices like a camera, a microphone, a keyboard, a website, or devices measuring physical quantities like temperature, pressure, distance, force etc. Obviously, the sensors need to be relevant to the data present in the environment that allow achieving the goal given to the system expected to learn from the analysis of the data.

In case of any collected data, structured or unstructured the perception capabilities have to be accordingly designed to allow for actual learning. In regard to structured data organised according to pre-defined models, they are most commonly used for the analysis of the relational databases. The unstructured data which has not any known or pre-defined organisation consist usually of randomly and context-free pieces as an image, a sound or a text.[46]

Machine learning does not necessitate to use the existing knowledge nor the careful identification of the relationship between variables. Thanks to this, it can refer to a wider spread of questions and offers deeper analysis compared to what is normally achievable by human judgement or by a statistical formula.[47] Indeed machine learning systems are faster and more efficient as when they are uploaded with new data they are able to search for new patterns and revisit earlier predictions.[48]

2.2.2 Machine reasoning

There are varying approaches and controversies around the problem of machine reasoning. One of them is a simplified description of an artificial intelligence system through its capabilities of perception, reasoning, decision making, actuation, verification, and embodiment. This allows to characterise the majority of the techniques that are currently used to build artificial intelligence systems. They all refer not only to the various capabilities but also to the walk through the stages of the system analysis. If agreed, they can be included in two main groups that refer to learning or to reasoning, the latter one is certainly at the core of the ethical dilemma as this is where the end of the process will result in the decision making.

The reasoning and decision making are the groups of techniques that include search, knowledge representation, reasoning, planning, scheduling, optimisation, including correcting and retracking. These techniques allow for the reasoning on

---

46 HLEG AI, 'A Definition of AI' (n 23) 2.
47 Geslevich-Packin, Lev-Aretz (n 31) 88.
48 Cary Coglianese, David Lehr, 'Regulating by Robot: Administrative Decision Making in the Machine-Learning Era' (2017) 105 Georgetown Law Journal, 1159.

the data coming from the agents and sensors. to do this, the data needs to be transformed to knowledge and as a consequence, the artificial intelligence systems are programmed to figure out how best to model this knowledge. This process is defined as knowledge representation. Once the knowledge has been modelled the system processes it. This reasoning phase includes interconnecting the searching, planning and scheduling, interfacing through symbolic rules, analysing a potentially large number of solutions. Then the optimising step leads to selection among all possible solutions best fitting to respond to a problem. Finally, the system decides what action to take. The reasoning and decision making are multi-layered and complex elements of the artificial intelligence systems combining the methods and techniques described here.[49]

The reasoning module that uses data and information collected by sensors and then processes them to select actions required to reach the solution aiming at a goal is at the core of an artificial intelligence system. This means that there is another sub-phase during which the data gathered by the sensors need to be processed and transformed into information which then the reasoning module can understand. In other words, the applications or sensors provide artificial intelligence system with the data referring to a given task which is then processed by the reasoning module. This module upon the information extracted from the data decides what is the best suitable action to achieve the goal given to the system. What may seem easy for humans to make the decision whether something needs an action, this may not be easy for a machine, as the information is rarely a simple 0–1 binary choice. The reasoning module has to be able to interpret the data to decide. This means that it needs to be able to transform data into information and to formulate and adjust such information in a simple way, which takes into account all relevant pieces of data. The reasoning module also has to process this knowledge and information to produce a numeric mathematical formula to decide what the best action is to be taken.

It is suggested that the understanding of the decision should be broad in the sense that it means any act of selecting the action to be taken by the machine. In particular, it should not be understood that artificial intelligence systems are fully autonomous.[50] In the majority of appliances using the AI the decision can be the suggestion or a recommendation provided to a human, who is usually the ultimate decision maker.[51]

When the decision is made, the artificial intelligence system can execute it through the actuators available to it. They could be physical or software-based. The AI system could produce a signal that activates the actuators or e.g. text generators—chatbots that respond to the requests of the other party either human or not, in case the action performed modified the environment, the next time the system will have to use its sensors again and perceive possibly different

49 HLEG AI, 'A Definition of AI' (n 23) 3.
50 Beever, McDaniel, Stamlick (n 13) 147.
51 HLEG AI, 'A Definition of AI' (n 23) 3.

information from the modified environment and then it will interpret it accordingly and perhaps differently.

Similar to human reasoning the artificial intelligence systems do not always choose the most appropriate or accurate action for the goal set for them. This may result from the fact, that they are capable of achieving only so-called bounded rationality. The limitations come from inadequate or insufficient resources, time, weaknesses or bugs of the programme or even scarcity of computational power.

There may be various grades of sophistication of the rationalising capabilities in the artificial intelligence systems. The very basic versions of systems modify the environment, but they are not capable of adjusting their recommendations or behaviours over time to improve accuracy in achieving their goals. Some more complex learning rational systems after taking a given action could evaluate the changed environment through their sensors or agents and thanks to more efficient computing modules determine the efficiency of their actions. Then they adopt the reasoning rules and decision-making methods to achieve better results.[52]

2.2.3 Robotics – embodied artificial intelligence

Robotics also called embodied AI can be described as the physically actioned AI. A robot is a physical machine designed to cope with the physical dynamics as well as the uncertainties and the complexities. Perception, reasoning, learning, action and interactions with other systems are the capabilities integrated into the control architecture of the robotic system. Complexities of the robotic systems come from the fact that apart from artificial intelligence, multiple other disciplines such as mechanical engineering, control theory and cybernetics play a role in robot design and operation. Examples of robots include robotic manipulators, autonomous vehicles, humanoid robots, robotic appliances, drones etc.[53]

Robotic artificial intelligence is a major complexity as it includes a variety of other subdisciplines and techniques. Robotics also relies on other techniques that do not belong to the artificial intelligence area. However, as the robotics is the ultimate embodiment of the AI it needs to be positioned within a wider discussion on the challenges to the AI deployment.[54]

---

52 Ibid.
53 Giovanni Comande, 'Multilayered (Accountable) Liability for Artificial Intelligence' in Sebastian Lohsse, Reiner Schulze, Dirk Staudenmayer (eds.), *Liability for Artificial Intelligence and the Internet of Things. Muenster Colloquia on EU Law and the Digital Economy IV* (Hart Publishing, Nomos 2019) 174.
54 This brief characteristic has been meant to be sufficient to place the robotics among the most crucial areas of analysis of the challenges for the AI by the multi-disciplinary and multi-stakeholder HLEG AI, which the main goal is to run the discussion about AI ethics, and AI policies. HLEG AI, 'A Definition of AI' (n 23) 4.

3 EU Policy Making in the AI Field

3.1 Opening remarks

The European Union in its policies aims at supporting the development of AI as a trusted tool, and in this context conducts a range of initiatives to assure that development of AI takes into account the ethical and societal values deriving from the founding Treaties and the Charter of Fundamental Rights. Therefore, the prerequisite expectation is that no matter how sophisticated the system would be the people should not only trust AI but also benefit from the use of it in their personal and professional lives. Aspirationally, the EU aims at creating an innovation-friendly ecosystem for AI. The EU policies not only expect from the AI developers to comply with the commonly accepted values but also strives to create a friendly environment where key players find the adequate infrastructure, needed research facilities, useful testing environments, available financial means, adjusted legal framework and matching skills levels the incentive to invest in systems that deploy AI. In the growing body of the EU policy documents, it is repeatedly underlined that the ambition for Europe is to become the world-leading market develops and deploys the ethical, secure and technologically cutting-edge AI. The desired global EU leadership in this field aims at promoting AI development with the human-centric approach.

Since the Digital Summit organised by the Estonian Presidency in September 2017, AI has been high on the agenda of the European Council and the Council of the EU. The crucial role in the policy making processes around AI is played by the Commission, and high-level expert groups operating under its auspices, whose activities and policy documents will be briefly analysed in paragraph 3.3 below. In general, the main goals of the plans of the coordinated EU policies on AI are to maximise the efforts that encourage synergies and exchange of knowledge and best practices across the EU. The idea is to collectively define the way forward that takes into account the ethical issues of the introduced solutions. The forward-looking goal of the coordinated policies is to achieve the EU impact to compete globally and operate under sound regulatory framework setting ethical standards respected by all stakeholders.

In April 2018, the European Commission in its communication 'Artificial Intelligence for Europe'[55] presented a proper European initiative on AI and indicated its major pillars. This Communication sets out a European initiative on AI, which aims to:

- Foster the EU's technological and industrial capacity and AI uptake across the economy, in both private and public sectors. This includes investments in research and innovation and better access to data.
- Prepare for socio-economic changes brought about by AI that will be impacting education, labour market and the social protection systems. This will demand anticipating upcoming changes and supporting the modernisation of existing set-outs.
- Ensure adjusted ethical and legal frameworks. They should be based on the European Union's values and in line with the Charter of Fundamental Rights of the EU. This will include forthcoming guidance on existing product liability rules, a detailed analysis of emerging challenges, and cooperation with stakeholders, through a European AI Alliance, for the development of AI ethics guidelines.

In view of accelerating the AI-related transformations, the EU member states together with Norway and Switzerland agreed to adopt a rolling coordinated plan which is expected to be monitored and reviewed yearly.[56] The first edition of this plan, adopted in December 2018[57] mainly refers to the EU level activities for 2019 and 2020 under this financial framework. This version of the plan is expected to be updated regularly until 2027 so to stay in line with the calendar of the EU multi-annual financial framework. The general desiderates of the European AI plan are not much different to general ideas around the common the EU policies that are expected to respond to the citizens' aspirations, societal needs and to foster competitiveness.

The European position in the AI industry is significant. The EU is one of the world hubs for AI researches. German Research Centre for Artificial Intelligence (DFKI) founded in 1988 is one of the world's largest research centres in the field of AI. Europe is also the seat for the scientific and engineering-focused established companies or start-ups. Despite the general perception, the EU is still the manufacturer of a third of the global production precision farming, security, health, logistics, transport, space, industrial and professional service robots increasingly relying on AI. Apart from this the EU develops and exploits platforms

---

55 Commission, COM (2018) 237 final (n 2).
56 The Member States' Group on Digitizing European Industry and AI and the Commission discussed between June and November 2018 possible strands for cooperation.
57 Commission, COM (2018) 795 (n 3)1. The Commission's plan will be discussed in more details in paragraph 3.3.

providing business-to-business services through applications targeting at smart enterprise and e-government solutions.[58]

Still, the main challenges for the EU is to be globally competitive in the AI technology deployment in the economy as only a fraction of its businesses have adopted digital strategies. This unfortunate data refers in particular to small and medium-sized businesses.[59] Only one in five of them was highly digitised. Furthermore, one-third of the workforce still does not possess basic digital skills.[60]

Progress in AI opens the door to new opportunities in areas such as personalised and precision healthcare, autonomous driving, fin-techs, advanced manufacturing, space-based applications, smart power grids, sustainable circular and bio-economy, improved detection and investigation of criminal activities (e.g. money laundering, tax fraud), media, etc.[61]

The effective implementation of AI in Europe will require the proper digital transformation by upgrading of the currently available infrastructure and completion of the regulatory framework for the Digital Single Market. Also, it demands the swift adoption of the Commission proposal for a European Cybersecurity Industrial, Technology and Research Competence Centre and the Network of National Coordination Centres.[62] Other required measures include: reinforced connectivity through spectrum coordination, very fast 5G mobile networks and optical fibres, next-generation clouds, as well as satellite technologies.[63] High-performance computing and AI will increasingly intertwine as we transit to a future using new computing, storage and communication technologies. Furthermore, infrastructures should be both accessible and affordable to ensure an inclusive AI adoption across Europe. The EU's small and young companies will need to be able to integrate these technologies into new products, services, processes and technologies. It will also require, including by upskilling and reskilling their workforce. Standardisation will also be a key for the interoperability and development of AI.

---

58 Commission, COM(2018)237 final (n 2) 3–5.
59 In 2017, 25% of EU large enterprises and 10% of small and medium-sized enterprises used big data analytics.
60 See, https://ec.europa.eu/digital-single-market/digital-scoreboard accessed 22 July 2020. According to McKinsey, 'Digital Europe: Realizing the Continent's Potential' (2016) https://www.mckinsey.com/business-functions/mckinsey-digital/our-insights/digital-europe-realizing-the-continents-potential# accessed 22 July 2020, European companies operating at the digital frontier only reach a digitisation level of 60% compared to their US peers.
61 Ugo Pagallo, Serena Quattrocolo, 'The Impact of AI on Criminal Law, and Its Twofold Procedures' in Woodrow Barfield, Ugo Pagallo (eds.), *Research Handbook on the Law of Artificial Intelligence* (Edward Elgar 2018) 387.
62 COM(2018) 630. The procedure is still ongoing: https://eur-lex.europa.eu/legal-content/en/HIS/?uri=CELEX:52018PC0630 accessed 22 July 2020.
63 Ex the EU-owned Global Satellite Navigation System Galileo.

A number of customs and paradigms will also have to change. It is also expected that data will either need to be processed locally (for example in connected automated driving that must be able to take swift decisions without waiting for an answer from a remote server) or much faster processes allowing for fast and smooth computing capabilities will be required. These changes in paradigms are already emerging and new technologies in energy-efficient computing architectures (such as neuromorphic and quantum) will be indispensable to ensure sustainable use of energy. There are already ongoing partnerships between the member states and the EU through joint undertakings such as ECSEL (electronic components and systems).[64] Key to processing big data and sustaining further developments in AI are EuroHPC (high-performing computing) and quantum flagship under the Research and Innovation Programme Horizon 2020.[65]

Building on its reputation for safe and high-quality products, Europe's ethical approach to AI is intended to strengthen citizens' trust in the digital development. Digital dependence on non-European suppliers and the lack of a high-performance cloud infrastructure that meets European standards and values can pose risks in terms of macroeconomic, economic and security considerations, jeopardise datasets and IP and inhibit innovation and commercial development of hardware and computing infrastructure for connected devices (IoT) in Europe. Without focusing exclusively on Europe, it is important to promote the development of such infrastructure in Europe as well. That is why, there is a need for the support of building open-source AI software libraries, taking into account the guidelines for trusted AI and in line with the latest achievements of research. By providing appropriate support for the development of such AI libraries, building on strong European expertise, enterprises and researchers will be able to use up-to-date software provided by software vendors operating in Europe who offer support and training, which will also contribute to increasing the competitiveness of European enterprises in this field. Also, the support is needed for the mechanism for advanced research, innovation and commercial development of hardware and computing infrastructure for connected devices and the Internet of Things (IoT) in Europe.[66]

The major policy works are developed around abovementioned three pillars of the EU's AI framework, which will be analysed in the following paragraph. Further in the chapter, we will discuss the role of the European Commission. Our goal is to put in an organised timeline various policy documents produced by the Commission, with the hope to clarify the policy regulatory processes step, by step. Finally, we will discuss the works of HLEG AI and European AI Alliance providing necessary support to the Commission, by sharing the expert

---

64 See, https://europa.eu/european-union/about-eu/agencies/ecsel_en accessed 22 July 2020.

65 See, https://ec.europa.eu/digital-single-market/en/blogposts/eurohpc-joint-undertaking-looking-ahead-2019–2020-and-beyond accessed 22 July 2020.

66 HLEG AI, 'Policy and Investment Recommendations' (n 5) 30.

knowledge and expanding participatory mechanisms which, by involving wide public are intending to shape trustworthy regulatory environment.

3.2 Three pillars of EU's AI framework

3.2.1 Boosting the EU's AI uptake in technological and industrial capacity

The first pillar of the EU's AI framework is relating to the need for increasing the AI uptake in technological and industrial capacity. AI sector is recognised as a 'key enabling' technology which may lead through necessary digital transformations, so much needed in all sectors of the European economy.[67] The adoption of AI should adapt to the demands of the rapidly evolving digital economy. An important part of the digitalisation is the attention that policymakers should pay to SMEs. Driving improvements in technology and services in all areas in the EU should happen on both sides of the supply and demand relations, through enabling policy and investment mechanisms. One of the priorities is that the public and private sector must seize the opportunities offered by both the development of innovative AI solutions and their application in different sectors. To facilitate and reinforce investment in AI, and to maximise its impact in both the public and the private sectors, joint efforts between the Commission, member states and the private sector are necessary. Only if the Commission and member states working together, will channel their investments in the same direction through joint programming and leverage significant private investments, will Europe as a whole have an impact and establish its strategic autonomy in AI. One of the tools that are used is Horizon 2020, which helps to pave the way to new partnership formulas on AI as it is addressed in different public-private partnerships including the robotics and big data and research and innovation agendas. The same refers to the academic research building the dedicated networks for facilitating the use of AI. The Commission declares its commitment to support joint measures together with member states, industry and academia on a common research and innovation agenda in AI. It aims at the development of the EU AI innovation ecosystem and at fostering close co-operation between all interested players to reinforce competitiveness across the whole AI value chain.[68]

The EU builds also sectoral multi-stakeholder alliances for key industries to promote AI ecosystems with the participation of relevant stakeholders. These alliances, as public-private partnerships bring together industry, research and academia, the public sector and civil society organisations, as well as policymakers to conduct a sector-based analysis of the challenges and opportunities generated

---

67 High-Level Strategy Group on Industrial Technologies, 'Report on Re-finding Industry' (n 2).
68 Commission, 'Annex to Coordinated Plan on AI' COM(2018) 795 final, 6–7.

by AI systems on a continuous basis.[69] There is an expectation they will take concrete actions to meet the sector-specific needs. This particularly refers to targeted policies and enablers to tackle.[70]

The EU should stay ahead of technological developments in AI and ensure that they are rapidly implemented throughout its economy. This means that increasing investment to strengthen basic research and scientific breakthroughs, improve AI research infrastructures, develop AI applications in key sectors, from health to transport, and facilitate the uptake of AI and access to data, is indispensable. Already mentioned, joint efforts by both the public sector at all levels as well as private sectors are needed to increase overall investment in line with the economic weight of the EU and investment on other continents. These investments will aim at consolidating research and innovation in AI, encouraging testing and experimentation, strengthening AI excellence research centres and starting efforts to bring AI to all potential users, with a focus on small and medium-sized enterprises.

So far, the public and private research and development investments in AI in Europe are counted in billions. According to pre-pandemic plans, the entire EU, both public and private sectors included, aimed at gradual increase of the AI investment to, at the range of at least EUR 20 billion by the end of 2020. It was then aimed for more than EUR 20 billion per year to be invested in the next years.

The works of the Commission and the EU member states intend to help to align and increase investment. This allows the EU to avoid risks of missing the opportunities AI offers, and not to let a brain drain and becoming a buyer of technological solutions developed elsewhere. The EU should foster its position of a research centre while bringing more innovations.

Member states should engage themselves and their economies in AI development. Their initiatives shall touch upon the stepping up of investments, strengthening research and innovation from the lab to the market, supporting AI research excellence centres across Europe, bringing AI to all small businesses and potential users, supporting testing and experimentation, attracting private investments, making more data available.[71]

Within the strengthening research and innovation from the lab to the market, there should be strong support given to AI technologies both in basic and industrial research. The guiding principle of all support for AI-related research shall be the development of 'responsible AI' following the human centricity paradigm.[72] This includes investment in projects in key application areas such as health, connected and automated driving, agriculture, manufacturing, energy,

69 Pasquale (n 45) 192.
70 HLEG AI, 'Policy and Investment Recommendations' (n 5) 15–17.
71 Commission, COM(2018)237 final (n 2) 6–12.
72 See, Commission's 'Responsible Research and Innovation' workstream: https://ec.europa.eu/programmes/horizon2020/en/h2020-section/responsible-research-innovation accessed 22 July 2020.

next-generation internet technologies, security, public administration and justice.

AI research shall also be supported by the creation of the Enhanced European Innovation Council (EIC) pilot.[73] This funding provider supports innovators, entrepreneurs, small companies and scientists who have innovative ideas with the potential and ambitions to scale them up internationally. The EIC pilot is dedicated to the ground-breaking, market-creating innovations and as such it is supposed to be facilitating AI development, to make this technology part of numerous projects, for business applications in health, agriculture, manufacturing etc. high reward research and innovation projects. The supported project should aim to demonstrate a new technological paradigm in such fields as human-centric AI. At the same time member states are supposed to implement innovative financial support facilities to help the digital transformation of small and medium-sized enterprises. Those include the integration of AI technologies into products, process and business models.[74]

In 2019, the European Commission brought together key new technologies stakeholders, to develop a common strategic research and innovation agenda for AI. It set up a Leaders' Group representing the stakeholders at CEO level from businesses and research organisations to develop the agenda and ensure the highest level of commitment to pave the way to new partnerships in AI. Funding in fundamental research is provided by the European Research Council, based on criteria around scientific excellence. The research actions under the patronage of Marie Skłodowska-Curie provide grants for researchers at all stages of their careers. There is also the initiative for supporting AI research excellence centres across Europe by building on Member States' efforts to establish AI-focused research centres. The Commission is willing to strengthen AI excellence centres across Europe and encourage and facilitate their collaboration and networking.

The EU would far more benefit of AI if it becomes available and accessible to all, including small businesses and potential users. Therefore, the Commission is supposed to facilitate access of all users, especially small and medium-sized enterprises, companies from non-tech sectors and public administrations. To achieve this goal, the Commission intends to support the development of an AI-on-demand platform built on the latest technologies. It will also encourage all to test them which aims at providing a single access point for all users to needed AI-based technologies. This includes knowledge, data repositories, clouds, high-performance computing power, algorithms and other tools. It should also offer support in analysing business rationalities behind AI in given circumstances and help them to integrate AI solutions into the processes of products and services inventing and disseminating.

---

73 See, https://ec.europa.eu/research/eic/index.cfm?pg=funding accessed 22 July 2020.
74 Geslevich Packin, Lev-Aretz (n 31) 100.

The Commission is also obliged to analyse systemic changes in value chains in order to anticipate the potential of AI for small and medium-sized enterprises by testing critical industrial applications of AI in non-technological sectors and strengthening the European centre for advanced production support for SMEs. Support for testing and experimentation of AI products and services is essential to bring them to market, to ensure compliance with security standards and rules and to ensure security as planned.[75] It should also enable policy makers to gain experience with new technologies in order to create an appropriate regulatory framework. The Commission is working on the establishment of testing and experimentation infrastructures open to companies of all sizes and from all regions. An initial series of test and experimentation infrastructures for AI products and services in the fields of health care, transport, infrastructure inspection and maintenance, agri-food and agile production is planned.

Apart from public resources coming from the Framework Programme for Research and Innovation (currently Horizon 2020), a sufficient level of private investment in AI transformation is crucial. The Commission needs to work with all financial institutions in Europe, private and public, like the European Investment Bank, to develop investment guidelines that take into account the Ethics Guidelines. They should lead to promoting financial support to sustainable business developments in general and in particular to ethical deployment of new technologies. The final form is to be determined. It can be a set of criteria in the societally accepted proofing of financial investments offered to supported projects. The adoption of the ethics guidelines by all stakeholders, notably by industry organisations, would indicate how technologies with humancentric values are critical. The European Strategic Investment Fund shall be engaged in order to attract private investment to support the development and deployment of AI as part of the wider effort to promote digitisation. This Fund is an initiative of the European Investment Bank Group and is the core of the investment plans for Europe. As such it is the natural stakeholder for providing financing to AI projects.[76]

It is worth mentioning about the Strategic Forum for Important Projects of Common European Interest, which has been launched by the Commission, in order to identify and ensure appropriate large-scale finance for projects of strategic importance for Europe including the integration of AI to strengthen the EU's industrial leadership.

When indicating major areas of investment, pertinent for AI industry and the European economy, at the same time we shall point at the research and innovation projects supporting AI applications that address societal challenges. This applies to sectors such as health, transport and agri-food. Apart from it,

---

75 Cristina Amato, 'Product Liability and Product Security: Present and Future' in Sebastian Lohsse, Reiner Schulze, Dirk Staudenmayer (eds.), *Liability for Artificial Intelligence and the Internet of Things. Muenster Colloquia on EU Law and the Digital Economy IV* (Hart Publishing, Nomos 2019) 89.

76 See, https://www.eib.org/en/efsi/what-is-efsi/index.htm accessed 22 July 2020.

there should be a strong support to the roll-out of AI across Europe through a toolbox for potential users, with a focus on small and medium-sized enterprises, non-technological companies and public administrations includes an AI on-demand platform providing support and easy access to the latest algorithms and expertise. There is a need to create a network of AI-focused digital innovation centres, which facilitate testing and experimentation, and the establishment of industrial data platforms will provide high-quality data sets.

Currently, we are witnessing the negotiations of the multiannual financial framework for the years 2021–2027. AI-related priorities, for the upcoming period, shall encompass:

- building and developing of a pan-European network of AI excellence centres.
- explainable AI is a crucial area for the research and development in the AI field.[77] It is strongly connected with legal and ethical compliance and the requirement of transparency. In order to increase the level of explainability and minimise the risk of bias or error, AI systems should be developed in a manner which allows humans to understand (the basis of) their actions AI;
- unsupervised machine learning, which is the type of machine learning that is not guided like in the case of supervised learning and is intended to bring order to data sets provided to AI systems and make sense of it. It is used to group unstructured data in accordance with its similarities and patterns;
- energy. Since certain blockchain applications which utilise mining consume high amounts of energy, the EU should give preference for such programmes that support newer energy-efficient infrastructures and applications. Therefore, the incentivising instruments are to focus on financing in innovative AI and blockchain companies, developing the EU investors networks concentrating on AI, multiplying member states investments by involving national banks willing to finance these technologies, incentivising private investments.[78]
- data efficiency, which is aimed at using less data in order to train AI algorithms; this investment priority is connected with the functioning of the data sharing centres closely linked with the AI-on-demand platform, which are to facilitate business and public sector development.
- new digital innovation hubs, world-leading testing and experimentation facilities in areas such as transport, healthcare, agriculture, food processing and manufacturing, tested in regulatory sandboxes, which are testing grounds for the areas that are still not regulated;
- adoption of AI by organisations across all sectors, including public interest

---

77 More on practical aspects of explainability, in the context of the medical sector, see, Andreas Holzinger et al., 'What Do We Need to Build Explainable AI Systems for the Medical Domain' (2017) 3–6 arXiv: 1712.09923v1 accessed 22 July 2020.
78 Pasquale (n 45) 102.

applications where the co-investment of the EU member states would be necessary;

- exploring joint innovation procurement for the use and development of AI;

The Commission plans to continue its support for technologies to enable AI in high-performance computing, microelectronics, photonics, quantum technologies, the Internet of things and cloud. These ideas are to coincide with energy-efficient agendas for turning the value chain greener.[79]

Another big challenge is to make more data available for the AI technologies that need a vast amount of data to be developed. The rule is that the larger a data set, the better even subtle relations in the data can be discovered. In principle, data-rich environments also provide for more opportunities. The algorithms first learn and then interact with its environment.[80] To illustrate it is enough to imagine that machines and processes until they are digitalised, they cannot be improved by AI for which they stay unavailable until they change their form for analogue to digital. Therefore, the availability of data is key for a competitive AI technology, that the EU should facilitate.

The Commission has made significant efforts recently to make public sector information and publicly funded research results available for re-use.[81] It is believed that due to the policy measure, the re-usability of such data will be improved, which then would help the body of data to grow. The challenge for public authorities is to find right policy measures to encourage also wider availability of privately-held data and to call on businesses to make available data for re-use.

The Commission has put forward a set of initiatives to enlarge the European data space. In February 2020, the European data strategy was adopted, aiming at creating a truly internal market for data, which would allow it to flow freely across the EU for the benefit of various stakeholders, like businesses, researchers and public administration.[82] Remaining initiatives on European data space, *inter alia* include: the adoption of the new directive on public sector information,[83] the update of the recommendation on access to and preservation of scientific information[84] or guidance on sharing private sector data in the economy.[85]

---

79 Commission, COM(2018)237 final (n 2) 6–12.

80 Borghetti (n 22) 70.

81 Such as data generated by the EU's space programmes (Copernicus, Galileo). Copernicus Data and Information Access Services: http://copernicus.eu/news/upcoming-copernicus-data-and-information-access-services-dias accessed 22 July 2020.

82 Commission, 'A European Strategy for Data' (Communication) COM(2020) 66 final.

83 Directive (EU) 2019/1024 of the European Parliament and of the Council of 20 June 2019 on open data and the re-use of public sector information (2019) OJ L172/56.

84 Commission Recommendation (EU) 2018/790 of 25 April 2018 on access to and preservation of scientific information (2018) OJ L 134/12.

85 Commission, 'Guidance on Sharing Private Sector Data in the European Data Economy' (Staff Working Document), SWD (2018)125 final.

All the EU programmes and initiatives, together with the network of Digital Innovation Hubs, are supposed to help to create the measures for start-ups and SMEs to easy funding and needed commercialising advice. Part of that should be supported in SMEs and start-ups to define their AI transition needs, build plans upon them, propose accessible financial schemes to facilitate their transformation, help to upskill the employees. This should include all sorts of business advice including investments and intellectual property rights.[86]

The network of Digital Innovation Hubs is to be used in the context of making available a legal and other needed support to implement trustworthy AI systems being in line with the Ethics Guidelines. It especially refers to providing technical know-how to SMEs that do not have sufficient funds and experience in this area.

Despite the possibilities AI could bring to the businesses, only a small fraction of them use AI actively in their current operations. Especially, it refers to small and medium enterprises that make up over 99% of Europe's businesses and account for about 56% of the EU's total turnover.[87] It is equally important as the large companies AI transformation.[88] Still, less than 75% of the EU businesses did not adopt any AI strategies or plans and just a small fraction of those which have piloted and tested their plans reported difficulties of scaling.[89] According to the EU policies all actors are supposed to join forces to bring AI technologies where most of its transformative power is expected.

The EU, in order to strengthen the discussed pillar of AI policy, intends to encourage partnerships of companies with training institutions to ensure that the content of the training programmes combine state-of-the-art knowledge with practical aspects of AI systems form development and testing to implementation and upscaling. All this is supposed to improve skills and to reskill the resources.

Another group of tasks on the Commission's agenda is boosting and scaling innovation and technology transfer in AI area. Both, academic and industrial researches foster AI innovation, with regard to the introducing this technology to market in view of providing benefits of consumers and business users. Such initiatives have to be institutionally supported by establishing clear competitive conditions, recognised and respected standards and access to fair, reasonable and non-discriminatory terms. This is understood it can be achieved by supporting

---

86 Jeremy A. Cubert, Richard G.A. Bone, 'The Law of Intellectual Property Created by Artificial Intelligence' in Woodrow Barfield, Ugo Pagallo (eds.), *Research Handbook on the Law of Artificial Intelligence* (Edward Elgar 2018) 412.

87 For more information, see the European Commission's latest annual report on SME's (2018–2019) https://op.europa.eu/en/publication-detail/-/publication/cadb8188-35b4-11ea-ba6e-01aa75ed71a1/language-en accessed 22 July 2020.

88 See Eurostat statistics on small and medium-sized enterprises' total turnover in the EU https://ec.europa.eu/eurostat/web/structural-business-statistics/structural-business-statistics/sme accessed 22 July 2020.

89 See for instance Artificial Intelligence in Europe, Outlook for 2019 and Beyond (EY 2018); PwC's Global Artificial Intelligence Study: Exploiting the AI Revolution (2017).

the growth of AI enablers and companies that provide reliable technology solutions. These can be start-ups and scale-ups, SMEs and larger companies. Also, similarly to other initiatives, the growth of AI enablers producing and exporting innovative technological products that compete on a global scale needs to be supported.[90]

The usual process of transition of AI solutions from research labs to testing environments and to commercial markets, according to the Commission needs institutional support. All elements of this chain should be supported to enable innovation and create a market of AI technology companies to create an attractive European AI brand. The friendly regulatory environment, administrative support and institutional guidance should be built to ensure the participation of industry in research and development. The prerequisites such as intellectual property rights protection, market competition and opportunities for global cooperation should be assured within this process. These prerequisites overlap with the third pillar of EU's AI which is an appropriate ethical and legal framework based on the European values.

Innovation can also be promoted through various types of competitions and challenge-driven research missions in AI in different sectors. Priority needs to be given to research challenges, data and applications and in all sectors in which Europe has a competitive advantage to scale Trustworthy AI. Also, in all these places where breakthroughs could happen thanks to the research efforts. This type of competitions can be directed towards applications focusing on a universal design approach and accessibility in the development of AI products and services. Such initiatives should become attractors of top talents from Europe and elsewhere, need to be financed by public schemes, with parallel support of the business in a view of creating social and economic good.

As the biggest economic impact is done by networks of individual companies, these ecosystems are built of different stakeholders including end-user facing and subcontracting companies, start-ups, scale-ups, SMEs, large companies but also research institutions. All of them set up public-private partnerships that foster sectoral AI ecosystems and bring the latest innovation from lab to market. The public sector participants both as market actors and as policymakers need also to be present there. The uptake and scaling of AI systems need to be seen in the context of 'enabling AI ecosystems'.[91]

---

90 Jacues Bughin et al., 'Notes from the AI Frontier: Modelling the Impact of AI on the World Economy' (McKinsey Global Institute 2018) https://www.mckinsey.com/~/media/McKinsey/Featured%20Insights/Artificial%20Intelligence/Notes%20from%20the%20frontier%20Modeling%20the%20impact%20of%20AI%20on%20the%20world%20economy/MGI-Notes-from-the-AI-frontier-Modeling-the-impact-of-AI-on-the-world-economy-September-2018.ashx accessed 22 July 2020.

91 Enabling AI ecosystems can be viewed as 'collaborative arrangements through which firms combine their individual offerings into a coherent, customer-facing solutions'. See Ron Adner, 'Match Your Innovation Strategy to Your Innovation Ecosystem' (2006) Harvard Business Review https://hbr.org/2006/04/match-your-innovation-strategy-to-your-

Identifying opportunities and challenges in AI sectors as well as the beneficial impact that can be achieved for society, private companies, public sector players and research institutions require data, infrastructure, skills, regulations and investments. The Commission conducts ongoing analysis to understand all needs of the sectoral AI eco-systems and to derive recommendations in terms of expected impacts and required enablers to be put in place.

The European agenda envisages that various institutions, member states and representatives of the private sector should create friendly funding conditions for trustworthy AI. It is clear Europe underperforms in early-stage innovations, digital technologies and AI investments. A coordinated effort is needed in the EU to ensure it can deliver the benefits that AI brings to society. It requires both a public funding mechanism as well as a general openness towards global competition. Europe has to build an environment of trust where all stakeholders are motivated to invest in AI technologies.[92]

Substantial funding in the technology-related programmes can help to manage the digital transformation. Although investment agencies may differ, their methods and instruments have to be adapted to the specificity of the AI needs. As dedicated long-term funding is needed for purpose-driven research on AI to maintain the competitiveness of the EU companies and, this funding should be made available to researches based on a collaborative approach. Those can help in creating significant projects on selected topics, instead of focusing on projects without international impact. Bringing research teams to work for joined goals is still difficult as a limited number of instruments are available at the EU level that could play an anchoring role for European researchers to stay and to attract the best ones from elsewhere. All the initiatives should be supported by structural funds for data infrastructure to coordinate data sharing and access. It is believed that making available data sources and redirecting funding flows to boost collaboration of public and private sector could become critical to enhance Europe's competitiveness.

AI is a group of technologies where volumes of investments make a difference in terms of innovation speed and market share.[93] With the digital economy characterised by diminishing returns for late entrants, it is a key for Europe to invest so as to have the possibility to capture large market shares and to make technology prevail.[94] Slow movers will have to catch up with established market

---

innovation-ecosystem accessed 22 July 2020. Ecosystems function conceptually as a means to understand the relationships between different organisations or parties that share a common motive, technology, platform or knowledge base. The AI ecosystem members are likely to have developed and deployed AI technology in different ways, to different extents and for different purposes.

92 HLEG AI, 'Policy and Investment Recommendations' (n 5) 26.
93 The forecast of the AI worldwide market value shows a fast growth, with AI reaching $118 billion by 2025 from $9.5 billion in 2018. See, Tractica, Artificial Intelligence Market Forecasts https://www.tractica.com/research/artificial-intelligence-market-forecasts accessed 22 July 2020.
94 Floridi, *The 4ᵗʰRevolution* (n 38) 31.

players.[95] In any case, the market for AI start-ups in the EU is rather limited and it is a key to ensure that the engines of the European economy shift to AI and benefit of it.[96]

Financing by the public is crucial for creating bigger funding pools and leveraging private investments. This is needed for accelerating the digital transformation of Europe partly through start-ups and SMEs. Co-financing of AI project is a key—member states need to combine such investments at European level to crowd-in additional means from the private sector. In further stages, such co-financing also has to address the larger investments targeting AI company growth. That all to ensure financing avenues for larger market deals that can help established companies to grow and scale-up in the transformation process in the digital economy.

The EU should remain an open economy and a lucrative investment environment for innovators and investors. This can happen only if there is a number of enabling elements that facilitate business decisions and promote investment in human-centred AI. It refers not only to the funds' and other support available but also to labour and immigration regime, legal certainty created through the regulations, the business-friendly attitude of regulators etc. That as an aggregate can provide the necessary level of attraction to bring in investors.[97] In the current context of uncertainties in world trade and protectionist measures on other markets, it is essential that the EU continues to build its free trade legal framework and investment facilities and at the same time takes decisive actions against unfair practices by third countries.[98]

3.2.2 Preparing for socio-economic change

Throughout history, the advent of new technologies — from electricity to the Internet—has changed the nature of work. It has brought great benefits to the society and economy. It has also caused concerns. The emergence of automation, robotics and AI is changing the labour market and it is essential for the EU to shape this change. These technologies can make life easier for humans. They can help them perform repetitive, strenuous and even dangerous tasks. They can also help to aggregate large amounts of data, provide more accurate information and propose decisions, including the use of AI to assist doctors in making diagnoses. Ultimately, they help to improve people's skills. Against the background of an ageing society, AI can provide new solutions to help more people, including

---

95 HLEG AI, 'Policy and Investment Recommendations' (n 5) 26.

96 Roland Berger, 'Artificial Intelligence – A strategy for European start-ups' (2018) https://www.rolandberger.com/fr/Publications/AI-startups-as-innovation-drivers.html   accessed 22 July 2020.

97 HLEG AI, 'Policy and Investment Recommendations' (n 5) 44–46.

98 European Political Strategy Center, 'EU Industrial Policy After Siemens-Alstom, Finding a New Balance Between Openness and Protection' (Brussels 2019) https://ec.europa.eu/epsc/sites/epsc/files/epsc_industrial-policy.pdf accessed 22 July 2020.

people with disabilities, to participate and stay in the labour market. As a result of AI deployment, new jobs and tasks will be created. At this stage for many of them, this is difficult or impossible to predict what they would be. Other jobs and tasks will be replaced. While at present it is difficult to quantify precisely the impact of AI on jobs, the need for action is clear. However, we may already point at some issues related to digital, AI-based transformation.[99] The problems of dehumanisation and commodification of human work may be identified as potential threats to be addressed by regulatory measures.[100] The risk of dehumanisation is associated in particular with the replacement of human workers by smart technologies (robots) in sectors like medicine or caregiving, where human-to-human, rather than human-to-machine interaction many times brings this intangible value of empathy which is needed and may not be truly replaced by efficient algorithms. In terms of the commodification of work through algorithmic technologies, we shall recall the problems related to the so-called gig-economy or platform economy. One of them is social invisibility which brings serious consequences to the social security of 'casual workers' providing services through platforms like Uber. They are many times self-employed, yet their performance is being monitored in a very meticulous way by the corporations staying behind given platforms. At the same time, those corporations are liberating themselves from any responsibilities for people working for them.[101]

AI impact on the labour market is strongly connected with the education and training policy. Since new jobs will be needed, the vocational and higher education programmes shall be adjusted in order to respond to the demand for new skills and capacities crucial for the new digitalised labour market. Digital transformation of the labour market, which AI technologies are part of, will bring changes in labour demand and supply.[102]

In education and training, there are overall three main challenges for the EU. Firstly, the challenge is to prepare the society as a whole i.e. to help to develop all sorts of digital skills which are complementary to and cannot be replaced by any machine such as critical thinking, creativity or management. Secondly, the EU has to focus on supporting workers in jobs which are likely to be the most transformed or to disappear due to automation, robotics and AI.[103] This means also to ensure access for all citizens, including workers and the self-employed, to appropriate and satisfactory social protection, in line with the European Pillar of

99 Comande (n 53)168.
100 Valerio de Stefano, 'Negotiating the Algorithm: Automation, Artificial Intelligence and Labour Protection' (2018) International Labour Office, Employment Working Paper No. 246, 5.
101 European Group on Ethics in Science and New Technologies, 'Future of Work, Future of Society' (Publications Office of the EU Luxembourg 2018) 12.
102 High-Level Expert Group on the Impact of the Digital Transformation on EU Labour Markets, 'Report on The Impact of the Digital Transformation on EU Labour Markets', (Publications Office of the EU Luxembourg 2019) 16–17.
103 Comande (n 53) 169.

Social Rights. It shall be stressed that the automation may impact financing schemes of social protection, necessitating a proper reflection on the suitability and sustainability of social security systems. Thirdly, the EU needs to train an adequate number of specialists in AI. Here the EU's long tradition of academic excellence can be helpful.

In order to look into the EU's initiatives of discussed problem, we need to go back to 2016 when the European Commission adopted the New Skills Agenda for Europe, which is the comprehensive plan to equip people with the right skills for the evolving labour market.[104] As a follow up on to this, the Council issued a Recommendation for the Member States on 'Upskilling Pathways: New Opportunities for Adults[105]'. The aim of this document was to popularise and improve basic literacy, numeracy and digital skills. A Recommendation was also adopted on key competences for lifelong learning. This focused mainly on the acquisition of digital competences, entrepreneurship and creativity as well as in sciences, technology, engineering and mathematics (STEM). The Commission also presented a Digital Education Action Plan[106] aiming at boosting digital skills and competences.

As it is believed now, while digitisation is going to affect rather the structure of the labour market through the automation of middle-skilled jobs, AI will have more impact on lower-skilled jobs.[107] The obvious and clearly unwilled consequence of this is that if it will not be addressed early and proactively, this may exacerbate inequalities between people, regions and industries in the EU. To avoid it, managing the AI transformation will mean, workers whose jobs are changing or may disappear due to automation should have every opportunity to acquire the skills and knowledge they need. If appropriately mastered, new technologies themselves can serve as support during the labour market transitions. This anticipatory approach and focus on investing in people are a cornerstone of a human-centric approach to AI and other digital technologies. As described earlier all this will be directly dependent on a significant investment. National schemes will be essential for providing such up-skilling and training. Adapting continuous learning systems to equip workers with tech-related skills could be assured through creating a right to continuous learning for all and implement it by appropriate laws and regulatory requirements.[108] This could relate to the need for career guidance and professional development for employees whose jobs are threatened by automation.[109] Europe should develop a

---

104 Commission, 'A New Skills Agenda for Europe. Working Together to Strengthen Human Capital, Employability and Competitiveness' COM(2016) 381 final.
105 Council Recommendation of 19 December 2016 on Upskilling Pathways: New Opportunities for Adults [2016] OJ C 484/ 1.
106 Commission, 'Communication on the Digital Education Action Plan' (Communication) COM(2018) 22 final.
107 Organisation for Economic Co-operation and Development, 'Automation, skills use and training' 2018.
108 See, Zech (n 32) 189.
109 Isabelle Wildhaber, 'Artificial Intelligence and Robotics, the Workplace, and Workplace-

similar syllabus and certification scheme for artificial intelligence. One of the ideas is to provide them with cross-recognised training certifications and developing a sort of 'professional passports' to ensure the portability of skills.

The role of the EU institutions will also be to support nurturing talent, diversity and interdisciplinarity.[110] All this to face the change of AI bringing about new job profiles, including in the area of developing machine-learning algorithms and other digital innovations.[111] This is another factor why Europe should strive to increase the number of people trained in AI and encourage diversity. More women and in general people from different backgrounds, including people with disabilities, must be involved in AI development, starting with inclusive AI education and training to ensure that AI is non-discriminatory and inclusive. Promoting an even more open and flexible approach to education and studies, including interdisciplinarity should also be supported. This could be achieved by encouraging earlier unmet joint degrees as a combination of law, psychology and AI. The importance of ethics in the development and use of new technologies should also be promoted and featured in programmes and courses. It is beyond just training the best talent, but it is also about creating an attractive environment for them to stay in the EU.

Initiatives to encourage more young people to choose AI subjects and related fields as a career should be promoted.[112] Supporting internships aimed at acquiring advanced digital skills, and a number of actions of the Digital Skills and Jobs Coalition aim at increasing competencies in coding skills and increasing the number of experts in digital.[113]

To ensure that workers have a chance to adjust and to have access to new opportunities will be crucial for people to accept AI. Like with any other new technology, it is important AI is not just imposed on society. It is the role of the EU and the countries, in dialogue with the social partners and civil society bodies, to jointly shape the process to ensure that its benefits are widely disseminated. The key is that the citizens are equipped to take full advantage of this technology and that a broader reflection on potentially deeper societal changes is taking place.

In view of the upcoming changes the Commission, in order to support the efforts of member states which are responsible for labour and education policies,

---

Related Law' in Woodrow Barfield, Ugo Pagallo (eds.), *Research Handbook on the Law of Artificial Intelligence* (Edward Elgar 2018) 583.

110 See, https://www.cognizant.com/whitepapers/21-jobs-of-the-future-a-guide-to-getting-and-staying-employed-over-the-next-10-years-codex3049.pdf accessed 22 July 2020.

111 Overall, the number of specialists in information and communication technologies in the EU has grown annually by 5% since 2011, creating 1.8 million jobs and rapidly increasing its share of total employment from 3% to 3.7% in just five years. There are at least 350,000 vacancies for such professionals in Europe, pointing to significant skills gaps. See, http://www.pocbigdata.eu/monitorICTonlinevacancies/general_info/ accessed 22 July 2020.

112 To achieve this the Commission has recently launched the 'Digital Opportunity Traineeships' https://ec.europa.eu/digital-single-market/en/digital-opportunity-traineeships-boosting-digital-skills-job accessed 22 July 2020.

113 See, https://ec.europa.eu/digital-single-market/en/digital-skills-jobs-coalition accessed 22 July 2020.

to adjust to the requirements of the AI technology, decided to set up dedicated training schemes. They are connected within with the blueprint on sectoral co-operation on skills.[114] This brings together businesses, trade unions, higher education institutions and public authorities.[115]

The EU is also intending to gather detailed analysis and expert inputs to anticipate the changes in the labour market and the skills mismatch across the EU. More specifically, the Commission plans to publish a foresight report on the impact of AI in education. Part of that is to launch pilots to predict the training requirements for future competence profiles and also to publish reports addressing the labour market impacts of AI. It is also to encourage business to education partnerships to take steps to attract and retain more AI talent and to boost continued collaboration.

Proposals under the next EU multiannual financial frameworks include strengthening support for the acquisition of advanced digital skills including AI-specific expertise. The Commission also intends to broaden the scope of the current European Globalisation Adjustment Fund (EGF) and beyond redundancies caused by delocalisation embrace also redundancies resulting from digitisation and automation.[116] The EU funds such as the European Social Fund or the abovementioned EGF should be even more responsive by dedicating more programmes to up-skilling strategies and making EGF intervention more preventive and less curative. Apart from this, it would require developing employment policies supporting and rewarding companies who are setting up strategic up-and reskilling plans. The organisations conducting strategic workforce planning for the existing workforce to upskill towards AI should be promoted. This should be organised with potential support from universities and consultancies. Ideally, employers should introduce new technologies with a disrupting impact on jobs only when they have initially properly worked on reskilling plans and alternatives for workers.[117]

Multiple reports on the expected development of the labour market, including 'The Future of Jobs Report' by the World Economic Forum, foresees a substantial reskilling need for every second employee within the next four years.[118] It repeats the need for education and training to be at the centre of all strategies to enlarge the talent pool for Europe. Continuous learning programmes will play a key role in supporting people in the process of anticipating, adapting, upskilling and retraining

---

114 See, http://ec.europa.eu/social/main.jsp?catId=1415&langId=en accessed 22 July 2020.

115 The cooperation now focuses on the automotive, maritime technology, space, textile and tourism sectors, and will address six other sectors in the future: additive manufacturing; construction; green technologies and renewable energy; maritime shipping; paper-based value chain; steel industry.

116 Commission, COM(2018)237 final (n 2) 12–14.

117 For more information, see http://www.ecdl.org accessed 22 July 2020.

118 World Economic Forum, 'The Future of Jobs' (2018) http://reports.weforum.org/future-of-jobs-2018/preface/ accessed 22 July 2020.

to take advantage of the opportunities created by new AI-related activities as part of broader career support mechanisms. Continuous training activities and vocational education to cope with the challenges of digital skills are intended to be central to the job retaining schemes. As much as the new social and behavioural skills needed in an environment where humans and machines will be working together.

To allow for it the critical skills should be defined in sensitive areas with human safety and security perceived as critical to assuring measures against skill deterioration.[119] It would also require addressing undesirable de-skilling through AI, in operations or processes that require human oversight or intervention. Encourage and support the development of new skills transfer and acquisition programmes to enable workers made redundant or threatened with redundancy as a result of automation and the increased use of AI to acquire new skills that would enable them to seek new forms of employment as the structure of the labour market should be reshaped in response to the increasing dependence on digital services and processes.[120] AI could also serve for forecasting algorithms to anticipate and timely address changes in the job market. The development of advanced skills and jobs could be fostered by the capacities offered by new technologies. At the same time, it can help to address one of the biggest challenges of the digital era, namely job insecurity and anxiety for the future enerations.

In Europe, governments, social partners such as employers, trade unions and vocational education and training providers are the main stakeholders defining training priorities, ensuring cross-sectoral and sectoral funding and delivering training to workers. The awareness of these stakeholders on the effects of AI on job markets is essential.

Yet another topic is helping public authorities to make well-reasoned policy decisions. Effective oversight of regulated entities deploying AI-enabled tools requires that supervisors are equally knowledgeable about AI and aware of the developing trends in their respective regulatory perimeter. There are multiple methods that do achieve it one of them is through setting digital affairs committees in national parliaments gathering politicians with diverse backgrounds including AI experts.

Public procurement processes of AI-enabled technology for education should include an assessment of embedded interests, ethics and social impacts.[121] Such products should not be used in educational institutions on the basis of free availability or promotional access by teachers or institutions but should be based on an assessment of their ethical consequences and commercial or other embedded considerations. Promoting critical and ethical awareness of available AI technology in education and considering the development of standards for AI tools in education should be built on key requirements for Trustworthy AI.[122]

119 Amato (n 75) 89.
120 Geslevich Packin, Lev-Aretz (n 31) 104.
121 Beever, McDaniel, Stamlick (n 13) 107.
122 HLEG AI, 'Policy and Investment Recommendations' (n 5) 35–37.

3.2.3 Ensuring appropriate ethical and legal framework based on EU's values

An environment of trust and accountability around the development and use of AI is a basic prerequisite for the successful deployment and acceptance of AI technologies in European society. The values set out in Article 2 of the Treaty on the European Union constitute the foundation of the rights enjoyed by those living in the Union.[123] In addition, the EU Charter of Fundamental Rights brings together all the personal, civic, political, economic and social rights enjoyed by people within the EU in a single text.[124] The EU has a strong and balanced regulatory framework to build on, which can set the global standard for a sustainable approach to AI technology. Below, we will just outline the major areas of EU law, which are already regulated at the EU level or need to be amended due to the AI specificity. The EU legal framework shall be developed further in our book, in parts which connect to the lawful AI and horizontal and sectoral regulations.

The Union has the highest standards in terms of personal data protection and safety and product liability. The General Data Protection Regulation (GDPR) ensures a high standard of protection of personal data, including the principles of data protection from the outset and by default.[125] It guarantees the free circulation of personal data within the EU. It includes provisions on decision-making based solely on automated processing, including profiling. In such situations, data subjects have the right to obtain meaningful information about the logic of the decisions.[126] The GDPR also gives individuals the right not to be subject solely to automated decision-making, except in certain situations.[127]

The Commission has also made a number of proposals in the context of the strategy for the digital internal market. This is an essential condition for the development of AI. The Regulation on the free movement of non-personal data[128] removes obstacles to the free movement of non-personal data and ensures that all

---

123   Article 2 of the Treaty on EU: 'The Union is founded on the values of respect for human dignity, freedom, democracy, equality, the rule of law and respect for human rights, including the rights of persons belonging to minorities'. The Member States share a 'society in which pluralism, non-discrimination, tolerance, justice, solidarity and equality between women and men prevail'.

124   Łukasz Bojarski, Dieter Schindlauer, Katerin Wladasch (eds.), 'The Charter of Fundamental Rights as a Living Instrument. Manual' (CFREU2014) 9–10 https://bim.lbg.ac.at/sites/files/bim/attachments/cfreu_manual_0.pdf accessed 22 July 2020.

125   Regulation (EU) 2016/679 of the European Parliament and of the Council of 27 April 2016 on the protection of natural persons with regard to the processing of personal data and the free movement of such data (GDPR) [2016] OJ L 119/1.

126   Articles 13 (2) f), 14 (2) g) and 15 (1) h) of the GDPR.

127   Article 22 of the GDPR.

128   Regulation (EU) 2018/1807 of the European Parliament and of the Council of 14 November 2018 on a framework for the free flow of non-personal data in the European Union [2018] OJ L 303/59.

categories of data are handled throughout Europe.[129] As such it increases confidence in the online world, like newly adopted Cybersecurity Act[130] and the proposed regulation on privacy and electronic communications also addresses this objective.[131] This is essential because citizens and businesses alike must be able to trust the technology with which they interact, have a predictable legal environment and be reassured of effective safeguards to protect fundamental rights and freedoms. To further enhance trust, people also need to understand how the technology works, so it is important to explore the explainability of AI systems. In order to increase transparency and minimise the risk of distortions or errors, AI systems must indeed be developed in such a way that people can understand the basis of their actions. Like any technology or utility, AI can be used for both positive and vicious purposes. While AI clearly creates new opportunities, it also brings challenges and risks. It refers to the areas of security and liability, criminal use or attacks, biases and discrimination.[132] The interactions between AI and intellectual property rights need to be considered, both from the perspective of IP agencies and users, in order to promote innovation and legal certainty in a balanced way.[133]

The ethical concerns addressing AI technologies result in the adoption of universal guidelines referring to the Charter of Fundamental Rights of the European Union[134] and also future EU regulation on ethical aspects of AI.[135]

The draft ethic guidelines address issues such as the future of work, fairness, safety, security, social inclusion and algorithmic transparency. More broadly, they look at the impact on fundamental rights, including privacy, dignity, consumer protection and non-discrimination. They also build on the work of the European Group on Ethics in Science and New Technologies and take inspiration from other similar efforts.[136] Companies, academic institutions, and other

---

129 Thomas Burri, 'Free Movement of Algorithms: Artificially Intelligent Persons Conquer the European Union's Internal Market' in Woodrow Barfield, Ugo Pagallo (eds.), *Research Handbook on the Law of Artificial Intelligence* (Edward Elgar 2018) 543.

130 Regulation (EU) 2019/881 of the European Parliament and of the Council of 17 April 2019 on ENISA (the European Union Agency for Cybersecurity) and on information and communications technology cybersecurity certification and repealing Regulation (EU) No 526/2013 (Cybersecurity Act) (2019) OJ L 151/15.

131 See, https://ec.europa.eu/digital-single-market/en/proposal-eprivacy-regulation accessed 22 July 2020.

132 Depending on the data input that is used to train AI systems, their outputs can be biased. See more in paragraph 4.5.6 below.

133 Using AI to create works can have implications on intellectual property, with questions arising for instance on patentability, copyright and right ownership, See more in paragraph 6.2.4.

134 HLEG AI, 'Ethics Guidelines for Trustworthy AI' (Brussels 2019).

135 See n 35.

136 At the EU level, the EU Fundamental Rights Agency carries out an assessment of the current challenges faced by producers and users of new technology with respect of fundamental rights compliance https://fra.europa.eu/en/project/2018/artificial-intelligence-big-data-and-fundamental-rights accessed 22 July 2020. The European Group on Ethics in Science and New Technologies also published a relevant 'Statement on

organisations from civil society bodies have been invited to contribute to the works of the Commission that continues working towards progress on ethics at international level.[137]

The Commission published a report on the broader implications for, potential gaps in and orientations for, the liability and safety frameworks for AI, Internet of Things and robotics.[138] It also supports research in the development of explainable AI and implements a pilot project proposed by the European Parliament on Algorithmic Awareness Building, gathers a sound evidence body and facilitates the framing of policy answers to the challenges posed by automated decision making, including distortions and discrimination.[139] Apart from this it supports consumer organisations and data protection supervising authorities at national and EU levels in building an understanding of AI-powered applications with the input of the European Consumer Consultative Group and of the European Data Protection Board.[140]

3.3 Role of the European Commission

3.3.1 Digital single market strategy

The foundation of European economic integration is an internal market, understood as an area without internal frontiers where free movement of goods, services, persons and capital and payment are assured.[141] The digitalisation of the economic processes has an obvious and transforming impact on how the internal market functions. Being aware of the challenges brought by the digital economy, the European Commission adopted 'A Digital Single Market Strategy for Europe'.[142] A notion of the digital single market covers internal/single market where

AI, Robotics and 'Autonomous' Systems (Brussels 2018) https://ec.europa.eu/info/news/ethics-artificial-intelligence-statement-ege-released-2018-apr-24_en accessed 22 July 2020. Examples of international efforts: Asilomar AI principles https://futureoflife.org/ai-principles/ Montréal Declaration for Responsible AI draft principles https://www.montrealdeclaration-responsibleai.com/ UNI Global Union Top 10 Principles for Ethical AIhttp://www.thefutureworldofwork.org/opinions/10-principles-for-ethical-ai/ IEEE, 'Ethically Aligned Design: A Vision for Prioritizing Human Well-being with Autonomous and Intelligent Systems' (2017) https://ethicsinaction.ieee.org/ all accessed 22 July 2020.

137 The European Commission's International Dialogue on Bioethics and Ethics in Science and New Technologies brings together the National Ethics Councils of EU Member States and of third countries, to work together on those matters of common concern.

138 Commission, 'Report on the Safety and Liability Implications of Artificial Intelligence, the Internet of Things and Robotics' COM(2020) 64 final.

139 See https://ec.europa.eu/digital-single-market/en/algorithmic-awareness-building accessed 22 July 2020.

140 Commission, COM (2018) 237 final (n 2) 14–17.

141 See, art. 26 TFEU.

142 Commission, 'A Digital Single Market Strategy for Europe' (Communication) COM (2015)192 final.

individuals and businesses can access and exercise online activities and where full respect of fair competition, high level of consumer protection and the principle of non-discrimination based on nationality is assured. The initial strategy adopted in 2015 was built on three pillars: improved access to online goods and services; assurance of proper conditions for the development of digital networks and services and maximise growth potential for European Digital Economy.[143] Even if Artificial Intelligence was not explicitly mentioned in the Strategy, various measures were intended for regulating the flow of data or online platforms using algorithms. At the same period, problems related to the development of AI-based technologies were noticed by the European Parliament which made wide-ranging recommendations on civil law rules on robotics and by the European Economic and Social Committee, which issued an opinion on the topic.[144]

In May 2017, the Commission provided a mid-term review of the Digital Single Market strategy.[145] This time, the Commission made a clear reference to the Artificial Intelligence, willing to build its capacities, by strengthening the EU's scientific and industrial potential in this field. As it was indicated, the EU was expected to take the leading position in the development of AI technologies, platforms, and applications, taking the benefit from the Digital Single Market, which is believed to be Europe's main asset and indeed a competitive advantage in a global economic play.[146] At the time the Commission did not take any straightforward commitment towards the comprehensive regulation of AI and merely stated that it would continue to monitor challenges and developments in this field.

The fast-growing technological progress and increasing use of AI-based technologies in different sectors of the economy and social life were noticed by the European Council, which at its summit in October 2017 gave a political impulse for launching a proper European initiative on AI, which was believed to be one of the foundations of Digital Europe. Treating it with the sense of urgency, the European Council formally invited the European Commission to draw necessary initiatives which would contribute to building a homogeneous European approach to Artificial Intelligence.[147]

European Commission's initiatives, which will be briefly outlined in the following paragraph, were complemented by various actions, taken jointly or

---

143 Ibid 3–4.
144 European Parliament, 'Resolution of 16.02.2017 with recommendations to the Commission on Civil Law Rules on Robotics' 2015/2103(INL); European Economic and Social Committee, 'Opinion on AI' INT/806-EESC-2016–05369-00-00-AC-TRA.
145 Communication, 'The Mid-Term Review on the Implementation of the Digital Single Market Strategy. A Connected Digital Single Market for All' (Communication) COM (2017)228 final.
146 Ibid.
147 European Council meeting (19 October 2017) – Conclusions, EUCO 14/17 http://data.consilium.europa.eu/doc/document/ST-14–2017-INIT/en/pdf accessed 20 July 2020.

individually at the Member States' level. The Member States build their own, national strategies for AI, which engage governmental, research and industry actors, assuring financing for AI technologies and building sound regulatory environment many times embedded in ethics.[148]

Apart from operating at the national level, the Member States are engaged in policy making processes taking place at the EU one. On 10 April 2018, 24 Member States and Norway signed a Declaration of cooperation on AI. This has been agreed to be an important step towards joining forces in order to build a common European approach towards AI, which would take into account the most pertinent social, economic, ethical and legal issues. The signatories states of this declaration confirmed their will to continue working together to build strong political commitment to ensure that the competitive market for the AI is created with investments proportionate to its economic importance. Also, the inclusive character of the digital transformation of societies was declared. In particular, making access to technologies at all levels should become a priority for member states. The citizens should be given a chance to acquire the competencies needed to actively participate in political and societal levies through the opportunities created by the digitalisation. Declaration also touched the issue of humancentric and values-based AI. The EU's sustainable approach to technologies should create a competitive edge resting in accordance with the basis of the Union's values, fundamental rights (set in art. 2 TEU) as well as ethical principles such as accountability and transparency. Finally, states noticed that the transformative technology, including AI-based systems, may raise new ethical and legal dilemma, one of them being a liability for the systems or their deployment. The abovementioned declaration marked a beginning of a strategic dialogue between the Member States and the European Commission, which led towards the adoption of several policy documents designing comprehensive regulatory approach towards AI.[149] It is worth noticing that among multiple other initiatives the Commission runs an AI Watch portal,[150] which is a platform where the Member States' initiatives and general uptake and impact of AI in Europe are supposed to be monitored. It is one of the elements of transparency necessary to build trustworthy and ethical regulation around all digital technologies and AI in particular.

---

148 Cyprus, Czechia, Denmark, Estonia, Finland, France, Germany, Latvia, Lithuania, Luxembourg, Malta, Netherlands, Portugal, Slovakia, Spain and Sweden are Member States which already adopted national AI strategies, either as an autonomous one or as parts of broader strategies of digitalization and digital transformation. In Austria, Belgium, Bulgaria, Croatia, Greece, Hungary, Ireland, Italy, Poland, Romania and Slovenia AI national strategies were supposed to be adopted in the course of the year 2020. For more detailed country reports, see https://ec.europa.eu/knowledge4policy/ai-watch_en accessed 20 July 2020.

149 See, https://ec.europa.eu/digital-single-market/en/news/eu-member-states-sign-cooperate-artificial-intelligence accessed 20 July 2020.

150 See, https://ec.europa.eu/knowledge4policy/ai-watch_en accessed 20 July 2020.

3.2.2 *AI communications and reports*

In response to the European Council's call to take up necessary initiatives on AI, the European Commission from the year 2018 drafted several policy documents. The first important strategic document was delivered on 25 April 2018, as the aftermath and a proposed framework for cooperation based on the Declaration of cooperation on AI. The European Commission presented a communication 'Artificial Intelligence for Europe', which marked a proper beginning of the European initiative on AI.[151] Its major goal is to maximise the impact of investments and cooperation at the EU and national levels to encourage synergies allowing to define the way forward to ensure the EU global competitiveness. EU initiative on AI defined, discussed above, the pillars of the EU approach which concern: strengthening the EU's technological and industrial capacity, preparing for socio-economic changes which are imminent in the context of the development of AI and finally regulating AI by an appropriate ethical and legal framework. Discussed communication provides an in-depth review of needed measures at the economic, social and legal level in order to control the development of AI technologies with a view to identify and maximise benefits of the EU's socio-economic interest. In an AI for Europe communication, the Commission stressed the need to prepare together with the Member States a coordinated plan on AI, which was delivered in December 2018.[152] The aim of that document, was to indicate the strategic framework, pointing at the most important areas which were to be taken into consideration by members states in the processes of drafting national AI strategies. First of all, the major goal of the plan concerned strengthening the Digital Single Market and elimination obstacles and market fragmentation. Also, the need to develop innovative public-private partnerships and financing schemes for start-ups and innovative SMEs together with building up the capacities of European research centres was stressed. In response to future changes which AI would bring to social structures and labour market, the importance of adapting education systems on all levels in order to better prepare the European society for AI was raised. Another area which was indicated as crucial for the AI sector is data management and data protection. The EU and its Member States are committed to pursue European model for data protection designed by the GDPR[153] and regulation on a free flow of non-personal data[154] and invent common tools which would support proper use of data within AI. The plan intends also to boost the private-public partnership. The EU together with

---

151 Commission COM(2018) 237 final (n 2).
152 Commission COM(2018) 795 final (n 3). The more detailed goals were included in the annex to the communication on the Coordinated Plan on AI. The annex indicates actions which were to be taken in 2019–2020 and prepared the ground for activities in the following years.
153 See n 125.
154 See n 128.

private sector actors intends to progressively increase AI use in public interest areas such as healthcare, transport, security, education, nature protection and energy. Further on it is envisaged to use the AI technologies in other areas such as manufacturing services, including e.g. financial services.

The more detailed analysis of the Coordinated Plan on AI allows stressing the most important regulatory priorities which shall define the European approach towards AI. The listed priorities cover:

- Boosting investments in AI technologies and applications to achieve reinforced excellence and trustworthiness through the ethical and secure by design approach.
- Assuring stability of regulatory environment for investments which will support experimentation and disruptive innovation in view of the wide use of AI by the European society.
- Developing and implementing industry-academia partnerships within research, development and innovation area.
- Adapting disseminating and learning programmes to prepare society for future AI deployments.
- Supporting the transformation of public administrations to make them frontrunners in the use of AI deploying systems.
- Promoting comprehensible ethical and respectful of fundamental rights guidelines for AI with a view to becoming a world leader in ethical, trusted AI and a setter of global ethical standards.
- Reviewing the existing legal frameworks at all levels to better adapt them to specific AI-related challenges.[155]

Finally, as it is mentioned above, the Commission stressed the necessity to adopt a common set of ethical guidelines which would ensure trustworthy, value-based and human-centred development of AI technologies. The task to complete these guidelines was entrusted to the High-Level Expert Group on AI (HLEG AI) (see paragraph 3.4 below). The Coordinated plan on AI together with its annex were to be implemented by the member states while drafting their national strategies on AI and also at the EU level, by its co-legislators (European Parliament and Council), who were invited to progress with the on-going legislative processes and include the AI-related policies in the context of the new multi-annual financial framework for 2021–2027.

In the discussed Coordinated plan for AI, there are two horizontal areas in which regulatory measures are particularly vital—setting ethical standards and assuring sound rules on safety and liability. In both cases in the policy-making processes, the European Commission decided to use knowledge and experience of experts who are members of specialised expert groups—already mentioned High-Level Expert Group on AI, which delivered Ethics Guidelines for Trustworthy AI[156] and the

---

155 Commission, COM(2018) 795 final (annex) (n 3) 1–3.
156 HLEG AI, 'Ethics Guidelines for Trustworthy AI' (n 134).

Expert Group on Liability and New Technologies—New Technologies Formation.[157] The latter group provides assistance to the European Commission in drawing up the guidance in developing principles that can be used for regulation of applicable laws at EU and national levels. The result of the Expert Group on Liability and New Technologies work is the report — Liability for Artificial Intelligence and other emerging digital technologies.[158]

The Commission's response to the work of abovementioned expert groups consisted in two documents — the communication — Building Trust in Human-Centric Artificial Intelligence[159] and the report on the safety and liability implication of AI, the Internet of Things and robotics.[160] In the first communication the Commission welcomed the ethical guidelines drafted by the HLEG AI and stressed its legal character as non-binding. Yet, the Commission treats the document as an important source of ethical rules and framework addressed to all stakeholders involved in building, developing and using AI technologies. Two paradigms have been particularly strongly underlined within this document — trust and human-centricity. The trustworthy AI is the one which puts human always in the centre of the technological progress and respects axiological foundations which correspond with the EU values rooted in human rights and freedoms.

In the report on the safety and liability implications of AI, the Internet of Things and robotics, the European Commission focused on key issues identified by the expert groups and other stakeholders and provided an evaluation of existing rules and provisions in this area (mostly the Machinery Directive[161] and the Product Liability Directive[162]), at the same time commencing the process of broader consultation.

It is worth mentioning that apart from the mainstream policy activities focusing primarily on Artificial Intelligence, the European Commission has not limited itself to this area only. It also ambitiously set up other expert groups which deal with more specific issues which connect to some extent to the AI-related regulatory areas. The first example is the Expert Group for the Observatory of the Online Platform Economy, which is exploring policy issues in

---

157 Expert Group on Liability and New Technologies was set up in March 2018 and is operating in two formations: the Product Liability Directive formation and the New Technologies formation.

158 See (n 7).

159 Commission, COM (2019) 168 final (n 6).

160 Commission, COM(2020) 64 final (n 138).

161 Directive 2006/42/EC of the European Parliament and of the Council of 17 May 2006 on machinery, and amending Directive 95/16/EC (recast) (2006) OJ L157/24.

162 Council Directive 85/374/EEC of 25 July 1985 on the approximation of the laws, regulations and administrative provisions of the Member States concerning liability for defective products (1985) OJ L210/29.

data access,[163] online advertising and the role of AI in the digital platform economy.[164]

Another expert body is a High-Level Expert Group on the impact of digital transformation on the EU labour markets which in April 2019 delivered the detailed report — The impact of the Digital Transformation on EU Labour Markets, which contains an analysis of current trends in the labour market, their implications, challenges and policy recommendations.[165]

With the appointment of the new Commission for the term of 2019–2024, the set of new priorities was announced.[166] One of them — 'a Europe fit for the digital age' — includes regulation of AI. In February 2020, the European Commission presented the new strategy for digital transformation — Shaping Europe's Digital Future.[167] In this document, once more it has been stressed that the technological development in the EU must be done the 'European way'. Digital solutions must correspond to European social model, European values and rules. The Commission has confirmed the digital transformation as a process evolving around key European features like openness, fairness, diversity, democracy and confidence. By building the digital world based on them, the EU will be setting trends and standards in this field globally. There are three main areas of the Commission's actions — technology which works for the benefit for people, competitive and fair economy and open, democratic and sustainable society. The Artificial Intelligence regulation was clearly included in the strategy with the White Paper on AI presented at the same time.[168] AI technologies and their regulation must be built on trust and should be grounded in fundamental rights and values, in particular the human dignity and privacy protection. The Commission has looked at AI from two perspectives — primarily from an individual one, observed from the perspective of the given citizen, whose rights should be protected and enhanced by the development of new algorithmic technologies. Another perspective is a collective one, of the society taken as a whole — here one may not only find good use of AI technologies for e-government but also for policies of sustainable development, with the European Green Deal whose goals may be attained with the use of AI.[169] The keyword

163 Nestor Duch-Brown, Bertin Martens, Frank Mueller-Langer, 'The Economics of Ownership, Access and Trade in Digital Data. Joint Research Centre Digital Economy Working Paper 2017-01' (European Union 2017) https://ec.europa.eu/jrc/en/publication/eur-scientific-and-technical-research-reports/economics-ownership-access-and-trade-digital-data accessed 22 July 2020.

164 See, https://ec.europa.eu/digital-single-market/en/eu-observatory-online-platform-economy accessed 20 July 2020.

165 See (n 102).

166 Commission, 'Commission Work Programme 2020' (Communication) COM(2020) 37 final.

167 See, https://ec.europa.eu/info/strategy/priorities-2019–2024/europe-fit-digital-age/shaping-europe-digital-future_en accessed 22 Julty 2020.

168 Commission, 'White Paper on Artificial Intelligence – A European Approach to Excellence and Trust' COM(2020)65 final.

169 Ibid 2.

used and repeated throughout the whole White Paper is trust. And the regulatory approach towards AI in Europe should intend to create the 'ecosystem of trust'. It means legal certainty, transparency, high ethical standards putting human always in the centre of the attention. An ecosystem of trust is a concept intended to work for the benefit of citizens, for companies and public entities and is supposed to be the bedrock of the future regulatory framework for AI. The White Paper marks the beginning of proper legislative works at the EU institutional level and touches upon all the most important aspects of the regulatory approach towards AI. Many of which are further discussed in our book in the following chapters dealing with general ethical standards, non-technical measures of regulation and sectoral and horizontal issues to be regulated.

3.4 High level expert group on AI

The European Commission during its policy making processes uses the support of different expert bodies and groups which are specialised in various aspects of the current regulatory topics.[170] Their role is consultative and they are set up in order to give advice and expertise to the Commission in relations to the preparation of legislative proposals and initiatives, as well as preparation of delegated or implementing acts.[171] The expert group system nowadays constitutes an element of the everyday EU policymaking, in which one can notice a phenomenon of expertisation of governance. Widespread use of expert groups by the European Commission has been meant to channel inputs from different stakeholders, academics and governmental entities.[172] In general, expert groups may be composed of five types of members. Type A members are individuals who act independently in the public interest and are appointed by their personal capacity. Type B members are individuals appointed to represent certain policy views common to given stakeholders' organisations. Type C members represent organisations like companies, associations, universities, NGOs, trade unions, research institutes, law and consulting firms. Type D members are those representing Member States' public authorities (national, regional or local) and Type E members represent other public entities — Union bodies, bodies of international organisations or third countries' authorities.[173] In the field of AI

---

170 More one the role, functions, types and impact of the expert groups in the Commission policy-making processes, Julia Metz, 'Expert Groups in the European Union: A Sui Generis Phenomenon?' (2013) 32 Policy and Society 268–276.
171 Commission Decision of 30 May 2016 establishing horizontal rules on the creation of Commission expert groups, Brussels, C(2016) 3301 final.
172 Eva Krick, Åse Gornitzka, 'The Governance of Expertise Production in the EU Commission's 'High Level Groups'. Tracing Expertisation Tendencies in the Expert Group System' in Mark Bevir, Ryan Phillips (eds.), *Decentring European Governance* (Routledge 2019) 105–106.
173 Commission Decision C(2016) 3301 final (n 171) art. 7.

with such complex regulatory issues covering technical, ethical, legal and social problems, there was a natural need to set up the body, supporting the Commission in its policy making duties relating to the implementation of the EU strategy on AI. The Commission in its strategy communication AI for Europe[174] already indicated at the High-Level Expert Group on AI as an auxiliary body providing necessary scientific, business-oriented and multi-stakeholder support. The members of this expert group were selected following the call for applications and the group started working in June 2018. The experts were nominated[175] based on their personal capacity. They represent academia (science and technology, legal and ethical experts), industry and civil society. The internal organisation of the HLEG AI reflects the tasks which it was mandated with and consists of two working groups. Working group 1 was responsible for drafting and proposing to the Commission AI Ethics Guidelines and Working Group 2 was focused on the Policy and Investment Recommendations. Both documents were delivered, respectively on the 8 April 2019 and on the 26 June 2019. Apart from those two major deliverables, the HLEG AI was mandated with the broader task of being the steering group of the European AI Alliance (see the following paragraph) and by doing so, managing the participatory mechanisms of AI regulations.

It should be noted that the HLEG AI co-operates with another permanent expert group — the European Group on Ethics in Science and New Technologies (EGE). It is an independent advisory body of the President of the Commission which already since 1991 have been assisting the Commission in legislative processes touching upon the ethical aspects of science and new technologies. EGE consists of 15 members appointed by the President of the Commission under the procedure and based on the conditions set in the Commission decision (EU) 2016/835.[176] Members of the EGE are expected to be internationally recognised experts with a sound record of scientific excellence and experience at the European and global level in the fields of law, natural and social sciences, philosophy and ethics. The EGE's advice to the Commission and to co-legislators (European Parliament and Council) towards the promotion of ethical EU policymaking takes the form of written opinions or statements which to date related to *inter alia* the EU food law, biomedical, bioethical and bio-technological aspects of the EU legislation.[177] Currently, the EGE is focusing on the topics of gene editing, artificial intelligence and the future of work, which

---

174 Commission COM(2018) 237 final (n 2).
175 At the beginning there were 52 members, currently there are 50. See, https://ec.europa. eu/digital-single-market/en/high-level-expert-group-artificial-intelligence accessed 22 July 2020.
176 Commission Decision (EU) 2016/835 of 25 May 2016 on the renewal of the mandate of the European Group on Ethics in Science and New Technologies, OJ L 140/21.
177 See more on the role of the EGE in the law-making process, Helen Busby, Tamara K. Hervey, Alison Mohr, 'Ethical EU law? The Influence of the European Group on Ethics in Science and New Technologies' (2008) 33 European Law Review 806–811.

makes it a natural partner for the HLEG AI. In March 2018 the EGE published its Statement on Artificial Intelligence, Robotics and 'Autonomous' Systems,[178] which was intended to be the basis for the reflection of HLEG AI while drafting its Ethical Guidelines.[179] The cooperation with two groups is also assured by the fact that one of the members of the EGE shall attend the meetings of the HLEG AI. While such close cooperation shall be assessed positively, since the coherent European vision of ethics within AI is crucial for sound regulation, there may be a problem with the true legitimacy of those groups and possible competition between the two. The legitimacy issue brings us to the common and on-going debate of 'the democratic deficit' of EU decision-making policies.[180] The constitutional status of the EGE is not very sound, since it does not have a proper legal basis in the Treaties, yet its impact on the legislative processes is undeniable.[181] The HLEG AI being part of the expert groups system managed by the Commission, may also raise concerns about the transparency of its works and the influence of the business lobbyist on HLEG's AI deliverables. The mitigating factor to those concerns is a balanced composition of the HLEG AI where there are not many disparities between the number of experts representing companies and those representing academia. However, there was an open critique raised by the EGE regarding works on the EU ethical framework on AI. On the 29 January 2019, two months before the delivery of the EU Ethics Guidelines by the HLEG AI, the EGE published a statement in which it expressed its concerns about the shortcomings of the processes leading to the adoption of EU Ethics Guidelines.[182] Even if the HLEG AI was not mentioned by its name, it was obvious that the remarks were addressed mostly to it. The first concern raised by the EGE related to a primacy given to technological progress versus ethical and social values. The EGE stressed that a human-centric AI shall be the one which priority human dignity and not merely a human wellbeing. Human dignity paradigm links the ethical standards with the fundamental rights which are at the heart of the European values. The EGE also noticed the problem of confusing legal obligations with voluntary commitments of the addressees of proposed guidelines, which may provoke the sensation that the risks are just partial and the compliance with the guidelines may not be properly enforced and monitored. Moreover, the critique concerned the composition of the HLEG AI and the fact that there was a need to properly balance the different voices of interest and expertise since such a body would be empowered with a rather fundamental task of deciding what would be good and ethical to the societies. Another element

---

178 The European Group on Ethics in Science and New Technologies, 'Statement on Artificial Intelligence' (n 136).
179 HLEG AI, 'Ethics Guidelines for Trustorthy AI' (n 134) 4.
180 Dorian Jano, 'Understanding the 'EU Democratic Deficit': A Two Dimension Concept on a Three Level-of-Analysis' (2008) 14 Politikon IAPSS Journal of Political Science 1.
181 See, Busby, Hervey, Mohr (n 177) 842.
182 See, https://ec.europa.eu/info/sites/info/files/research_and_innovation/ege/ege_ai_letter_2019.pdf accessed 22 July 2020.

which was questionable was the short timeline — from the constitution of the HLEG AI until the delivery of the Ethic guidelines only 10 months were to pass. Such a short period for preparing such a vital, universal and future-shaping document might have raised doubts about the profoundness of the reflection which may be detrimental to the credibility of the document and legitimacy of the whole process. The EGE called for more reflected approach, engaging societal stakeholders in more meaningful deliberation and dialogue, which the EGE itself saw as a facilitator of.

The abovementioned letter, on one hand, showed the symptom of the competition between the two bodies, with the EGE feeling to be left on the margin of the mainstream works on ethical guidelines. On the other hand, the concerns raised were accurate and consequently were duly taken into consideration while progressing with the works of the EU ethical framework for AI.

3.5 Participatory democracy in the field of AI on European level (European AI Alliance)

Given the scale of the challenges associated with transformations, AI is bringing in every sphere of societal life, the full mobilisation of various participants. Among these, there are businesses, consumer organisations, trade unions, and other representatives of civil society bodies. The EU facilitates therefore the creation of a broad multi-stakeholder platform, the European AI Alliance, to work on all aspects of AI. The European Commission also facilitates interactions of the Alliance with the European Parliament, member states, the European Economic and Social Committee, the Committee of the Regions as well as international organisations. AI may play a key role in facilitating participatory democracy. The Alliance can help to direct, channel and structure this role.

It is intended to be a space for sharing best practices, encourage private investments and activities related to the development of AI. It will involve all relevant stakeholders to gather input, exchange views, develop and implement common measures to encourage the development and use of AI.[183] It is also meant to be a vehicle to collect views and demands in relation to wider societal expectations thus creating an additional channel of participatory influence on decision-makers in particular in relation to deployment of new technology.

Yet, it is another instrument of two-directional communication of society with regulators. It assures the consolidation of EU institutions within their policies and decisions making process. The adopted approach is aimed at the more systematic monitoring and periodic ex-post evaluation of regulatory measures giving chance for stakeholders' consultations at the same time. This type of consultation system of the EU institutions should be adapted in particular in the AI age. Important ethical questions should be asked within this process. Broad consultation of civil society should be deployed within this process. In this

---

183 Commission, COM(2018)237 final (n 2) 18–19.

context, the European AI Alliance is further developed and relied on as an important channel.

The role of it as a medium to institutionalise a dialogue on AI policy with affected stakeholders would be to define red lines and discuss AI applications that may generate risks of unacceptable harms. Eventually, it should also point out applications that should be prohibited or tightly regulated or in specific situations where the risk for people's rights and freedoms would be too high and the impact of this technology would be unfavourable to individuals or society as a whole.[184] If the future is to be built in non-negotiable values as democracy, the rule of law and fundamental human rights, the AI systems should be deployed to continuously improve and defend the democratic culture and enable an environment where innovation and responsible competitiveness can thrive.[185]

The major concerns for the participatory debate should be the use of AI systems in situations relating to the democratic processes. This includes opinion-formation, political decision-making or electoral contexts.[186] Moreover, AI's social impact should be considered.

184 HLEG AI, 'Policy and Investment Recommendations' (n 5) 41.
185 Roger Brownsword, *Law, Technology and Society. Re-imagining the Regulatory Environment* (Routledge 2019) 116.
186 Floridi (n 38) 181

4 Values first – ethic guidelines for trustworthy AI as a bedrock of regulatory approach

4.1 Opening remarks

All efforts relating to the regulation of AI are steered by the socio-political processes, which intend to respond to the question where we are right now and where we want to be in the future with digital technologies. The fact that they are developing very rapidly is undeniable. The new, innovative technologies are mostly driven by the private sector, where corporate needs and resources fuel R&D. It is a private business, sometimes together with academia, that is shaping the societal applications and perceptions towards AI. The biggest tech companies (Amazon, Apple, DeepMind, Google, Facebook, IBM and Microsoft) in 2016 formed the Partnership on AI to Benefit People and Society (now Partnership on AI), which goal is to shape best practices, research and public dialogue about AI. Right now, the Partnership on AI counts more than 100 partners including companies (tech, telecom, consulting, media), academia institutions (universities, research institutes), NGOs or UN's organisations.[187] However valid and important is the input of such multi-stakeholder bodies, leaving the task to regulate AI (also from an ethical point of view) solely to private, non-governmental entities, which lack proper legitimacy and political accountability, could be considered as doubtful and dangerous for the democratic processes, values and fundamental rights. Thus, there is a pressing need, not only in Europe, to create a 'good AI society', which is designed by the multi-stakeholder—governmental and non-governmental—effort taking holistic approach built upon certain universal and sound foundations.[188]

Within the European Union, as was indicated above, it was decided to commence the true legislative process around AI from setting firm ethical standards. Such a choice is prompted by the fact that the laws and regulations in the time of fast progressing technological development, many times, if not always, are reactive to reality.[189] The regulation is usually a mere response to existing social

---

187 See, https://www.partnershiponai.org/partners/ accessed 22 July 2020.
188 Corinne Cath et al., 'Artificial Intelligence and the 'Good Society': The US, EU, and UK Approach, Science and Engineering Ethics' (2017) 24 Science and Engineering Ethics 507–508; Turner (n 25) 209–210.
189 Kris Broekaert, Victoria A. Espinel, *How Can Policy Keep Pace with the Fourth Industrial*

phenomena. Having this in mind, it is needed to turn to the notions which are universal, long-lasting, flexible in the sense of its endured applicability. Ethics embedded in values being central for the European project is a natural bedrock upon which horizontal and sectoral regulations in the field of AI should be built. There are three most important focal points of ethical standards-setting for AI. These are human centricity, the ethics by design approach and trust as a major condition for socially and legally acceptable AI. Each of them is discussed below.

4.2 Humancentric AI

Human centricity is a point of departure for ethical AI. It is thus necessary to reflect on the content of this notion, its practical importance and the ways it may be achieved.

The human centricity of AI can be defined as a concept that places human-being at the centre of any reflection about the Artificial Intelligence, its development, features and use. The human-centred approach is nowadays omnipresent in business, design and marketing. It is in natural opposition to technology-centred approach, where systems have priority in the design process and human operators or users are considered only at its final stages. There is a belief in such an approach that machines are superior in its technological excellence and the role of an individual is merely passive in the sense that one can only follow and operate technological devices.[190] The human-centred approach comes as an alternative, placing individual human being, his needs and preferences at the heart of design, marketing and business strategies. It intends to improve user experience and satisfaction by conducting design thinking processes using participatory or empathic mechanisms.[191] Such an understanding of human-centricity, however valid for design concepts nowadays, shall be considered as a rather technical and tool-oriented feature. Once the human-centricity is discussed from the viewpoint of the ethical or regulatory perspective towards AI, a more universal and value-based position should be adopted. In this sense, the AI technologies should not be a goal for themselves, but they should always have a subordinate position versus humans—their freedom, needs, wellbeing and integrity. Human centricity should not just reflect human needs met by new technologies, but it should also be the concept which can guarantee the safeguard of individuals' rights and increase of human well-being. Human-centricity should guarantee that humans enjoy a supreme and unique moral status in the civil, political, social and economic sense. It should thus work as a shield against tech industries' attempts to maximise their

---

Revolution https://www.weforum.org/agenda/2018/02/can-policy-keep-pace-with-fourth-industrial-revolution/ accessed 22 July 2020.
190 T. Hancke, C.B. Besant, M. Ristic, T.M. Husband, 'Human-centred Technology' (1990) 23 IFAC Proceedings Volumes, 59–60; Susan Gasson, 'Human-centered vs. User-centered Approaches to Information System Design' (2003) 5 The Journal of Information Technology Theory and Application 31–32.
191 Beever, McDaniel, Stamlick (n 13) 108.

profits by abusing certain fundamental rights and values like privacy, free will, dignity or even human life.

Human-centricity not only implies attention to individuals but also to the well-being of society at large and the environment that humans live in.[192] In fact, it should be noted that human-centric AI is strongly connected to fundamental rights and requires collective approach grounded in societal and constitutional rules in which individual freedom and respect for human dignity is meaningful and does not merely focus on purely individualistic account of the human. Thus, human-centricity should be taken into account in particular when proceeding with labour market transformations impacted by the diffusion of AI systems, which should not disrupt negatively workplace, adequate social protection, collective representation rules and other social benefits which are offered to European employees. Also, value-based human-centricity should be pursued in e-government and e-democracy. This is one of the most vulnerable sectors where the technology should be serving civic society, allowing for trustworthy participation in political processes and respect of democracy and the rule of law.[193] The question of human-centricity here starts with the accessibility of the AI-based digital public services. The good governance and right to a good administration should be assured by making the e-public services optional and not obligatory for citizens, who due to the digital illiteracy or economic situation might not be able to use advanced technological tools. Human-centricity, in this sense, should reflect the principles of non-discrimination and equality of citizens and should respect the necessity of inclusiveness of citizens in the political and administrative processes.[194]

From a regulatory perspective, assuring human-centricity may take different forms. In the vast majority of cases, it would necessitate some efforts taken at the early designing stages to follow the 'ethics in design' paradigm (see paragraph below) in order to comply with the respect of the fundamental ethical values and rights. The difficulty with this approach stems from the fact that assuring human centricity would depend on algorithm developing entities, whose rights may be protected by trade secret rules or intellectual property rights.[195] Even if there are ethical guidelines or at some point also binding legislation regulating the proper development and use of AI algorithms, the true challenge starts with the assurance of compliance and control over adopted rules and safeguard mechanisms driven by transparency and explainability.

192 HLEG AI, 'Policy and Investment Recommendations' (n 5) 9. See also, Mark O. Riedl, 'Human-centered Artificial Intelligence and Machine Learning' (2018) 33 Human Behaviour and Emerging Technologies 34. The author links humancentricity with the need for the AI systems to be capable of producing explanations that non-expert users can understand- thus explainability is one of the components of the human-centred approach.
193 Brownsword (n 185) 112.
194 HLEG AI, 'Policy and Investment Recommendations' (n 5) 9.
195 Cubert, Bone (n 86) 415.

A regulatory approach towards humancentric AI may consist in adopting the policy, legislative and investment incentives of deployment of AI-based technologies, which are beneficial for humans. Such an approach can promote automation of some dangerous tasks and jobs which put humans at risk. Responsibly developed AI technologies may increase the health and safety standards and reduce exposure of humans to work-related accidents, harmful substances or difficult environmental conditions. Paradoxically, the human-centricity in this sense would mean the primacy of technology which could lead to the replacement of humans by machines and would stress the value of automation based on AI.[196]

Human-centricity may also result in taking very restrictive measures, limiting or even prohibiting the development and deployment of, particularly perilous technologies applied in some sensitive industries. One of the examples of such an approach is an attempt to regulate the production and use of lethal autonomous weapon systems, which are understood as 'a weapon systems without meaningful human control over the critical functions of selecting and attacking individual targets'.[197] Currently there is a global debate taking place whether this kind of weapons shall be merely regulated or prohibited. The more detailed analysis of the problem will be developed in paragraph 7.2.5 of this book.

One of the most important legal and ethical problems touching upon the paradigm of the human-centricity is the legal personhood of AI. This is a question that has been largely debated in academia, considering different aspects of the establishment of legal personality for AI systems (including robots).[198] Once an entity possesses legal personhood, it has rights and obligations prescribed by law which signifies the ability to know and execute its rights as a legal agent and is subject to legal sanctions.[199] The concept of legal personhood when applied to natural persons is determined by fundamental assumptions regarding understanding human beings as sentient, conscious and rational agents. The legal personhood of legal entities (business entities like corporations, foundations) is dictated by the necessity to recognise their power and legal status to perform economic acts and to have legal credibility.[200] The most recent debate around legal personhood of AI autonomous systems was triggered by the resolution of

---

196 HLEG AI, 'Policy and Investment Recommendations' (n 5) 9.
197 See, European Parliament, 'Resolution of 12 September 2018 on Autonomous Weapon Systems' (2018/2752(RSP), OJ C433/86.
198 Turner (n 25) 173–205; S.M. Solaiman, 'Legal Personality of Robots, Corporations, Idols and Chimpanzees: A Quest for Legitimacy' (2017) 25 Artificial Intelligence Law 155; Joanna J. Bryson, Mihailis E. Diamantis, Thomas D. Grant, 'Of, for, and by the People: The Legal Lacuna of Synthetic Persons' (2017) 25 Artificial Intelligence Law 273; Ugo Pagallo, 'Apples, Oranges, Robots: Four Misunderstandings in Today's Debate on the Legal Status of AI Systems' (2018) Philosophical Transactions Royal Society A 376; Gunther Teubner, 'Digital Personhood? The Status of Autonomous Software Agents in Private Law' (2018) Ancilla Iuris, https://www.anci.ch/articles/Ancilla2018_Teubner_35.pdf accessed 25 May 2020.
199 Solaiman (n 198) 157–158.
200 Robert van den Hoven van Genderen, 'Do We Need Legal Personhood in the Age of

the European Parliament adopted in 2017 on civil law rules on robotics.[201] The European Parliament addressed to the Commission the recommendation to create a specific legal status for robots, by granting to at least the most sophisticated autonomous robots the status of electronic persons liable for damages they may cause, and possibly applying electronic personality to robots which make autonomous decisions or interact with third parties independently.[202] The academia's response to this document focuses mostly on the necessity of managing existing and future gaps in responsibility and avoiding situations in which it would be difficult to determine liability for damages caused by the autonomous systems.[203] Gunther Teubner points at the dynamics of digitalisation, which are constantly creating 'responsible-free' spaces.[204] He notices the insufficient character of existing legal conceptual instruments and tools, which do not fully respond to changing and progressing reality. The author is critical towards idea of granting full legal personhood to digital entities and proposes more nuanced approach build upon the distinction of three types of new digital risks that need to be accommodated by the private law. Namely autonomy risk, association risk and network risk. Only for the first category of risk, it could be adequate to grant autonomous software agents the partial legal personhood, which would result in giving rise to their liability as legally capable assistants to companies.[205] Association risk and network risk would need to create new solutions, building legal subjectivity of members of the human-machine association or searching for it through elements of a risk pool.[206]

Theoretically, there are different considerations for accepting the autonomous legal status of AI, drawing inspirations from the particular legal status of children, who lack certain rights and obligations enjoyed by adults or from company law and corporate legal personality, whose scope nowadays is extensive enough for corporations to own property, conclude contracts or to be held liable.[207] In this sense, it is possible to accept the concept of grounding AI legal personality solely on its obligations, rather than rights. Apart from abovementioned accountability gap which may be one of the reasons to consider the AI legal personhood, there are also other justifications related to the distribution of the works of AI creativity or promotion and enhancement of innovation and economic growth.[208] The

---

Robots and AI' in Marcelo Corrales, Mark Fenwick, Nikolaus Forgó (eds.), *Robotics AI and the Future of Law* (Springer 2018) 20–21.
201 See (n 144).
202 European Parliament' resolution on civil law rules on robotics (ibid), § 59 (f).
203 van den Hoven van Genderen, 'Legal Personhood in the Age of Artificially Intelligent Robots' (n 11) 217.
204 Teubner (n 198) 38.
205 See also, Zech (n 32) 195.
206 Teubner (n 198) 77–78.
207 Ryan Abbott, Alex F. Sarch, 'Punishing Artificial Intelligence: Legal Fiction or Science Fiction' (2019) 53 UC Davis Law Review 1, 376.
208 Turner (n 25) 185–188.

possibility of transposing the idea of 'limited liability' to the AI-based systems and granting them such a limited legal personality could work as a firewall between individual AI engineers and designers and the AI systems designed by them, which may cause harms. It could be particularly valid in case of the systems featured with a high level of independence in decision-making.[209] Notwithstanding the general logic of limited liability, one should remember about the 'piercing of corporate veil' principle, which could be transposed to 'digital persons' and allowing for pursuing claims not against a 'digital person' itself but against the natural or legal person behind it.[210]

Despite stated reasons justifying the acceptance of some level of legal personality for AI systems, there is a strong and predominant criticism at the European level towards this idea. Such criticism is deeply rooted exactly in a human-centric approach and the concern for maintaining the law's coherence and capacity to defend natural persons.[211] The controversy over discussed problem has driven AI and robotics experts, industry leaders, lawyers, medical and ethics experts to draft an open letter to the European Commission expressing great concern about the abovementioned European Parliament's resolution.[212] The open letter raises valid points against granting AI-driven technologies proper legal status.[213] Firstly, such a status of robots may not be derived from the natural person model, since machines or data-driven algorithms may not be granted fundamental rights (ex. dignity), right to citizenship or social rights (ex. right to remuneration and fair working conditions). Also, it may not be grounded in the legal entity model, nor in an Anglo-Saxon trust model which presumes the human factor behind the representation and responsibility of the management of robots.

The negative approach towards establishing a legal personality for AI was also articulated in two major policy documents, which most likely will influence the EU regulatory approach towards this problem. Firstly, the HLEG AI, in its Policy and Investment recommendations, in general terms, has clearly advised policy makers to refrain from establishing legal personhood for AI systems or robots.[214] The reasons for such a position were dictated by the concerns about the respect of principles of human agency, accountability and responsibility together with the concerns of infliction of serious moral hazard.[215]

---

209 Ibid.
210 Expert Group on Liability and New Technologies – New Technologies Formation, 'Liability for Artificial Intelligence and Other Emerging Digital Technologies' (n 7) 38.
211 Bryson, Diamantis, Grant (n 198), Solaiman (n 198) 176–177.
212 See, http://www.robotics-openletter.eu/ accessed 22 July 2020.
213 The open letter uses as synonymous notions of 'electronic person', 'autonomous', 'unpredictable' and 'self-learning' robots.
214 HLEG AI, 'Policy and Investment Recommendations for Trustworthy AI' (n 5) 41.
215 Comande (n 53) 167.

In the same line, the Expert Group on Liability and New Technologies—New Technologies Formation, in its report 'Liability for Artificial Intelligence and other emerging digital technologies',[216] stated that there should be no need to give autonomous systems a legal personality, since granting it could raise a number of ethical issues. The arguments presented in the report were focused solely on the issue of civil liability and did not develop the company law aspects of AI technologies, like the possibility to admit an AI to act as a member of a board. Experts believed that harm caused by even fully autonomous technologies could be reducible to risks attributable to natural persons or existing categories of legal persons. Thus, from a purely practical perspective, there should be no pressing need nowadays to pursue revolutionary legal concepts, raising serious ethical concerns.

4.3 Ethics by design

Ethics by design is a key concept in the European approach towards AI, where ethical and legal rules shaping trustworthy and humancentric algorithmic society are implemented already at the outset of the design process. The concept 'by design' is not a novel one and is universally used as a standard for safeguarding privacy and data protection. Privacy by design is one of the major elements of the data protection system, confirmed by the GDPR.[217] It promotes proactive and preventive approach consisting in the adoption of appropriate procedures and data protection standards at the moment when the means for data processing are being determined and designed and then throughout the stages of the data processing itself, assuring full lifecycle protection.[218] Translation of such an approach to the AI-related technologies imposes on developers, designers and engineers the main responsibility of assuring the compliance with ethical and legal standards set by legislators or regulators. Similarly to privacy in design principle, ethics should be embedded into the design and treated as a default setting. In the case of AI technologies, ethics by design principle is particularly burdensome and difficult to be met. It is associated with methods and algorithms design which is needed to provide autonomous digital agents (AI algorithmic solutions or embodied AI (robots)) with the capability to make ethical decisions which correspond to humancentric standards and ethical, moral and legal rules pertinent to the society. The ethics by design in AI for it to be truly implemented needs a mental and strategic shift among researchers, developers and corporations from ensuring a better performance to ensuring the trust of developed technologies.[219] Looking at this principle from the regulatory perspective, we

---

216 See (n 7)
217 See art. 25 GDPR.
218 Ann Covoukian, 'Privacy by Design. The 7 Foundational Principles. Implementation and Mapping of Fair Information Practices' https://iapp.org/media/pdf/resource_center/pbd_implement_7found_principles.pdf accessed 22 July 2020.
219 Virginia Dignum et al., 'Ethics by Design: Necessity or Curse?' (2018) AIES Proceedings of the 2018 AAAI/AM Conference o AI, Ethics, and Society, 6.

shall stress that European approach towards ethical and trustworthy AI is currently based either on existing legislation on fundamental rights, consumer protection, product safety and liability rules or on still non-binding Ethical Guidelines for Trustworthy AI.[220] Thus, ethics by design as a rule imposed on developers and deployers of AI, if there is no coherent, solid and binding European regulatory framework, may encounter difficulties to be fully enforced. At present, there is a fragmentation in the internal market, with just a few member states (Germany, Denmark or Malta) already adopting some solutions regarding ethical AI.[221] Such a situation in a natural way calls for the EU-wide horizontal approach, which was stressed by the Commission in its White Paper on AI.[222] Legislative process, at the time of writing these words, officially has not been launched yet, however, in April 2020 the European Parliament published a draft report with recommendations addressed to the Commission, which contains the proposal of the regulation on ethical principles for the development, deployment and use of AI, robotics and related technologies.[223] Even if these are recommendations by the European Parliament, which the Commission is not bound with, they are worth mentioning, since they reflect the current state of European legislative debate around AI. Regardless of the scope of possible amendments introduced during the proper ordinary legislative procedure, proposed provisions represent the general logic of the future regulation. Recommended provisions are built around the most important principles which stress human-centricity, risk assessment, safety and security, trust, transparency, non-bias and non-discrimination, social responsibility, gender balance, environmental protection, sustainability, privacy, good governance. Those principles are believed to be followed by the developers, deployers and users and their compliance shall be enforced by national AI supervisory authorities together with the European Agency for AI, which are to be established respectively in every member state and at EU level. Adoption of binding legislation setting common ethical standards together with assuring compliance mechanisms shall strengthen the successful application of the 'ethics by design' principle.

4.4 Foundations of trustworthy AI

4.4.1 Opening remarks – why trust matters

The trust is a prerequisite to ensure a human-centric approach to AI. There is a widespread conviction that trust in AI may only be achieved by fairness, accountability, transparency and regulation.[224] For the new technologies to be

---

220 Amato (n 75) 81.
221 Commission, COM(2020)65 final (n 168) 10.
222 Ibid.
223 See (n 35).
224 European Parliamentary Research Service, Scientific Foresight Unit (STOA), 'The Ethics of Artificial Intelligence: Issues and Initiatives', PE 634.452 March 2020, 29.

trusted, they need to be trustworthy. The notion of trust, being multidisciplinary and multifaceted, in the most general terms presupposes that one party is accepting and is willing to rely on the actions of the second party. The trust may have different aspects and may exist in various social contexts. It may be perceived either as a particular personal feature of an individual, but it can also be seen as a conviction applied towards social structures and behavioural intention.[225] The multidisciplinary character of trust consists of the fact that it is of interest to psychology, management and communications, sociology, economics or political science.[226] For law and regulatory systems, the object of trust are not people, but institutions and social structures. Such an institution-based trust means that individuals believe, with the sense of security that there are favourable and assuring conditions put in place which protect individuals' lives. The trust in this sense focuses on an impersonal object rather than on interpersonal relations. Trust to technology, devices, machines, Internet solutions is just another aspect of such an institution-based trust. To achieve trust, the trustworthiness of new technologies, including AI, should be ensured. People nowadays show acceptance towards the use of robots and AI technologies in sectors which cause some difficulty to human capabilities. At the same time, due to the natural lack of empathy and emotions on the side of AI-driven devices, people tend to have reservations towards their use in education, healthcare, care for children of disabled.[227] The biggest challenge is to identify the ways in which AI technologies may be developed across industries with the due respect to values close to each democratic society. It is a matter of effectiveness of new technologies, but also a matter of proper functioning of social, political and economic structures, which rely on them.

Since trust is a precondition for ensuring a people-centred approach to AI, the most important premise of the AI regulatory environment is the belief that AI should not be an objective in itself, but a mechanism to serve people, with the eventual aim of improving human well-being.

It is believed that trustworthiness may be achieved by building a strong legal, ethical and value-based environment around AI. The values and principles which are pertinent to our modern, democratic societies shall be fully integrated into the design, development, deployment and use of AI. Evidently, building trust is an extremely difficult and long-lasting process. AI-based technologies which use machine learning and reasoning mechanisms, being capable of taking decisions without human intervention, raise several issues which can undermine trust. Soon this type of functionality will become standard in many types of goods and

---

225 D.Harrison Mcknight, Norman L. Chervany, 'Trust and Distrust Definitions: One Bite at a Time' in R. Falcone, M. Singh, Y.H. Tan (eds.), *Trust in Cyber-societies: Integrating the Human and Artificial Perspectives* (Springer 2001) 28.

226 Ibid. See also, J. Patrick Woolley, 'Trust and Justice in Big Data Analytics: Bringing the Philosophical Literature on Trust to Bear on the Ethics of Consent' (2019) 32 Philosophy and Technology 111–134.

227 Special Eurobarometer 382, 'Public Attitudes Towards Robots' (2012) 32–37.

services, from smartphones to automated cars, robots and online applications. Nevertheless, decisions made by algorithms can result from data that is incomplete and therefore not very reliable, cyber attackers can manipulate them, or they can be biased or simply wrong. An unreflective application of the technology during its development would therefore lead to problematic results and to a reluctance on the part of citizens to accept or use it. These issues direct the ethical and regulatory reflection towards transparency, explainability, the use of biased, incomplete or manipulated data, which is the driving force of AI. The European policy making bodies noticed the problem of trust towards AI. The initial works, predating the proper legislative procedures, are focusing on the assurance of trustworthy AI. HLEG AI, in Ethics Guidelines, together with the European Commission in its White Paper on AI,[228] intend to create the ecosystem of trust which would build the needed acceptance of citizens towards technologies surrounding them. Without trustworthy technologies, the possible progress would be hindered and its socio-economic benefits might be merely contingent and limited. As the Ethics Guidelines state, the trust towards AI does not only concern the technology's inherent properties, but also broader, holistic social systems, actors and processes which relies on AI applications. The elements of this systems cover individuals, governments, corporations, but also infrastructure, software, protocols, standards, governance and oversight mechanisms, existing legislation, incentive structures, auditing procedures, best practices reporting and others.[229] In order to achieve trust, the focus should not only be put on the technical aspects of systems used but also stressed is the need to build diversity in terms of gender, racial or ethnic origin, religion or belief, disability and age at every stage of AI development. AI applications should empower citizens and respect their fundamental rights. They should aim to enhance people's abilities, not replace them, and also enable access by people with disabilities.[230]

The Ethics Guidelines postulate the development of three major components of trustworthy AI. It should be legal, ethical and robust. Trying to determine the understanding of trustworthiness is difficult. The task of translating it into the language of law and regulation seems even more complicated. Nevertheless, it was decided to make such an attempt by creating a definition of the trustworthiness of systems based on artificial intelligence by listing their specific features and criteria. These three components (legal, ethical and robust) are the framework for the seven key requirements for determination of trustworthy AI. These include human agency and oversight; technical robustness and safety; privacy and data governance; transparency; diversity, non-discrimination and fairness; societal and environmental well-being and accountability. These requirements are intended to apply to all AI systems regardless of the settings and

---

228 HLEG AI, 'Ethics Guidelines for Trustworthy AI' (n 134); Commission, COM(2020) 65 final (n 168).
229 HLEG AI, 'Ethics Guidelines for Trustworthy AI' (n 134) 4.
230 Commission, COM(2019)168 final, (n 6) 1-2.

industries. Yet, the modalities of application of those requirements shall be sector-specific, proportionate and shall reflect and be dependent on the impact of AI technologies on human lives. The more dangerous and impactful are the technologies, the stricter application of requirements shall be.[231] Although the guidelines drafted by the HLEG AI are non-binding and formally do not create new legal obligations, much of the already existing EU legislation reflect these requirements.[232]

The full effectiveness of those components can only be assured once they work together and overlap in their operation. The trustworthy AI approach is intended to promote responsible and sustainable AI innovation in EU, which would guarantee that AI systems from the moment of their design, through development and use are lawful, ethical and robust. AI, according to the European approach, should be worthy of individual and collective trust.

A trustworthy approach assuring that AI systems' design, development and use are lawful, ethical and robust are key to unlock responsible competitiveness. The EU guidelines intended to foster responsible AI innovation in Europe, seek to make ethics a core pillar for developing a unique approach to AI. All this in view of enabling benefit, empowerment and protection of individual and common societal good. Ensuring trustworthiness of AI systems will secure the confidence that appropriate measures are in place to safeguard against their potential risks. As impacts of the use of AI systems do not stop at national borders, neither do their impact. Global regulatory measures are therefore required to secure trustworthiness of AI systems as regards opportunities and challenges they bring forth. Despite how idealistically this sound, all stakeholders should, therefore, be encouraged to work towards a global framework for trustworthy AI. This should be built on international consensus while upholding fundamental rights-based approach.[233]

4.4.2 Lawful AI – fundamental rights and beyond

The law and ethics are intertwined one with another. In the field of AI, this connection is of particular importance, since ethics is considered to be the bedrock of any regulatory measures. It is understood that compliance with the law is merely necessary, but insufficient; thus, the ethical approach to AI provides extra advantage.[234] Yet, one should remember, that even though to some extent ethics and law are in certain relation one to another, in the theory of law those two notions are separate and exclusive. Even though the law and ethics provide

---

231 Ibid.
232 Ibid 3–4.
233 HLEG AI, 'Ethics Guidelines for Trustworthy AI' (n 134) 4–5.
234 Luciano Floridi et al., 'AI4 People – An Ethical Framework for a Good Society: Opportunities, Risks, Principles and Recommendations' (2018) 28 Minds and Machines 694–695.

both positive and negative obligations, it is possible that norms may be at the same time ethical but illegal, legal but unethical, ethical and legal and illegal and unethical.[235] An addressee of legal and ethical norms are either bound to act in a given manner or to refrain from taking a particular action. Norms of positive character may indicate the preferred behaviour or may categorically imply the necessary action. In the case of AI technologies, the compliance with the law and legally binding obligations falls under the first condition of trustworthy AI and is essential for building so much demanded ecosystem of trust.

At the European level, the adoption of AI-oriented set of horizontal binding legal acts is expected within the next following months (2021–2022). The lack of a particular legislative framework designed for the AI industry does not mean that algorithmic technologies escape regulation. AI systems operate within the existing regulatory framework which is governed by the multilevel legal system in which there is already a number of binding rules adopted at international, European and national level. International law framework is rather general and relies on the UN Human Rights treaties[236] and Council of Europe conventions with the most important one—European Convention on Human Rights.[237] At the fora of both abovementioned organisations, the works are taking place which focus on AI's ethical dimension and its implication on fundamental rights. In August 2018, at the UN General Assembly Special Rapporteur for the promotion and protection of the right to freedom of opinion and expression, submitted its report relating to the human rights legal framework for artificial intelligence.[238] The document explores the potential impact of AI on the rights to freedom of opinion and expression and contains recommendations addressed both to states and companies. Recommendations focus on the regulatory measures to cover public and private sector engagement in design, deployment and use of AI technologies and to connect it in an efficient way with human rights principles and ethics. Interestingly the Special Rapporteur stressed the relation between fundamental rights and ethics, giving priority to the former. He stated that 'human rights law provides the fundamental rules for the protection of

---

235 See, Guido Noto La Diega, 'The Artificial Conscience of Lethal Autonomous Weapons: Marketing Ruse or Reality' (2018) 1 Law and the Digital Age, 3. Author in a concise way recalls Hans Kelsen's separation theory, Hans Kelsen, *General Theory of Law and State* (A. Wedberg tr., Harvard University Press, 1945) 363, 410–411.

236 Ex. International Bill of Rights, International Covenant on Civil and Political Rights, International Covenant on Economic, Social and Cultural Rights, International Convention on the Elimination of All Forms of Racial Discrimination, Convention on the Elimination of All Forms of Discrimination against Women, Convention on the Rights od the Child, see https://www.ohchr.org/EN/ProfessionalInterest/Pages/UniversalHumanRightsInstruments.aspx accessed 22 July 2020.

237 See, https://www.echr.coe.int/Documents/Convention_ENG.pdf accessed 22 July 2020.

238 Report of the Special Rapporteur, 'Promotion and protection of the right to freedom of opinion and expression', A/73/348, see https://freedex.org/wp-content/blogs.dir/2015/files/2018/10/AI-and-FOE-GA.pdf accessed 22 July 2020.

individuals in the context of AI, while ethics frameworks may assist in further developing the content and application of human rights in specific circumstances[239].

The Council of Europe's engagement in AI regulation consists of various policy and analytical documents, governing the general impact of human rights on the algorithmic system,[240] together with the ones touching upon more specific aspects of AI legality, like non-discrimination in AI and Algorithmic Decision-Making,[241] bioethics and new technologies,[242] children's rights on the Internet,[243] culture,[244] democratic processes with standards for e-voting[245] and European Electoral Performance Index, education, freedom of expression and diversified cultural offer,[246] fight against crime, including cybercrime,[247] gender equality[248] and justice[249] and data protection which at the Council of Europe's level is regulated by the modernised Convention for the protection of individuals with regards to the processing of personal data.[250]

Internationally adopted instruments regulating human rights are addressed to states which are obliged to facilitate their implementation in the private sector. It is necessary that AI developed in this sector shall meet the same standards as the one in the public sector. Nowadays, there is also a strong conviction that private corporations are expected to assure compliance and respect for human rights. The UN Guiding Principles on Business and

239 Ibid.
240 Recommendation CM/Rec(2020)1 of the Committee of Ministers to member states on the human rights impacts of algorithmic society (Council of Europe 2020).
241 Frederik Zuiderveen Borgesius, *Discrimination, Artificial Intelligence, and Algorithmic Decision-Making* (Council of Europe 2018) 1–51.
242 Rapporteur Report, '20th Anniversary of the Oviedo Convention', Strasbourg 2017 https://rm.coe.int/oviedo-conference-rapporteur-report-e/168078295c accessed 22 July 2020.
243 Guidelines to respect, protect and fulfil the rights of the child in the digital environment, Recommendation CM/Rec(2018)7 of the Committee of Ministers (Council of Europe 2018).
244 E-relevance of Culture in the Age of AI, Expert Seminar on Culture, Creativity and Artificial Intelligence, 12-13 October 2018, Rijeka, Croatia https://www.coe.int/en/web/culture-and-heritage/-/e-relevance-of-culture-in-the-age-of-ai accessed 22 July 2020.
245 Recommendation CM/Rec(2017)5 of the Committee of Ministers to member States on standards for e-voting (Council of Europe 2017).
246 Entering the new paradigm of AI and Series Executive Summary (2019) December, https://rm.coe.int/eurimages-executive-summary-051219/1680995332 accessed 22 July 2020.
247 See, https://www.coe.int/en/web/cybercrime/resources-octopus-2018 accessed 22 July 2020.
248 See, https://www.coe.int/en/web/artificial-intelligence/-/artificial-intelligence-and-gender-equality accessed 22 July 2020.
249 European Commission for the Efficiency of Justice (CEPEJ), *European Ethical Charter on the Use of AI in Judicial Systems and Their Environment*(Council of Europe 2019).
250 CM/Indf(2018)15-final, 18 May 2018.

Human Rights[251] together with the Council of Europe Recommendation on human rights and business[252] provide in this sense, the obligation for member states to apply necessary measures which require business enterprises in general, but also the ones involved in design, development, deployment and use of AI, to apply human rights due diligence through ought their operations.

Developers, deployers and users of AI technologies who operate in the European Union fall under the scope of the system of the EU law, which is directly applicable and consists of primary and secondary law. The former covers founding treaties (the Treaty on EU and the Treaty on the functioning of EU[253]) and the Charter of Fundamental Rights of the European Union.[254] Crucial for legal and ethical AI is compliance with legally binding rights guaranteed by the EU Treaties and the EU Charter. It also shows the complexity and multifaceted character of the regulatory environment. Fundamental rights which are enshrined nowadays in legally binding acts of international, European and national origin, impose obligations on states, but to some extent also on developers, deployers or users of AI technologies, which shall make those technologies lawful, hence meeting the first component of trustworthy AI. At the same time, fundamental rights, due to their strong axiological load, can be understood as reflecting moral, universal entitlements of all individuals, regardless of their legally binding status. Thus, compliance with fundamental rights may also form part of the second component of trustworthy AI—ethical AI.[255] On the top of it, once the EU institutions adopt the regulation on a framework of ethical aspects of AI[256] ethics will become part of a legally binding, directly applicable and effective legal act. Thus, the interconnection between law and ethics in the field of AI will become even stronger, since ethical rules will have the status of legal rules.

The EU Treaties and the EU Charter provide a comprehensive system of fundamental rights protection at the EU level, which relies on art. 6 TEU, confirming that the EU Charter has the same legal value as the treaties (art. 6.1 TEU) and that the fundamental rights as guaranteed by the European Convention of Human Rights and resulting from common constitutional traditions of all member states constitute general principles of the EU law (art. 6.2 TEU). Apart from the protection of fundamental rights, axiological foundations

---

251 UN Guiding Principles on Business and Human Rights. Implementing the UN 'Protect, Respect and Remedy' Framework (2011) https://www.ohchr.org/documents/publications/guidingprinciplesbusinesshr_en.pdf accessed 22 July 2020.
252 Human rights and business, Recommendation CM/Rec(2016)3 of the Committee of Ministers to member states (Council of Europe 2016). See also, in relation to AI, 'Unboxing Artificial Intelligence: 10 steps to protect Human Rights', Recommendation by the Council of Europe Commissioner for Human Rights (Council of Europe 2019) 9.
253 Consolidated versions of the Treaties (2012) OJ C326/13.
254 Charter of Fundamental Rights of the EU (2012) OJ C326/391.
255 HLEG AI 'Ethics Guidelines for Trustworthy AI' (n 134) 10.
256 See (n 35).

of the EU legal system rely on values stated in art. 2 TEU, namely human dignity, freedom, democracy, equality and the rule of law. The bundle of the abovementioned values provides the most important guidance for identifying universal and abstract ethical principles and values, which shall be taken into consideration while building trustworthy and human-centric AI.

When discussing the specificity of fundamental rights protection at the EU level, we shall state that the EU Charter's field of application is limited to areas of the EU law. Thus, the more comprehensive protection is guaranteed by the European Convention on Human Rights, which covers areas that fall outside the scope of the EU law. Once the Charter contains rights which correspond to the ones enshrined in the Convention, their scope and meaning shall be the same as laid down by the Convention and interpreted by the European Court of Human Rights. Another interpretative reference relates to the constitutional traditions common to member states—once Charter recognises rights resulting from such traditions, their meaning shall be harmonious with them.[257]

As is mentioned in the Ethics Guidelines for Trustworthy AI, among the set of fundamental rights covered by international human rights law, the EU Treaties and the EU Charter, one can identify the group of fundamental rights, which have particular importance for the development, deployment and use of AI systems. It is worth mentioning that ethical reflection which accompanies the enforcement of fundamental rights by AI sector may give rise to a more insightful view on existing and future challenges of constantly developing technology. AI systems can, at the same time, empower and obstruct fundamental rights. In situations where there are serious risks of the negative impact of AI on fundamental rights, the proper assessment mechanisms should be undertaken. Already at the design and development stages, there should be an *ex ante* assessment evaluating if the risks are serious and whether they could be mitigated of justified. Also, fundamental rights assessment shall encompass the possibility of external feedback regarding AI systems' compliance with fundamental rights.[258] Such a feedback could be delivered by the regulators of the AI sector operating either on national or supranational (ex the EU) levels.

The core of the AI-related fundamental rights, which in particular necessitate proper risk assessment, encompasses the respect of human dignity, freedom of the individual, respect for democracy, justice and the rule of law, equality, non-discrimination and solidarity and citizens' rights.[259]

The respect of human dignity strongly linked with the abovementioned human-centric approach towards AI is a crucial value of European integration

---

257 See art. 52.3. and 4 of the Charter.
258 HLEG AI, 'Ethics Guidelines for Trustworthy AI' (n 134) 15–16. See also, 'Algorithms and Human Rights. Study on the human rights dimensions of automated data processing techniques and possible regulatory implications' (Council of Europe study DGI[2017] 12) 40.
259 HLEG AI, 'Ethics Guidelines for Trustworthy AI' (n 134) 9–11.

and holds the central place in the constitutional traditions of all member states. The contemporary European attachment to the respect of human dignity is marked with the historical context of the World Word II and the then collapse of the humanistic values which had been building the European socio-cultural heritage.[260] Nowadays, human dignity faces new challenges dictated by the development of new technologies, yet the general meaning of this principle remains intact—every human being possesses an 'intrinsic value', which should never be undermined or repressed by others—be it individuals, public or private institutions or new, algorithmic technologies.[261] The respect of human dignity presupposes that people are moral subjects and as such deserve to be treated with respect. Human dignity may thus oppose such AI systems which manipulate, segregate, threaten or expose humans to danger. Thus, in reference to 'ethics by design' principle AI systems shall be developed and designed in a way that protects humans—their physical and mental health but also a cultural sense of identity.[262] The respect for human dignity is strongly connected with the principle of freedom of the individual. Every human being is free to make decisions regarding his life. Individual freedom assumes that those decisions are free from manipulation, are taken in a conscious way in a process which is exempt from threats and intimidation. The threats which AI technologies bring to this principle concern the problem of self-determination. Issues of hidden nudging,[263] AI-based profiling using personal data, an obscurity of algorithms may limit the freedom of choice of individuals. The discussed freedom is a foundation of other rights and freedoms which include freedom to conduct a business, the freedom of the arts and science, freedom of expression, the right to private life and privacy, and freedom of assembly and association.[264] Human dignity and individual freedom are also strongly connected to the principles of equality, non-discrimination and solidarity. Those principles in an AI context shall guarantee that the system's operations cannot generate unfairly biased outputs. This means that the data fed to AI systems should be as inclusive as possible, respecting potentially vulnerable groups like workers, women, persons with disabilities, ethnic minorities, children, consumers or others at risk of exclusion.[265]

260 Paweł Łuków, 'A Difficult Legacy: Human Dignity as the Founding Value of Human Rights' (2018) 19 Human Rights Review 314–315.
261 Christopher McCrudden, 'Human Dignity and Judicial Interpretation of Human Rights' (2008) 19 European Journal of International Law 655–724; Laura Valentini, 'Dignity and Human Rights: A Reconceptualisation' (2017) Oxford 37 Journal of Legal Studies 862–885.
262 Eric Hilgendorf, 'Problem Areas in the Dignity Debate and the Ensemble Theory of Human Dignity' in Dieter Grimm, Alexandra Kemmerer, Christoph Möllers (eds.), *Human Dignity in Context. Explorations of a Contested Concept* (Hart Publishing, Nomos 2018) 325 ff.
263 See, Yeung (n 12).
264 HLEG AI, 'Ethics Guidelines for Trustworthy AI' (n 134) 9–11.
265 Ibid.

Another bedrock principle refers to the constitutional law's respect for democracy, justice and the rule of law and citizens' rights. The law shall authorise all governmental powers and shall set democratic standards based on the equality, checks and balances and independence of justice. The relationship between technology and democracy is particularly tense nowadays. With a growing number of AI-powered systems used in democratic processes, there is a pressing need for assuring that AI technologies, many times resting in the hands of just a few global internet corporations (like Microsoft, Facebook, Google, Twitter, Amazon or Apple) are being used to foster democracy and its processes, rather than to undermine it. The influence of these corporations consists of the provision of AI-based systems building information society. The services of social media platforms are nowadays one of the major tools used in political and electoral campaigns. They are the source of knowledge for voters, platforms for deliberation, tools enabling participatory mechanisms. As P. Nemitz indicates, the cumulation of power in the hands of just a few is visible through their financial power, the power over infrastructures for democracy and discourse, the power over individuals exercised through profiling and personal data collection and finally the power expressed through the fact that the biggest corporations are the centres of AI innovation.[266] The AI-related challenges to democratic mechanisms, on the one hand, consist of the omnipresence of social media and its impact on electoral processes. On the other hand, the ever-growing use of e-government tools and algorithmic decision-making mechanisms used in the public sector towards citizens also necessitate regulated environment, where explainability is a crucial condition. The exercise of citizens' rights like the right to vote, the right to good administration, access to public documents, and the right to petition the administration may be enhanced by AI systems which may improve the efficiency of government in the provision of public goods and services to society. Yet the regulation, sound legal provisions should shield the democratic processes and citizens from AI-based intrusion, through another variation of 'by design' concept. 'Rule of law by design' shall be assured in order to build trust for AI. Also, there is a need for setting up methods of validation if the government's decisions using AI technologies were opaque and biased against individuals and that rely on data-driven systems were biased against individuals compared to other similar decisions, given that access to one's own personal data is not enough to ensure the analysis of fair and just decisions that are in accordance with legal standards.

Apart from the EU primary law, which as was explained above, is more horizontal and value and fundamental rights-oriented, the AI industry operating in the EU shall follow the rules of the EU secondary law. Even if the proper AI-oriented secondary legislation hasn't been adopted yet, there is already a substantial set of the EU regulations and directives touching upon different aspects of the AI industry. Thus, the EU has a strong regulatory framework that

---

266 Nemmitz (n 3) 7.

will set the global standard for human-centric AI. These include the General Data Protection Regulation,[267] which ensures a high standard of protection of personal data and requires the implementation of measures to ensure data protection by design and by default. The Regulation on the free flow of Non-Personal Data[268] removes barriers to the free movement of non-personal data and ensures the processing of all categories of data anywhere in Europe. The recently adopted Cybersecurity Act will help to strengthen trust in the online world, and the proposed ePrivacy Regulation[269] also aims at this goal. Apart from privacy and cybersecurity regulation, there are: Product Liability Directive,[270] anti-discrimination Directives,[271] consumer law[272] and Safety and Health at Work Directive.[273]

4.4.3 Ethical principles

The trustworthiness of AI requires not only compliance with the law. It is less so because, as we have already pointed, laws are not always reacting to technological developments on time. Legal norms sometimes are blind to changing the ethical sensitivity of societies or simply they are not rightly suited to addressing certain issues. For AI systems to be trustworthy, means they should, most of all, be ethical. This translates into being in line with ethical norms.[274] To begin with, it is worth to remind that AI ethics is a sub-field of applied or descriptive ethics. It focuses on ethical issues raised by the development, deployment and use of AI. It refers to the question of how AI can advance or raise concerns to the good life of individuals also if it can enhance the quality of life or human autonomy and freedom necessary for a democratic society.

Ethical reflection on the digital transformation of AI can serve multiple purposes. Firstly, it can stimulate reflection on the need to protect individuals and groups at the most basic level. Secondly, it can stimulate new kinds of innovations that seek to foster ethical values, such as those helping to achieve the UN Sustainable Development Goals.[275] Those are firmly embedded in the EU Agenda 2030.[276] If the descriptive ethics' ultimate goal is to refer to a postulate of determining what is good, or rather to differ what is good from what is not,

---

267 See (n 125).
268 See (n 128)
269 COM(2017) 10. See also (n 131).
270 See, (n 162)
271 See, paragraph 6.2.1 below
272 See, paragraph 6.2.2 below
273 Council Directive 89/391/EEC of 12 June 1989 on the introduction of measures to encourage improvements in the safety and health of workers at work (1989) OJ L183/1.
274 HLEG AI, 'Ethics Guidelines for Trustworthy AI' (n 134).
275 See, https://www.un.org/sustainabledevelopment/sustainable-development-goals/ accessed 22 July 2020; Commission, 'Reflection Paper. Towards a Sustainable Europe by 2030' COM(2019)22.
276 See, https://ec.europa.eu/environment/sustainable-development/SDGs/index_en.htm accessed 22 July 2020.

trustworthy, i.e. ethical AI can contribute to improving individual flourishing and the societal common good. It can support generating prosperity, value creation and sustainable wealth growth. It can help to achieve a fair and just society, by helping to increase citizens' health and wellbeing and by fostering equality in the distribution of economic, cultural, educational, social and political opportunities.[277]

It is therefore imperative to understand how the direct AI development, deployment and use can contribute to building better lives. The use of AI systems, like any other powerful technology, raises ethical challenges. Those relate to their impact on individual and collective decision-making capabilities and even potentially their safety. Inevitable future delegating of decisions to AI systems will impact people's lives. Still, the humankind should assure they do not delegate control over them so they are aligned with values that should never be compromised and that they are able to act accordingly. Separately, suitable accountability processes should be assured as well. The EU, as much as the rest of the world, is confronted with the need for a normative vision of an AI-immersed future it wants to realise. Furthermore, it has to understand which notion of AI needs to be studied, developed, deployed and used in Europe to achieve that a vision.

A domain-specific ethics code—however consistent, developed and fine-grained may be—can never function as a substitute for ethical reasoning itself, which must always remain sensitive to contextual details that cannot be captured in general Guidelines. Beyond developing a set of rules, ensuring Trustworthy AI requires us to build and maintain an ethical culture and mind-set through public debate, education and practical learning.[278]

Multiple organisations have grounded their models of desired ethical frameworks for AI systems on fundamental rights.[279] For example, the European Group on Ethics in Science and New Technologies proposed a set of principles, based on the fundamental values enumerated in the EU Treaties and Charter.[280] These ethical principles could be useful in designing specific regulatory instruments that despite the evolving technical parameters of changing technologies can help to interpret fundamental rights and guide the rationales for them. Recently, the AI4People's group has surveyed several ethical frameworks adopted at different fora[281] and tried to find some level of coherence between them, by grouping various sets of ethical principles into four major categories, commonly used in bioethics: beneficence, non-maleficence, autonomy and justice.[282] Under the umbrella of beneficence fall more detailed principles of

---

277 Geslevich Packin, Lev-Aretz (n 31) 106.
278 HLEG AI, 'Ethics Guidelines for Trustworthy AI' (n 134) 9.
279 Reliance on fundamental rights also helps to limit regulatory uncertainty as it can build on the basis of decades of practice of fundamental rights protection in the EU, thereby offering clarity, readability and foreseeability.
280 See (n 253 and 254).
281 See (n 136).
282 Floridi et al. (n 234) 695–699.

protection of well-being, preserving dignity and sustaining the Planet. Non-maleficence translates into the protection of privacy, security, 'capability caution' and prevention of harm.[283] Autonomy gives individuals the power to decide and justice, which is usually invoked in reference to the distribution of resources, aims at promotion of prosperity and solidarity.[284]

At the EU level, Ethical guidelines distinguish four principles of ethical AI, which are: respect for human autonomy, prevention of harm, fairness and explicability. These are exemplary ethical principles, rooted in fundamental rights which have to be taken into account and that must be respected in order to ensure that AI systems are trustworthy. Furthermore, if seriously thinking on trustworthy, thus ethical AI, these imperatives should be agreed and assured by AI practitioners to adhere to them. The principles listed above represent some of the fundamental rights as they appear in the EU Charter. Respect for human autonomy is linked to the right to human dignity and liberty (Art. 1 and 6 of the Charter). The prevention of harm is connected to the protection of physical or mental integrity (Art. 3). Fairness is closely linked to principles of non-discrimination, solidarity and justice (Art. 21 and). Finally, explicability is closely linked to the rights relating to justice (Art. 47). As we can see, to a large extent discussed ethical principles are reflected in existing legal requirements and hence also fall within the scope of the first component of Trustworthy AI which is lawfulness. However, even though many legal obligations reflect ethical principles, alignment to ethical principles goes beyond just formal compliance with laws.[285]

If looked at the principle of autonomy of human beings as one of the fundamental rights of the EU, respect for the freedom of people should be observed in every form.[286] Humans must be able to keep full and effective self-determination over themselves and be able to control AI systems so that this as ultimately assured. AI systems must never be able to subordinate, coerce, deceive, manipulate, condition or herd humans. In contrary, they should augment, complement and empower individual and collective human cognitive, social and cultural capacities as well as human centricity and human choice. As AI systems will fundamentally change the labour sphere, securing human oversight over work processes is necessary in assuring ethical AI systems. The requirement of human agency and oversight will be developed in paragraph 4.5.2 below.

Another ethical principle is the assurance that AI systems should never be a cause and exacerbation of harm, which can come in different forms. Harms can be individual or collective and can include harm to social, cultural and political environments. AI systems should not adversely affect human beings, individually, but also different social groups. More specifically, it should entail the protection

---

283 Brownsword (n 185) 306.
284 Ibid.
285 See, more on this topic, Luciano Floridi, 'Soft Ethics and the Governance of the Digital' (2018) 31 Philosophy & Technology 1–8.
286 Burri (n 129) 549.

of human dignity and mental and physical integrity. In order to assure it, AI systems must be safe and secure, technically robust and not open to malicious use. Preventing harm also entails respect for the natural environment and all living beings. Particular attention should be paid in this respect to situations where AI systems can cause or exacerbate adverse impacts caused by asymmetries of power of information. Specifically, it refers to relations between governments and citizens, businesses and consumers and employers and employees.

The AI systems fairness refers to both a substantive and a procedural dimension. The substantive dimension of fairness implies a commitment to equal and just treatment ensuring that individuals and groups are not biased discrimination and stigmatised. The fair AI should foster equal opportunity in access to education, goods, services and technology. Also, fairness means that AI systems should be in line with the principle of proportionality between costs and benefits, means and ends, and consider carefully how to balance competing interests and objectives. Measures taken to achieve an end should be limited to what is strictly necessary. It also entails that when several measures can be used to achieve the same goal, preference should be given to the one which is less harmful to fundamental rights and ethical norms (e.g. AI developers should always prefer public sector data to personal data). Proportionality may also refer to the relation between user and deployer in a way that there should be a balance between the rights of companies (including intellectual property and trade secrets) on the one hand, and the rights of the user on the other.[287]

The procedural dimension of fairness entails the ability to block, contest, protect and seek redress against decisions made by AI systems and by the humans operating them in case that principle is not respected. Those remedies can be enforced through the collective rights of association and to join a trade union in a working environment.[288] Anybody, individually, collectively and institutionally accountable for the decision should therefore be identifiable as well as their decision-making processes should be traceable and explicable.

Explicability means that AI-related processes need to be transparent, their capabilities and purposes communicated, and decisions explainable. It is crucial for building trust in AI systems by those that are affected by them. Sometimes an explanation of why a model has generated a particular output, and what combination of factors contributed to that, may not be possible. These so-called, black-box algorithms require special attention.[289] In their cases other explicability measures may be required. Examples of them are traceability, auditability and transparent communication on system capabilities.[290]

---

287 Gerald Spindler, 'User Liability and Strict Liability in the Internet of Things and for Robots' in Sebastian Lohsse, Reiner Schulze, Dirk Staudenmayer (eds.), *Liability for Artificial Intelligence and the Internet of Things. Muenster Colloquia on EU Law and the Digital Economy IV* (Hart Publishing, Nomos 2019) 131.
288 See, art. 12 of the EU Charter.
289 Pasquale (n 45) 191.
290 The degree to which explicability is needed is highly dependent on the context and the

In case of tensions that may arise between the ethical principles, the EU fundamental commitment to democratic mechanisms, free and open participation of individuals and societies into the political processes as well as clear accountability methods should serve as a help. Also, the advantages of AI systems should always exceed the foreseeable risks. If AI practitioners are not able to find the right solution based on the principles above, they should approach ethical dilemmas and trade-offs via evidence-based and rationalized reflection and not by intuition or random discretion.

While bringing substantial benefits to individuals and society, AI systems also pose certain risks and may have a difficult to anticipate, identify or measure negative impact. Therefore, adequate and proportional, procedural and technical measures should be a prerequisite to mitigate these risks.[291]

4.4.4 Robust

Even though it is ensured that the AI systems are aligned with the universally expressed expectation that they are designed, deployed and used lawfully and ethically, individuals and society must also be confident that due to their imperfections they will not cause harm. Such systems should perform in a safe, secure, predictable and reliable way.[292] The technical and human steered safeguards and controls should be foreseen and built into them to prevent any adverse impacts. In that respect it is important to ensure that AI systems are robust. Robustness is just a general notion to describe a cluster of features that altogether are responsible for technical, functional and operational correctness and reliability of the trustworthy AI systems.[293] This refers to a technical aspect. From the technical perspective robustness is to ensure the systems are appropriate in a given context, application domain or life cycle phase. Computer science research focuses on the guarantees of robustness. They include verification, validity, security and control. Verification cover methods which yield high confidence that systems follow formal constraints. Validity, closely linked with verification, allows to ensure that system which meets the formal constraints, does not produce unwanted outcomes. Security focuses on the prevention of intentional manipulation by unauthorised entities and control allows for meaningful human control over AI system once it is deployed.[294]

---

severity of the consequences if that output is erroneous or otherwise inaccurate. For example, little ethical concern may flow from inaccurate shopping recommendations generated by an AI system, in contrast to AI systems that evaluate whether an individual convicted of a criminal offence should be released on parole.

291 HLEG AI, 'Ethics Guidelines for Trustworthy AI' (n 134) 11–14.
292 Cubert, Bone (n 86) 418.
293 Geslevich Packin, Lev-Aretz (n 31) 91.
294 Stuart Russel, Daniel Dewey, Max Tegmark, 'Research Priorities for Robust and Beneficial Artificial Intelligence' (2015) 36 AI Magazine 107–108.

From the social perspective, the robustness of AI systems is considered in the context and environment in which it operates. Robustness of AI systems is therefore closely connected and complement to their coherence with ethics.[295]

4.5 Implementing trustworthy AI

4.5.1 Opening remarks

Setting up even the most comprehensive legal, ethical and technical framework intended to assure trust of AI technologies is not enough. Trust can be truly achieved once such a framework is properly implemented, accepted and internalised by relevant stakeholders. As stated in paragraph 4.4.1, the major conditions of trustworthy AI—lawfulness, ethicality and robustness- are translated into specific requirements. They are thought to be applicable to all entities touched by AI and at all stages of the AI system's life cycles. The stakeholders involved in the process of implementation of the trustworthy AI are: developers (including researchers, designers), deployers (public or private organisations using AI systems technologies within their operations and offering products and services to the public), end-users (individuals who engage with the AI system, directly or indirectly) and the broader society—all others who are directly or indirectly affected by AI systems. Each of these groups have different duties, some have rights. At the initial stage, developers should implement and apply the requirements to design and development processes. They are a crucial element of this chain of stakeholders, responsible for enforcement of ethics by design paradigm. Deployers need to make sure that AI based systems they use and products and services they provide comply with the requirement. Finally, end-users and broader society shall exercise their right to be informed about these requirements and expect that they are duly respected.[296] The most important requirements which refer to: human agency and oversight; technical robustness and safety; privacy and data governance; transparency; diversity, non-discrimination and fairness; societal and environmental well-being and accountability, will be discussed below. When reflecting on their scope and intensity, one should state that their proper relevance will be sector-specific and would depend on the personal scope of application. Once they directly or indirectly affect individuals' rights and integrity, there will be stronger pressure on relevant actors to assure compliance with them.

4.5.2 Human agency and oversight

Human agency and oversight are strongly connected with the idea of human centricity of AI. This requirement is intended to provide control mechanisms over AI systems, so that they assure the wellbeing of the individuals. Human

---

295 HLEG AI, 'Ethics Guidelines for Trustworthy AI' (n 134) 7.
296 Ibid. 14–15.

agency is related to the autonomy of users. They should be able to make in-formed autonomous decisions regarding AI systems. It presumes a given level of self-awareness of users, their knowledge and digital literacy. Thus, it may be difficult to achieve, given different degrees of accessibility to digital technology. In theory, users should be provided with the knowledge and tools to follow and interact with AI systems, which in return should support users in making better, more informed choices in accordance with their goals.[297] The important concern here is related to the problem of the opacity of AI systems. The question arises how to assure human agency and autonomy when systems many times work in ways that are simply inaccessible and opaque to an average human under-standing? How to reconcile unequal levels of human knowledge which result from various factors, like age, wealth or social and political conditions, with the expectation that AI systems shall be subject to human autonomy? These ques-tions are particularly valid, once we conclude that AI systems influence human actions through Big Data driven decision-making mechanisms. They target in-dividual's choice in personalised ways, using nudging techniques (or hy-pernudging) which result in shaping individual user's understanding and perceptions of the surrounding world.[298] Algorithmic decision-making processes may use sub-conscious processes, including various forms of manipulation, de-ception and omission of important information. The problem with the access to knowledge on how AI driven systems/engines operate, which should be crucial to assure user's autonomy, is also related to the dominance of global corpora-tions standing behind global networked market. The regulatory framework's role is to find the balance between privileged epistocratic holders of advanced tech-nological AI knowledge and unprivileged regular users, whose technological awareness may be weak.[299] One of the human autonomy guarantees should be the rule that once the decision is based only on automated processing, it should not produce adverse legal effects towards affected users.[300]

Another element of the discussed requirement is human oversight. It is closely linked to the human agency yet refers to more specific control measures that should be enforced in order to assure trustworthy AI. When human agency for the reasons stated above may be difficult to achieve, human oversight consists in various measures imposing explainability or adaptability mechanisms. Human oversight may be implemented through design and technical capacities of given system, providing proper governance tools. They depict the relations and in-teractions between humans and algorithmic systems (be it embodied or non-embodied). There are different modalities of such mechanisms, expressing different levels of human review of decisions taken by AI systems. Four major

297 Beever, McDaniel, Stamlick (n 13) 111.
298 Yeung (n 12) 20.
299 John Danaher, 'The Threat of Algocracy: Reality, Resistance and Accommodation' (2016) 29 Philosophy and Technology 255
300 HLEG AI, 'Ethics Guidelines for Trustworthy AI' (n 134) 15–16.

approaches towards human oversight could be distinguished: human-in-command, human-in-the-loop, human-on-the-loop or human-out-of-the-loop. Human-in-command (HIC) approach entails the strongest human oversight and refers to the capability to oversee the overall activity of the AI system. HIC allows for the very broad influence of human, taking into consideration the economic, societal, legal and ethical impact of a system under control. The human intervention may consist of the ability to decide when and how to use the system in any particular situation. This can take various types of decisions, including the limitation of the use of an AI system in a given situation; introduction of human discretion during the use of the system, or assurance of the ability to override a decision made by a system. Human-in-the-loop (HITL) model refers to the approach where there is a strong interaction between humans and AI. Humans are directly involved in training and tuning of data used by the AI system and decision is taken by it only when the human agent requests it or demands it. The system works based on many times manual human control. Once there is a proper human intervention, the additional data is incorporated in the decision-making process and the algorithm is able to perform a particular operation automatically in the future. HITL is a way to assure a better accuracy to algorithmic decision-making. Human-on-the-loop (HOTL) approach supposes human intervention during the design cycle of the system and monitoring the system's operation. HOTL allows system to work autonomously, by constantly sorting and tuning collected data, identifying patterns and proposing given decisions, which could be implemented by humans, who would be able to override it. Finally, human-out-of the-loop (HOOTL) systems would leave all decisions to machines with no possibility of human oversight or override.[301]

The type of applied human oversight mechanisms shall depend on the AI system's application area and potential risk. Some systems make human involvement easier than others. Some data-mining systems are capable of being interpreted and understood by human beings. While some rely on such complex factors which are non-interpretable and too difficult to grasp. For the former, there is a possibility of assuring the oversight mechanisms, which would enable accountability and transparency of the system in question. For the latter, human agency and oversight are limited, which also impacts explainability.[302] The less oversight a human can exercise over an AI system, the more extensive testing and stricter governance is required. Public authorities shall have the power to exercise their oversight in line with their mandates.[303]

301 Commission COM (2019) 168 final (n 6) 4; See also, Danielle Keats Citron, Frank Pasquale, 'The Scored Society: Due Process for Automated Predictions' (2014) 89 Washington Law Review 6–7; Danaher, 'The Threat of Algocracy' (n 299fdopeo9) 248.
302 Tal Z. Zarsky, 'Governmental Data Mining and Its Alternatives' (2011) 116 Penn State Law Review 292–293.
303 HLEG AI, 'Ethics Guidelines for Trustworthy AI' (n 134) 14–15.

4.5.3 *Technical robustness and safety*

Technical robustness and safety are other components of trustworthy AI. Algorithms need to be secure, reliable and as much as it is possible, free from erroneous outcomes. The important technical requirement concerns the resilience from cyber-attacks, hacking and data manipulation.

Attacks may take the form of 'data poisoning', model leakage or may target the software or hardware infrastructure. Under attack, the AI system's data, as well as the system itself, can be changed, leading it to make different decisions, or causing it to shut down. Thus, AI systems should be equipped with fallback plans assuring general safety in case of difficulties. This means that in problematic situations AI systems should not harm individuals nor the environment and that mechanisms of mitigating unintended consequences and errors are put in place. There is hence a need to establish a proper process of risk assessment across various application areas. The level of safety measures should be proportional to the scope of the risk posed by an AI system, which in turn depends on the system's capabilities.[304]

Technical side of AI should also guarantee accuracy, reliability and reproducibility of judgements and decisions taken by the system. It means that data and information upon which algorithm is build should be able to be classified in a proper way and the system should have an ability to make correct predictions, recommendations, or decisions based on data or models. The accuracy is particularly important once the AI system has a direct impact on human lives. Reproducibility and reliability are technical conditions of trust. The system needs to be reliable and work in various situations with a range of inputs. It needs to assure repetitive outcomes, namely it needs to behave in the same way, once operating under the same conditions.

4.5.4 *Privacy and data governance*

Data is a foundation of nowadays economy and is believed to be the most valuable commodity.[305] Data is also the absolute bedrock of the algorithmic society. Without going too much into technical aspects of the discussed topic, AI systems operate based on data, which is processed and applied within them. All individuals who use the Internet, social media provide data describing their behaviours and habits to the algorithmic systems.[306] Owing to it, AI systems may reason and deduce individuals' preferences and depending on the type of system, may influence economic, social, cultural or political choices. Not only amount of data is important to the functioning of a given AI system, but also its quality,

---

304 Ibid 16–17.
305 The Economist, 'The world's Most Valuable Resource Is No Longer Oil, but Data' (2017) https://www.economist.com/leaders/2017/05/06/the-worlds-most-valuable-resource-is-no-longer-oil-but-data accessed 22 July 2020.
306 Floridi, *The 4th Revolution* (n 38) 105.

which impacts systems' performance. The quality of data consists of its legal, unbiased character, free from errors or mistakes, establishing its full integrity. The quality of data needs to be addressed prior to training of AI system with any given data set. Building algorithms upon erroneous and malicious data may distort the system's behaviour. That is why relevant data needs to be tested, reported and documented at all stages of AI systems' lifecycle. Due to expressed reasons, privacy and data protection are crucial requirements for trustworthy AI and shall be guaranteed extensively. All individuals shall have full control over their data and have the conviction that it is not used to harm them in any way. Thus, access to data must be strictly governed.[307] Data protection and its fair use are one of the major expressions of right to privacy. It is a fundamental right, is especially connected to and at the same time affected by AI systems and overall by digital technologies.

In the most general terms, the privacy deserves protection due to the fact that every human being must have the right to the exclusive control of one's life in the spheres that do not relate to others. Privacy is thus a sphere which is free from another peoples' interference.[308] As such, can be opposed to the sphere of public activity. Whatever is kept private, is reserved to oneself. Each human being shall have the power to decide how much and to which extent would like to share with others. Privacy is hence strongly connected to human autonomy. The broad right of privacy covers several components among which one can mention the secrecy of correspondence, personal data protection or the protection of the household. Privacy can be broken down into three elements: the first—relational—relays on the mentioned power of an individual to decide about the scope of information related to him or her to be made public; the second—informative—regards the capacity to control the disclosure of personal and private information and the third—physical—allows for the rationed access to oneself.[309]

Both privacy and data protection are strongly exposed to the digital world. Many times, users of Internet and new technologies are voluntarily, yet not always consciously stripping themselves from privacy by exposing their preferences, lifestyles, intimate details through social media and search engines.[310] The new challenges like for example COVID-19 pandemic—also stresses the privacy—quarantine and contact-tracing applications, however dictated and to some

---

307 HLEG AI, 'Ethics Guidelines for Trustworthy AI' (n 134) 17.
308 Marek Safjan, 'Prawo do ochrony życia prywatnego' in *Szkoła Praw Człowieka* (Helsińska Fundacja Praw Człowieka Warszawa 2006) 211.
309 Renata Dopierała, *Prywatność w perspektywie zmiany społecznej* (Nomos 2013) 20–23. See also, Agata Gonschior, 'Ochrona danych osobowych a prawo do prywatności w Unii Europejskiej' in Dagmara Kornobis-Romanowska (ed.), *Aktualne problemy prawa Unii Europejskiej i prawa międzynarodowego – aspekty teoretyczne i praktyczne* (E-Wydawnictwo. Prawnicza i Ekonomiczna Biblioteka Cyfrowa. Wydział Prawa, Administracji i Ekonomii Uniwersytetu Wrocławskiego 2017) 242–243.
310 Pasquale (n 45) 61.

extent justified by the public health protection, raise at the same time serious concerns of excessive intrusion into privacy.[311]

The discussed requirement which is being one of the building blocks of trustworthy AI is strongly enforced at European level. Right now, the European Union through GDPR and Directive on privacy and electronic communication[312] sets global standards of data protection.[313] More detailed analysis of the European approach towards data protection, providing horizontal regulation, also impacting AI will be delivered in paragraph 6.2.3 below.

4.5.5 Transparency

One of the major concerns and critics of algorithmic society is based on the claim that it operates as a 'black box' society.[314] AI-based systems and solutions involved in decision-making processes are being used in financial sector, judicial systems, political processes. Algorithms make decisions. But these are developers behind them, commissioned by businesses, financial institutions or governmental entities, who know how they are made. End users are faced with obscure and opaque technologies, which are not understandable to them and raise concerns of abuse. The problem here is related to two contradictory spheres—on the one hand, the AI industry is not assuring full transparency of their technologies, hiding behind trades secrets or nondisclosure agreements. On the other hand, it is the individual users whose lives are growingly open. People leave traces of their online presence through cookies, Facebook or Instagram likes, shares and viewed content. We are tracked by the geolocation mechanisms. By doing all this, we provide data to algorithms—the question is to whom the data will be available, for how long, and how it is intended to be used. There is hence a tension—the businesses—they have knowledge from which they draw power and are not eager to share neither one nor another. Individuals—they are subjects of algorithmic decisions, which they don't understand, yet they should know how an algorithm reached given outcome. The lack of understandable explanations hinders trust. So, for the system to be trusted it should be explainable, traceable and transparent. The transparency shall refer to the data used, the system itself and the business models applied. The starting point for the assessment of discussed requirement shall be communicated. Humans shall be aware and duly informed that they are dealing and interacting with AI systems, which must be identifiable.

---

311 See, https://www.europarl.europa.eu/news/en/headlines/society/20200429STO78174/covid-19-tracing-apps-ensuring-privacy-and-data-protection accessed 22 July 2020.
312 Currently there are legislative works taking place intending to replace the directive by the ePrivacy Regulation (see n 131).
313 Paul M. Schwartz, 'Global Data Privacy: The EU Way' (2019) 94 New York University Law Review 771.
314 As Frank Pasquale states in his 'The Black Box Society" (n 45) 3, the term 'black box' is used aa a metaphor to describe a system whose workings are mysterious, where we can observe its inputs and outputs, but we cannot tell how one becomes the other.

Once the AI practitioners and users are informed about dealing with AI systems, there should be strong pressure on their traceability, explainability and transparency. In general, the goals of transparency differ depending on the interests of the given subject—be it developer, deployer, user, the general public or governmental entities. According to Weller, there are eight major types and goals of transparency.[315] Type 1 refers to the developer's intention to understand how their system works—what works fine and what are shortcomings. Type 2, from the user perspective—the goal is to provide a sense on the system operation, which leads to trust in technology. Type 3—for the society—to understand and become comfortable with a given system, overcoming the fear of unknown. Type 4 is for the user's understanding of why particular decision was made and to enable its meaningful challenge. Type 5 of goal provides the expert—regulator the ability to audit given decision which is crucial in terms of determination of accountability and legal liability. Type 6 is intending to facilitate monitoring and testing for safety standards. Type 7 and 8 are beneficiary for deployers and transparency in theses senses intends to make a user comfortable with a decision so he or she continues to use given system and to lead user into some preferred behaviour.[316]

Traceability should be understood as a feature allowing for proper documentation of the used data sets, the applied processes and protocols of algorithmic decision-making. Regulatory bodies established both at the EU and national levels,[317] should be empowered to demand proper records of AI-operations and decisions in order to assure traceability at all the stages.[318] Discussed feature enables identification of the reasons for erroneous AI-decisions, which could be crucial for assuring accountability of relevant entities. As such, it can also have a preventive character helping the avoidance of future mistakes. Traceability facilitates auditability as well as explainability, which concerns the ability to explain technical processes, but also areas of application of given AI systems, which may be related to human decisions.[319] Technical explainability is strongly linked to the understanding of AI mechanisms. To explain it means to provide a statement that makes something clear, that tells how something works and makes something easier to understand.[320] Explainability shall therefore allow for the review of the technical processes of the technologies. As it is pointed in HLEG AI's Ethical Guidelines the discussed requirement may

---

315 Adrian Weller, 'Transparency: Motivations and Challenges' (2019) arXiv:1708.01870v2 accessed 22 July 2020, 2–3.
316 Ibid.
317 See, European Parliament, 2020/2012 (INL) (n 35). One of the aims of the proposed regulation is the establishment of the European Agency for Artificial Intelligence, together with supervisory authorities in each member state which shall be responsible for assuring compliance with ethical principles and for setting standards for the governance of AI.
318 Virginia Dignum et al., 'Ethics by Design' (n 219) 64.
319 HLEG AI, 'Ethics Guidelines for Trustworthy AI' (n 134) 17.
320 See, Oxford Learner's Dictionary https://www.oxfordlearnersdictionaries.com/definition/english/explanation accessed 22 July 202.

be an object of some trade-offs concerning either enhancing of the system' explainability at the cost of its accuracy. More understandable are simpler machine learning systems, based for example, on decision trees or algorithms allowing for visibility of AI systems.[321] On the other hand, explainability may suffer due to increased levels of the system's accuracy.[322] This is particularly problematic for more complex, yet powerful mechanisms used in neural networks.[323]

The hiddenness of AI systems is particularly dangerous once those systems have a significant impact on individuals' lives (ex. by governmental, administrative, judicial decisions). Hiddenness concerns are, of course, strongly linked to data collection and processing. This is recognised and called by John Danaher as one of the 'threats of algocracy'.[324] The term algocracy itself is used by the author to describe the particular type of governance which is organised and structured based on computer-programmed algorithms. It structures and constrains the ways in which humans within those systems interact one with another, the relevant data and the broader community affected by those systems.[325] Whenever someone has to do with algocratic systems it should be possible to demand a suitable explanation of the AI system's decision-making process. In particular, such a requirement is valid for the AI-based governmental decisions producing legal effects or affecting individuals in a significant way. In this case, their addressees shall be able to evaluate and possibly challenge them. To do so, there is a presumption of explainability.[326] Yet, there is a question, whether this requirement is feasible at all. The very possibility and degree of explainability depend on several factors—a type of AI system and the potential knowledge together with the technological literacy of an AI user. The lowest level of explainability is with totally opaque systems. These are the ones where mechanisms mapping inputs and outputs are invisible to users. Such systems rely on genuine 'black box' approach, many times dictated by the licencing agreements. More approachable are interpretable and comprehensible systems. The former consisting of mechanisms where a user can see, verify and understand how inputs are mapped to outputs. Here the preconditions are transparency of a model and certain level of user's understanding of mathematical mapping details. Comprehensible systems emit symbols (like words or visualisations) together with its outputs, which allows users to relate properties of the inputs to their

321 Harry Surden, 'Ethics f AI in Law: Basic Questions' in Forthcoming chapter in *Oxford Handbook of Ethics of AI* (2020) 731 https://ssrn.com/abstract=3441303 accessed 22 July 2020.
322 HLEG AI, 'Ethics Guidelines for Trustworthy AI' (n 134) 17.
323 Ron Schmelzer, 'Understanding Explainable AI' https://www.forbes.com/sites/cognitiveworld/2019/07/23/understanding-explainable-ai/#25a1dc6b7c9e accessed 22 July 2020.
324 Danaher, 'The Threat of Algocracy' (n 299) 249.
325 Ibid 247.
326 HLEG AI, 'Policy and Investment Recommendations for Trustworthy AI' (n 5) 20.

outputs.[327] From the technical point of view the Explainable AI (XAI) currently is becoming an emerging field in machine learning, which would help to address the questions of why AI system make particular decisions; why AI system does not take different ones and what are the errors and how to correct them.[328] Legal and ethical perspective is still full of doubts—the main problem is how to enforce explainability without losing or reducing instrumental gains of AI systems. What would be the corporate reaction to the stricter legal rules imposing explainability as a condition *sine qua non* for admitting AI systems to the market? Also, there are doubts on reviewability and the extent to which AI systems may rely on interpretable processes. Danaher points at the risk of replacing algocracy by the threat of epistocracy.[329] An average user-consumer does not have a background knowledge to understand and review algorithmic processes. Thus, in order to assure explainability, individuals would have to rely on human epistemic elites, who design, programme and engineer AI systems.

4.5.6 Diversity, non-discrimination and fairness

Bias is another buzzword of AI and is related to the problem of fairness and non-discrimination. Bias, understood through its negative connotations, refers to unfair belief or behaviours that one address towards a particular individual or a group.[330] Biased and discriminatory outcomes of AI systems are not hypothetical.[331] They are the nowadays technological reality with various racial or gender AI-based discrimination cases confirmed.[332] The problem of bias of AI systems, in the field of computer science and the industry is approached through the principle of fairness.[333] In this field there are two major concepts: individual and

---

327 Derek Doran, Sarah Schulz, Tarek R. Besold, 'What Does Explainable AI Really Mean? A New Conceptualization Perspectives' (2017) arXiv:1710.00791 accessed 22 July 2020.

328 Schmelzer (n 323).

329 Danaher, 'The Threat of Algocracy' (n 299) 259.

330 Ayanna Howard, Jason Borenstein, 'The Ugly Truth About Ourselves and Our Robot Creations: The Problem of Bias and Social Inequity' (2018) 24 Science and Engineering Ethics 1522.

331 Geslevich Packin, Lev-Aretz (n 31) 88.

332 Several examples of discriminatory AI can be given: facial recognition technologies deployed by the police in the UK, which were discriminatory towards women and certain racial groups, predictive policing algorithms that turned out racist or Google Photos which tagged photos with descriptors and for the black user's photos depicting her and her friend there was tag "gorillas"; See Robin Allen, Dee Masters, 'Artificial Intelligence: the right to protection from discrimination caused by algorithms, machine learning and automated decision-making (2019) ERA Forum https://doi.org/10.1007/s12027-019-00582-w accessed 22 July 2020; Rafhaële Xenidis, Linda Senden, 'EU Non-discrimination Law in the Era of the Artificial Intelligence: Mapping the Challenges of Algorithmic Discrimination' in Ulf Bernitz et al. (eds.), *General Principles of EU law and the EU Digital Order* (Kluwer Law International 2020) 151.

333 See, Solon Barocas, Moritz Hardt, Arvind Narayanan, 'Fairness and Machine Learning. Limitations and Opportunities' https://fairmlbook.org/ accessed 22 July 2020, Catherina

group fairness. The individual fairness occurs once individuals of equal or similar status, receive similar algorithmic output. Group fairness is achieved through statistical parity when the distribution of outcomes is the same for each group.[334] Legal approach focuses more on the non- discrimination, which in EU law plays a particular role, being one of the general principles of the EU law and regulated extensively both in the primary (non-discrimination based on nationality) and in the secondary legislation.[335] Therefore, AI should be developed with due regard to all grounds that are protected from discrimination in the EU law. Fairness and non-discrimination are interrelated. Once the system is fair, based on just, un-biased and integral data, it will not produce discriminatory outco. Fairness is obviously not only a technological issue but is of interest to ethics and in con-sequence to law.[336] Fairness and justice are the crucial notions of applied ethics and play fundamental role in a reflection on ethical decision-making.[337] For both notions, which many times are treated interchangeably, important is the as-sumption that one needs to be treated as one deserves. Fairness is more con-nected to the impartiality and judgments which are made without reference to one's feelings and interests, while justice being connected to rightness of given decisions or judgments. Both intend to assure equality of treatment. And such an equality of treatment shall be crucial for an algorithmic decision as well. The bias of AI systems leading to the breach of fairness leading to unequal treatment/discrimination is related to the data sets used by AI systems and/or codes de-signed to train them in an improper way. There is already quite an extensive scholar reflection on the sources of discrimination of AI systems, which is summarised by Xenidis and Senden.[338] Worth mentioning, due to its clarity, is the taxonomy proposed by Hacker[339] who distinguishes two major causes of bias in algorithms: biased training data and unequal ground truth. Biased training may occur when data is incorrectly handled (ex through incorrect labelling of data or sampling bias, when some social or ethnical groups are misrepresented)

Xu, Tulsee Doshi, 'Fairness Indicators: Scalable Infrastructure for Fair ML Systems' (2019) Google AI Blog https://ai.googleblog.com/2019/12/fairness-indicators-scalable.html accessed 22 July 2020.

334 Philipp Hacker, 'Teaching Fairness to Artificial Intelligence: Existing and Novel Strategies against Algorithmic Discrimination under EU Law (2018) Common Market Law Review 1175.

335 More detailed analysis of the EU non-discrimination law will be provided in Chapter 6 of the present book.

336 Beever, McDaniel, Stamlick (n 13) 137.

337 Manuel Velasquez, Claire Andre, Thomas Shnaks, S.J., Michael J. Meyer, 'Justice and Fairness' https://www.scu.edu/ethics/ethics-resources/ethical-decision-making/justice-and-fairness/ accessed 22 July 2020.

338 Xenidis, Senden (n 332) 154–155.

339 Hacker (n 334) 1146–1150. For a more detailed analysis of bias sources, see Solon Barocas, Andrew D. Selbst, 'Big Data's Disparate Impact' (2016) 104 California Law Review 671.

or is subject to historical discrimination, which perpetuates existing types of bias through self-learning algorithms.[340]

The problem of unequal ground truth bias is linked to the so-called proxy discrimination (or statistical discrimination), which occurs when neutral practice disproportionately harms members of a protected class.[341] The ground truth in machine learning is the best available approximation of reality, which is expressed in empirically observable data. When such a ground truth is not evenly distributed between protected groups and is based on existing stereotypes (ex like the one stating that men drivers have more accidents than women drivers) we face bias.[342] Often, these biases reach algorithmic process unintentionally, by mistake or through subconscious (implicit) human bias.[343]

Once taking a closer look to AI systems and possible biased outcomes produced by them, one may ask a question about the decision-making processes which do not rely on technology but on human actors. Judges deliberating over judicial decisions, bank officers making decisions about loans, police officers running investigations, governmental administrative organs deciding in individual cases impacting citizens. Do they or were they free from bias? Were they always taking fair and just decisions deprived of any stereotyping? The answer is, of course, negative. Humans are subject to different types of conscious or unconscious biases, which may lead to overly favourable or indirectly discriminatory treatment of different societal groups. As Surden indicates, taking an example of decisions taken within justice systems, the legal system itself is also subject, just like AI systems, of particular structural design choices which empower certain groups while hindering the others. Complex legal language, opening hours of courts or other administrative bodies—these are just two examples of such choices which may give privileges to citizens with higher social status (more flexible jobs, better educational background).[344] The important point is that it is extremely difficult to determine whether human-based bias is less dangerous for the reliability of decision than algorithmic bias. The argument claiming that AI systems may improve the consistency of rendered decisions shall be addressed with caution and shall focus on the careful implementation of AI-based systems, with full awareness of their limitations and with the human centricity as a major ethical goal.

From the EU policy making perspective, the fight with algorithmic bias may consist of different forms. Such concerns should be tackled from the beginning of the system' development. From the technical point of view, the very much stressed conditions are the establishment of diverse design teams and setting

340 Hacker (n 334) 1147.
341 Anya E.R. Prince, Daniel Schwarcz, 'Proxy Discrimination in the Age of Artificial Intelligence and Big Data' (2020) 105 Iowa Law Review 1257.
342 Hacker (n 334) 1148, Xenidis, Senden (n 332) 154–155.
343 Hacker (n 334) 1149.
344 Surden (n 321) 729.

mechanisms for stakeholders' participation in AI development.[345] It would be beneficial to demand their regular feedback at all stages of the AI system's lifecycle, to provide necessary information and consultations to those affected directly or indirectly by AI systems.[346]

Thus, inclusion and diversity are the most important elements preventing AI systems from producing discriminatory outcomes. They not only cover designing teams but also should be construed in a way which allows full accessibility of AI systems, regardless of users' age, gender, disabilities or belonging to some minority groups. This is particularly important for the public services using AI and would necessitate an approach based on the universal design covering all needs of different societal groups. In particular, there is a call to establish a European Strategy for Better and Safer AI for Children, in line with the European Strategy for a Better Internet for Children,[347] designed to empower children, while also protecting them from risks and potential harm.

4.5.7 Societal and environmental well-being

Apart from all other factors, if AI is to be regarded as trustworthy, its impact on the environment and other living beings should be taken into account. This means all humans, including current and future generations, should be respectful for and benefit from biodiversity and a habitable environment. Sustainability directed and environmentally responsible AI systems, as another form of human tools, are, therefore, a necessity. This applies specifically to AI solutions addressing global concerns. As a consequence of this, the impact of AI systems should be considered not only from an individual perspective, but also from more general perspectives of societies.[348] In light of the principles of fairness and prevention of harm, the wider humankind natural environment should be considered as stakeholders throughout the AI systems. Sustainability and ecological respect by AI systems should be encouraged. Therefore, the research should be boosted into AI solutions addressing areas of global concern to the benefit all human beings, including the natural environment of future generations. AI systems are tackling some of the most pressing societal concerns, yet it has to be ensured that this occurs in the most environmentally friendly way possible. The entire AI systems supply chain, should be assessed in this regard, through a critical examination of the resource usage and energy consumption, waste limitation and reuse. Measures securing the environmental friendliness of AI systems should be encouraged necessary elements for the Trustworthy AI.

---

345 Commission, COM (2019) 168 final (n 6) 6.
346 HLEG AI, 'Ethics Guidelines for Trustworthy AI' (n 134) 19.
347 Commission, 'European Strategy for a Better Internet for Children' (Communication) COM(2012)0196 final.
348 Commission, COM(2019)168 final (n 6) 6.

Ubiquitous exposure to social AI systems is observed in all areas.[349] It refers to education, culture, labour, care, research and entertainment.[350] The ultimate effects of that may vary the conception of social relationships. As AI systems can be used to enhance social capacities, they can also contribute to their deterioration affecting people's physical and mental wellbeing. The effects of these systems must, therefore, be carefully monitored and considered.

The same refers to societal perspective on AI systems and their impact on institutions, democracy, political choices, execution of power and society at large. Therefore, the use of AI systems should be carefully scrutinised, particularly in situations relating to the democratic process including both political decisions and the electoral contexts.[351]

AI systems are able to provide tools safeguarding the integrity of institutions, the privacy of individuals as well as the environment.[352] They can do it by detecting and proving discrimination, rooting out privacy infringing content or improving the detection of pollutants and their sources. At the same time, they could cause adverse impacts to individuals, society and the environment. Discriminations, biases, privacy infringements, social or economic exclusions or environmental infringement are just a few examples of those.[353] The reflections on trustworthiness should therefore also be discussed from the point of view of adequate protection against such impacts.

One of the strong temptations for governments willing to assure safety is building pervasive surveillance systems based on AI. This could become threat if pushed to extreme levels. Trustworthy AI means they should not be engaged in mass surveillance of individuals by governments. On the contrary the, governments should deploy and procure only such AI systems that are designed to be respectful of the law and fundamental rights and aligned with ethical principles.

Equally, commercial surveillance of individuals and societies should be countered. This refers in particular to consumers whose fundamental rights of privacy as well as a free and informed choice are respected. It also concerns all sorts of nominally free services. As underlined earlier, consideration should be given to power asymmetries between institutions, businesses and individuals. Disproportionalities that may be built derive from economic, data and computing inequalities. The minimum way to counter them should be an introduction of the mandatory self-identification of AI systems, whenever they

---

349 This denotes AI systems communicating and interacting with humans by simulating sociality in human-robot interaction (embodied AI) or as avatars in virtual reality. By doing so, those systems have the potential to change our socio-cultural practices and the fabric of our social life.
350 Geslevich Packin, Lev-Aretz (n 31) 108.
351 HLEG AI, 'Ethics Guidelines for Trustworthy AI' (n 134) 19.
352 Floridi, *The 4th Revolution* (n 38) 119.
353 S. J. Blodget-Ford, 'Future privacy: a real right to privacy for artificial intelligence' in Woodrow Barfield, Ugo Pagallo (eds.), *Research Handbook on the Law of Artificial Intelligence* (Edward Elgar 2018) 317.

interact with a human and whenever there is a reasonable likelihood that end users could not be able to recognise that, deployers of AI systems should be responsible for the full transparency by disclosing that the system is non-human. The AI solutions should address sustainability challenges, by enacting circular economy plans by those responsible for their design, deployment and use. Companies should be institutionally incentivised to reduce the carbon footprint of data centres and devices, big-data-driven AI and modern computing architectures to ensure that AI products and services do not have an undue sustainability impact.[354]

The EU should establish monitoring mechanisms to analyse continuously, measure and score the societal impact of AI. This could help tracking the positive and negative consequences of AI appearances on society and allow to adapt or redirect strategies and policies ongoingly. All relevant EU agencies should be included in this mechanism to ensure that the information generated is trusted, of high and verifiable quality, sustainable and available so that ultimately AI-based solutions themselves could help the monitoring and measuring their societal impact.[355]

There are some specific elements of the societal wellbeing. One of them is monitoring the development of personalised AI systems built on children's profiles. With particular care, they should ensure their alignment with fundamental rights, democracy and the rule of law. The discussions on introducing a legal age at which children could receive a clean data slate of any public or private storage of data related to them as children is very relevant in this context.

For AI systems deployed by the private sector, specific measures should be considered. For example, in case of safety-critical applications, the need to introduce a mandatory obligation to conduct a Trustworthy AI assessment is necessary. Apart from that, other measures might be needed, like: stakeholder consultations with relevant authorities; traceability; auditability and ex-ante oversight requirements.[356] If harmful irregularities are detected an obligation to enable effective and immediate redress should be introduced.[357]

In conclusion, Trustworthy AI is useful mean to enhance individual and societal well-being. This is understood as directly linked with the sustainability expectations towards them and could be instrumental in safeguarding societal and natural environment. It requires growth and competitiveness, to generate beneficial progress and it requires inclusion, to allow everyone to benefit therefrom. Technology is a crucial driver of innovation and productivity. AI is one of the most transformative technologies of our time. However, using

---

354 HLEG AI, 'Policy and Investment Recommendations' (n 5) 11–12.

355 Ibid 14.

356 With due regard to the UN Convention on the Rights of persons with disabilities https://www.un.org/development/desa/disabilities/convention-on-the-rights-of-persons-with-disabilities.html accessed 22 July 2020.

357 HLEG AI, 'Policy and Investment Recommendations' (n 5) 40.

Trustworthy AI to enhance the wellbeing implies important execution pre-requisites. In particular it refers to securing individual and societal empowerment and protection. Individuals need to be aware of and understand the capabilities, limitations and impacts of AI. They also must have the necessary education and skills to be able use the technology, to ensure that they can benefit from it. They should be prepared for a transformed labour environment with prevalent AI systems. And as discussed above they need adequate protection from any adverse impact that AI can bring.[358]

4.5.8 Accountability

The final requirement of accountability is in close relation to all abovementioned ones and in particular with the principle of fairness. To ensure accountability for AI systems and their outcomes auditability is the key as the assessment of ethical requirements by internal and external auditors and the accessibility of reviews and evaluation reports strongly contributes to the trustworthiness of the technology. Availability for audits should especially be ensured in safety-critical applications, when it comes to those affecting fundamental rights. Also, foreseeable or pre-dictable adverse effects of AI systems should be identified, assessed and mini-mised. For the traceability reasons, they should be documented, as well. The impact assessments methodologies should be implemented to facilitate this process, however it is commonly agreed that these assessments should be pro-portionate to the risks the AI systems could bring. The requirements should be balanced in a rational and methodologically explainable manner. In case of ne-gative impact occurrence, accessible mechanisms should be foreseen to ensure adequate redress.[359]

In terms of auditability, which entails the assessment of algorithms, data and design processes, they do not necessarily imply that every piece of information on business models and intellectual property related to the AI systems have to be always openly available. In fact, many times, due to the specificity of IP rights and trade secrets protecting AI systems, the auditability may encounter important limitations. However, evaluation by auditors and the availability of evaluation reports from the reviews help to create trustworthiness of the technology. Independent audits are particularly critical when they refer to fundamental rights.

To build the trustworthiness of AI systems, there is a need for establishing reporting mechanisms which would touch on actions or decisions that contribute to given system outcomes. Also, the response tools which would address the consequences of such outcomes, have to be ensured. Due protection has to be available for whistle-blowers, NGOs, trade unions and all others who identify, assess, document and strive to minimize potentially negative impacts of AI sys-tems. The use of impact assessments models prior to, during and after the end of

---

358 Ibid 47.
359 Commission, COM(2019)168 final (n 6) 6.

the processes of the development, deployment and use of AI systems could be helpful to minimise potentially negative impact. The takeaways and action plans of these assessments have to be proportionate to the risk that the AI systems may pose. Differently should be treated systems that have the capacity of impacting human life and wellbeing (ex. medical devices powered by algorithms) from applications used in popular media platforms (like Netflix), which simply profile the offered content according to user's preferences.

In the process of building the trustworthiness of AI systems, the requirements described here may evoke mutual tensions and then implicate necessity to face inevitable trade-offs. They should be addressed in a rational and methodological manner, entailing that relevant interests and values are identified. If a conflict between them arise, trade-offs should be acknowledged and evaluated from the point of view of risk they pose to ethical principles. In situations in which no ethically acceptable trade-offs can be identified, the AI system should not proceed in that form. The decision-maker should be accountable for the implementation of all the requirements and for continuous review of the appropriateness of trade-offs. If necessary, changes should be made to the systems in question. Furthermore, when negative impact of AI systems occurs, accessible mechanisms should be foreseen for adequate redress. Knowing that redress is possible when things go wrong is a key accountability for designers, developers and deployers to ensure trust.[360]

To implement the above requirements, both technical and non-technical methods can be employed. These encompass all stages of an AI system's life cycle. An evaluation of the methods employed to implement the requirements, as well as reporting and justifying changes to the implementation processes, should occur on an ongoing basis.[361] AI systems are continuously evolving and acting in a dynamic environment. The realisation of Trustworthy AI is, therefore, a continuous process.

There are multiple non-exclusive methods that can be implemented to help to assure the trustworthiness of AI systems. They can be either complementary or alternative to each other, since different requirements and sensitivities may refer in a given case. Selecting and using them is the accountability of the designers, developer and deployers of the AI systems. Some of them are of technical nature and are meant to ensure trustworthy AI and may vary in level of maturity.

Requirements for trustworthiness should be reflected in procedures which should be anchored in the AI system's architecture. This could be accomplished through a set of desired behaviours, the white list type of rules, that the system should always follow. Again, it is for the designers, developers and deployers to establish appropriate toolbox used for the ethical scrutiny. Also, the restrictions on behaviours or states that the system should not transgress, could be enumerated in the blacklists sort of procedures. It is a good practice to ensure monitoring of the system's compliance with these rules by a separate codified process.

---

360 HLEG AI, 'Ethics Guidelines for Trustworthy AI' (n 134)19–20.
361 Wildhaber (n 109) 583.

Accountability may be promoted by the efficient implementation of 'by-design' schemes. The values-by-design methods provide links between the abstract principles which the system is required to respect and the specific implementation decisions. As we discuss in the present book, for AI there are various 'by-design' rules to be implemented—privacy-by-design, ethics- by-design, security-by-design, rule of law-by-design—are just a few principles that need to be embedded in the system form the moment it is designed. To be trustworthy AI systems need to be ethical, secure in its processes, data and outcomes which are used should be resistant to malicious attacks and wrongdoings of any origin. Finally, the systems should not be designed in a way that may undermine the fundamentals of democratic systems. In 'by-design' method the compliance with norms implemented into the design of the AI system is a key. In practice implementation of this method is not much different to compliance assurance processes referring to any other areas. Namely, the responsible entities have to identify and assess the impact of their AI systems from the outset. Together, with this they must recognize the norms their AI system ought to comply with.

Another precondition allowing to assure accountability stems from the presumption that for a system to be considered trustworthy, it should be understood why it behaved a certain way and why it provided a given interpretation. Explainable AI (XAI) concept tries to address this issue to understand the system's underlying mechanisms better. Processes with neural nets can result in parameters set to numerical values difficult to correlate with end results. Scaringly, small changes in data values might result in dramatic changes in interpretation. It can happen that this vulnerability is exploited by attackers on the system. In this respect, methods involving XAI research are vital to explain the system's behaviour to users and to select and deploy reliable technology.

Due to the non-deterministic and context-specific nature of AI systems, traditional testing is not enough. Failures of the concepts and representations used by the system may only manifest when a programme is applied to sufficiently realistic data. Consequently, to verify and validate processing of data, the underlying model must be carefully monitored during both training and deployment for its stability, robustness and operation within well-understood and predictable bounds. It must be ensured that the outcome of the planning process is consistent with the input and that the decisions are made in a way allowing validation of the underlying process.

Trustworthiness is never a static feature. Therefore, it has to be tested and validated as early as possible and as frequently as needed. This is a question of accountability to assure the systems behave as intended in their life cycles and in particular after deployment. Multiple metrics should be developed to cover the categories that are being tested for different perspectives and checks themselves should be conducted by diverse groups of testers. They should include red teams deliberately attempting to break the system to find vulnerabilities and bug bounties that use outsiders to detect and report system weaknesses.

Appropriate quality of service indicators should be determined to ensure whether the AI systems have been tested and developed with respect to security and safety requirements. These indicators are measures to evaluate the algorithms and typical software metrics of functionality, performance, usability, reliability, security and maintainability.[362]

4.6 Assessing trustworthy AI

4.6.1 Assessment by developers and deployers of AI

Assessment of trustworthiness particularly applies to AI systems that directly interact with users and is primarily addressed to developers and deployers. The assessment of accordance with law is a normal responsibility for the function of legal compliance. The other elements of trustworthiness of AI systems need to be assessed in the specific contexts in which they operate. The assessment of those elements should be implemented though a governance structure embracing operational and management level.

The assessment list and governance structure should be a double fold qualitative and quantitative process. A qualitative process ensures representability, where a limited number of entities from different sectors and of different sizes should provide in-depth feedback. A quantitative part of the assessment process implies that all interested stakeholders could provide feedback through an open consultation. Then the results should be integrated into the assessment list with the aim to achieve a framework that can be horizontally used across all applications and hence offer a foundation for ensuring Trustworthy AI in all domains. Once such assessment is performed, it would serve as a foundation for a sectoral and application-specific framework that could be further developed.[363]

Using the assessment results should require attention to the areas of concern as well as to the questions that for some reasons could not be answered. To avoid such a problem in advance, it is important to assure the diversity of skills and competences in the team developing and testing the AI system. To achieve this, it might be recommended to involve stakeholders from inside and outside the organisation. Ideally, the assessment itself should guide AI practitioners to achieve Trustworthy AI. The assessment should refer and be logged to the specific use in a proportionate way to be useful in addressing the raised concerns. It should encourage reflection on the potential steps that should be taken, so that trustworthy AI achieved. Many AI practitioners already have existing assessment tools and software development processes in place to ensure compliance also with non-legal ethical standards. The assessment should not be carried out as separated exercises but could be incorporated into their broader ongoing practices.[364]

---

362 HLEG AI, 'Ethics Guidelines for Trustworthy AI' (n 134) 21–22.
363 Ibid 24.
364 Ibid 25–26.

4.6.2 Governance structure of evaluation process

The assessment process could be managed through varying structures. It could be done by incorporating it into existing governance mechanisms, or by implementing new processes. That choice should always depend on the internal structure of the entity and be proportionally adjusted to its size and resources. Research demonstrates that, as in other general compliance reviews, the management attention at the highest level is needed to achieve change.[365] It also demonstrates that involving all stakeholders boosts the acceptance and the relevance of the introduction of any new technological and non-technological process.[366] Different governance models may, for instance, entail the presence of an internal and/or external ethical (and sector-specific) expert. Boards might be useful to highlight areas of potential conflict and suggest ways in which that conflict might best be resolved. As such boards should serve as escalation bodies for evaluating all AI innovations in case issues and concerns are detected. Meaningful consultations and discussion with stakeholders, including those at risk of being adversely affected by an AI system, are useful too. Such an approach is in accordance with general good management principles according to which there should be an involvement of those who are impacted by the possible introduction of AI systems via information, consultation and participation procedures.

The role of the top management in the assessment of trustworthiness is to set the tone and determine the necessity in discussing and evaluating the AI systems' development, deployment or procurement. Boards can effectively perform oversight tasks, focusing in particular on the following areas: AI technical expertise, infrastructure oversight, legal and ethical compliance and the AI impact on the business and industry. In order to assure effective oversight, the members of the board need to have knowledge about AI itself. They need to be fully informed and aware of the technical aspects of AI technologies used or produced by the company, but also, should have insight into the ethical and legal challenges.[367] To support the management, controlling functions like compliance, legal or corporate responsibility department should monitor the use of the

---

365 See, https://www.mckinsey.com/business-functions/operations/our-insights/secrets-of-successful-change-implementation accessed 22 July 2020.

366 See, for instance, Alex Bryson, Erling Barth, Harald Dale-Olsen, 'The Effects of Organizational Change on Worker Well-Being and the Moderating Role of Trade Unions' (2013) 66 ILR Review; Uwe Jirjahn, Stephen Smith, 'What Factors Lead Management to Support or Oppose Employee Participation—With and Without Works Councils? Hypotheses and Evidence from Germany' (2006) 45 Industrial Relations: A Journal of Economy and Society 650–680; Jonathan Michie, Maura Sheehan, 'Labour Market Deregulation, "Flexibility" and Innovation' (2003) 27 Cambridge Journal of Economics 123–143.

367 International Corporate Governance Network, 'Artificial Intelligence and Board Effectiveness' (February 2020) https://www.icgn.org/artificial-intelligence-and-board-effectiveness accessed 22 July 2020.

assessment and the implementation of recommendations coming from it. They should update the standards or internal policies on AI systems and ensure that the use of such systems complies with the current legal and regulatory framework as well as the policies of the organisation. The product and service development department should use the assessment to evaluate AI-based products and services and log all the results of the controls introduced in this respect. These results should be discussed at management level so that it could be approved. The similar role should be given to the quality assurance or department or to its equivalent. It should ensure and check the results of the assessment and escalate issues higher up in case the results are not satisfactory or there are no needed results implemented.[368] There are also other departments like HR and procurement that within their scopes of tasks should be engaged in evaluating the assessment reports.

For the purposes of ethical compliance, organisations should establish governance frameworks ensuring accountability for the ethical dimensions of decisions associated with the development, deployment and use of AI systems or more broadly with development, deployment and use of any cyber technologies. This should start from appointing a person in charge of ethical issues related to technologies as well as ethics panels, boards, committees. The role of them should be to supervise and advice. Also, dedicated systems of certifications and bodies can play a role in support of this task. Separately more should be done to build efficient communication channels with within and across the industries and with the regulators, opinion makers and other interested groups. They should allow for sharing best practices, knowledge, experience and proven models, discussing dilemmas or reporting emerging ethical problems. This set of mechanisms can only be supplementary to the legal and regulatory scrutiny and supervision.[369]

4.6.3 Weaknesses of compliance assessment

There are no thoroughly conceptualised and universally accepted guidance for stakeholders on how to ensure a Trustworthy AI. The same refers to the lack of guidance on how to ensure the implementation of ethical and robust AI. Even though a number of legal obligations has already captured some of those requirements, the legal uncertainty exists regarding the extent to which such legal obligations are already in place. There is also a lack of guidance on standards in terms of the development and the use of the assessment measures that could be available to assure the trustworthiness of AI systems.[370]

---

368 HLEG AI, 'Ethics Guidelines for Trustworthy AI' (n 134) 24–25.
369 Ibid 23.
370 HLEG AI, 'Policy and Investment Recommendations' (n 5) 43.

4.7 Relations between law and ethics in the field of AI – a critical look

In light of discussed Ethical Guidelines on Trustworthy AI, there is a need to summarise the complex relationship between law and ethics. As we stated, the legal and ethical requirements, even if connected to each other, shall be considered as separate ones. As the AI4 Peoples report on good governance indicates, law and ethics in the field of AI can interact with each other in three ways.[371] First, describes the influence of ethical principles on hard law, adopted as top-down measures. However, in this context it is not always possible to accommodate ethical rules within existing binding law framework. The best example to show the tension is the requirement of transparency, which is absolutely crucial from the viewpoint of trustworthiness, being one of the fundamental ethical principles. It is extremely difficult and sometimes even impossible to comply to it in case of IP protected rights or national security rules, which per se are shielded from the transparency, safeguarding either an intellectual asset of the company or the common weal of public security, which deserves a privileged position in the hierarchy of societal values. The second type of relation between ethical principles and binding legislation consists of the lack of conflict between one and another, thus peaceful co-existence of the two realms of ethics and law.[372] Finally, the third type is prompted by the fact that AI is such a disruptive technology that presupposes co-existence of not only law and ethics, but also within ethical principles allows for the distinction of the ones adopted by different governmental and non-governmental fora. Different economic operators, societal associations and social partners are constantly developing their own values, which are put against not only legal requirements but also defined and regulated ethical norms.

In the context of these considerations, we shall define the effort taken at HLEG AI while drafting ethical guidelines on AI, as an attempt to place what is supposed to be ethical AI in the context of existing and possible future legislation and show how to complement and strengthen legal and regulatory environment.[373]

---

371 Ugo Pagallo et al., 'AI4 People. Report On Good AI Governance. 14 Priority Actions, a S.M.A.R.T. Model of Governance, and a Regulatory Toolbox' (2019) 11 https://www.eismd.eu/wp-content/uploads/2019/11/AI4Peoples-Report-on-Good-AI-Governance_compressed.pdf accessed 22 July 2020.
372 Beever, McDaniel, Stamlick (n 13) 51.
373 Ibid.

5 Non-technical Methods of Achieving Trustworthy AI

5.1 Regulatory perspective

5.1.1 Risk-based approach v. precautionary principle-based approach

There is a variety of non-technical methods that could be valuable in securing and maintaining Trustworthy AI. These should be assessed on an ongoing basis. The regulation to support AI's trustworthiness already exists today, for example, in the shape of product safety and liability frameworks. That regulation if accordingly revised, adapted or introduced, could be a safeguard and an enabler, and as such, becomes an efficient method of achieving trustworthy AI through the non-technical method.[374]

Regulatory instruments allowing to control and supervise the changing technological landscape is usually constructed upon a risk-based or principle-based approach. In terms of the risk-based approach, the character, intensity and timing of regulatory intervention should be dependent of the type of risks created by an AI system.[375] Regulations, therefore, being results of the conducted analysis should be in line with an approach based on principle proportionality and precautionary. During that analysis, various risk classes should be distinguished, measured and categorised. This can, for instance, be done based on their impact and determination, whether they are acceptable or unacceptable, and/or their probability of occurrence. The higher the impact and probability of an AI-created risk, the stronger the appropriate regulatory response should be. The risk itself should be understood broadly, covering the harmful impact on individuals and societies taken as a whole. The risks may have tangible character (ex. leading to harms on the environment or

---

374 HLEG AI, 'Ethics Guidelines for Trustworthy AI' (n 134) 22.
375 Ernst Karner, 'Liability for Robotics: Current Rules, Challenges, and the Need for Innovative Concepts' in Sebastian Lohsse, Reiner Schulze, Dirk Staudenmayer (eds.), *Liability for Artificial Intelligence and the Internet of Things. Muenster Colloquia on EU Law and the Digital Economy IV* (Hart Publishing, Nomos 2019) 121.

human life) or may be intangible (taking the form of detriments to democracy or the rule of law).[376]

This means that in the case of AI applications that generate unacceptable risks, a precautionary principle-based approach[377] should be reflected in regulations that refer to them.[378] These precautionary measures should be adopted when there is a threat of potential harm to environmental, human or societal good. Decisions about the types, severities and probabilities of unacceptable risks must be taken as a result of open, transparent and accountable deliberations. The EU's legal framework and obligations under the Charter of Fundamental Rights have to be taken into account within these deliberations.

Particularly strong attention should be focused, and the due consideration should be given in the analysis of the level of autonomy in AI-based decision-making while designing the regulatory framework. This depends in particular on whether the autonomy refers to information source only, a support function, or is a feature of entire systems excluding any human involvement. In any case, the autonomy should be under tight regulatory scrutiny when it comes to developing and deploying AI systems.[379] To assure this new regulatory measure, governance mechanisms should be put in place to adequately protect the societies and individuals from adverse impacts to enable oversight, and if needed enforcement, without blocking potential innovation at the same time.[380]

Setting up an institutional structure for Trustworthy AI to fill an existing governance gap by the EU should be structured around contributing to developing framework and policies ensuring that AI is lawful, ethical and robust, providing guidance so that AI applications comply with relevant laws and regulatory requirements, assisting in the application of a risk-based approach that includes an assessment of the intensity, probability and unacceptability of AI-created risks, overseeing applications that can have a significant systemic impact, assisting in standards-setting, promoting intra-EU cooperation, hosting a repository of best practices and contributing to preparing for socio-economic changes brought about by AI.[381]

---

376 More on threats, risks and harms and wrong related to AI technologies, Karen Yeung (rapporteur), 'A Study of the implications of advanced digital technologies (including AI systems) for the concept of responsibility within a human rights framework', DGI(2019) 5 (Council of Europe 2019) 28–43.

377 Precautionary principle-based approach is commonly used in the regulation of environment; Didier Bourguignon, 'The precautionary principle. Definitions, applications and governance' (European Parliament 2016).

378 The European Commission has held that 'whether or not to invoke the Precautionary Principle is a decision exercised where scientific information is insufficient, inconclusive, or uncertain and where there are indications that the possible effects on the environment, or human, animal or plant health may be potentially dangerous and inconsistent with the chosen level of protection'. Commission, 'Communication on the Precautionary Principle', COM(2000)0001 final.

379 HLEG AI, 'Policy and Investment Recommendations' (n 5) 38.

380 Ibid 49.

381 Ibid 41–42.

Although proud for its regulatory environment conceived to stimulate competition and innovation and safeguarding fundamental rights at the same time, the new challenges raised by AI require reflection on the adequacy of the current EU regulatory regime and governance structure. It means that trustworthy AI necessitates an adjusted regulatory and governance framework. This should be a framework that promotes development and deployment of AI that ensures and respects fundamental rights, the rule of law and democracy and safeguards individuals and society from unacceptable harm. Ensuring an appropriate regulatory and governance framework that maximises the benefits of AI and that prevents and minimises its risks a complex task. Separately, when trying to establish it, independent oversight mechanisms have to be established. There is a view that an expansion of the institutional capacities, expertise and instruments of policymakers is also needed.[382]

Prior to doing so, systematic mapping and evaluation of the existing EU laws and other regulations relevant to AI systems are needed. The questions asked within the process of mapping these regulations refer in the first instance to promotion and assurance of the ethical principles within these regulations. They also refer to existing frameworks for monitoring, information-gathering and enforcement and if they are capable of providing effective oversight to ensure that objectives could be effectively met.[383]

The European Commission in its White Paper on AI indicates at the risk-based approach as the method for determining if the regulatory intervention is proportionate. There should be a clear differentiation of AI applications based on their high risk or low-risk character. The high-risk AI application shall be the one which meets two cumulative criteria: it is employed in a sector where the risk, in general, are more likely to occur (transportation, healthcare, energy, parts of the public sector). New regulation on AI shall exhaustively list such sectors. The second condition refers to the use of AI application in a given sector in such a way that significant risks are likely to happen. Such a risk assessment could be based on the impact of the affected parties (ex. if AI application poses a risk of injury or death).[384] Such a risk evaluation would impact the intensity of regulatory approach. If an AI application falls under the category of high risk, all the mandatory requirements of the future regulatory framework should apply. For non-high-risk applications, voluntary measures could apply.

5.1.2 *Principle based approach v. prescriptive and casuistic rules*

Another type of approach to regulating AI consists in referring to the principles that should be respected while conceiving and applying the technology. This process is based on analysis to what extent current regulations are principles-based

---

382 HLEG AI, 'Policy and Investment Recommendations' (n 5) 37.
383 Ibid 38.
384 Commission, COM(2020) 65 final (n 168) 17–18.

and how strongly these principles respond to the technological challenges. This examination of the existing regulations within this approach should be conducted ongoingly. It should be evaluated if AI systems create risks that are adequately addressed by current legislation. The detailed provisions might refer to particular problems like identifying, tracking, profiling and nudging if they are illegitimate or illegal. The use of such technologies for that purpose could take place only on an exceptional basis if the selected conditions, such as national security, happen. Even in these conditions, this should be evidence-based, necessary and proportionate.[385] Apart from the evaluation of the static institutional structures of the existing regulatory environment, it is crucial to examine it also from the dynamic, functional viewpoint. It would mean investigations on competences, capacities and resources that could assure meaningful and effective information-gathering, monitoring and enforcement of legal standards providing effectiveness.[386] The priority criterion for these investigations should be respected for fundamental principles the technologies should be compliant with.

As a result of such regulatory assessment from the perspective of the principles, achieving trustworthy AI by these instruments would require a sequence of interlinked actions. One of them should be harmonising regulatory implementation and enforcement mechanisms across the EU so that their provisions are coherent and non-precluding.[387] If willing to create a true European Single Market for trustworthy AI, regulatory interventions at the national level should be satisfying the principles of subsidiarity, necessity and proportionality.[388] Moreover, interested stakeholders should be encouraged to participate in this process, funding to enable civil society organisations to participate contributing to the Guidelines' piloting process should be guaranteed and ensuring an appropriate follow-up should be arranged.

Policymakers and regulators must adopt a tailored approach so that the EU moves towards the new economic and technological Single European Market for AI. This is a complex and multifaceted undertaking which includes the avoidance of market fragmentation while maintaining a high level of protection of individuals' rights and freedoms. To do so, they should consider a big picture by

---

385 It also extends to biometric AI-powered methods of emotional tracking, empathic media, DNA, iris and behavioural identification, affect recognition, voice and facial recognition and the recognition of micro-expressions. HLEG AI, 'Policy and Investment Recommendations' (n 5) 40.

386 Ibid.

387 Amato (n 75) 92.

388 Fragmentation of rules at Member State level should be avoided and the creation of true systems and services should be prioritised At the same time, there may be specific sectors where additional regulatory requirements apply compared to the future horizontal policy framework for AI in the EU: sectors such as banking, insurance and healthcare are already exposed to significant regulatory requirements that are likely to overlap with the emerging policy framework for AI. In these sectors, as well as any other sector that will feature such overlaps, it is essential that the European Commission performs regular fitness checks to ensure that legislation is proportionate, clearly designed and effectively implements.

looking at AI's overall impact. In very practical terms, it means the underlying logic of the particular segments should be analysed in terms of impacts and enablers like governance and regulatory measures that are needed.[389]

However, in the general context of rapid technological change, unnecessarily prescriptive regulation should be avoided. It might therefore be optimal to adopt a principled-based approach to regulatory reviews and outcome-based regulatory requirements to policies. All of them subject to tight, controls, monitoring and enforcement. If the European Commission grounds its policy measures on AI in EU values and principles, it should translate the aspirational goal of trustworthy AI into a concrete set of indicators. That could serve as a reference while monitoring the convergence of the EU market towards the set policy goals. It should be noted that the regulation proposal on ethical aspects of AI drafted by the European Parliament and addressed to the Commission, represents such a principle-based approach.[390]

However, even in the principle-based approach, the adoption of a segment-specific methodology should be considered. When developing the regulatory framework for AI, the necessary measures to protect individuals, societies, markets or any valuable specificities against potential harm should be secured. In consequence, any AI-related products and services developed and deployed in the B2C, B2B and P2C contexts should differ depending on a merit a tailored approach.

Organisations and stakeholders can sign up to the Guidelines and adapt their charter of corporate responsibility, Key Performance Indicators ('KPIs'), their codes of conduct or internal policy documents to add the striving towards Trustworthy AI. An organisation working on or with AI systems can, more generally, document its intentions, as well as underwrite them with standards of certain desirable values such as fundamental rights, transparency and the avoidance of harm.[391]

5.2 Standardisation and certification

Many of the goals and requirements of Trustworthy AI may be in practical terms achieved by standardisation and certification. Since AI has a global impact which causes global challenges, there is a need for international standards which would help to attain major AI policy goals, and in the particular ethical dimension of AI. Currently, two major international standards bodies are working on AI standards. The first one is a joint committee ISO/IEC JTC 1[392] established between ISO (International Organization for Standardisation, being responsible for developing and publishing international standards in various areas of socio-

---

389 HLEG AI, 'Policy and Investment Recommendations' (n 5) 48.
390 European Parliament, 2020/2012(INL) (n 35).
391 HLEG AI, 'Ethics Guidelines for Trustworthy AI' (n 134) 22.
392 See, https://www.iso.org/isoiec-jtc-1.html accessed 22 July 2020.

economic life) and IEC (the International Electrotechnical Commission). Within ISO/IEC JTC 1, there is a Standards Committee on AI (SC42). The second international body developing AI standards is the IEEE SA[393] (Institute of Electrical and Electronics Engineers Standard Association), within which there are working groups on AI standards series.

The advantages of international standards consist of their capacity for guiding and channelling the development and deployment of new technologies and defining their social impact. Such standards also provide a platform for the experts' voices to be heard and duly taken into consideration. Experts involved in standardisation processes have influence over standards which have factual and sometimes also legal impact on a global approach to a given problem. Also, in particular for AI research organisations, international standards bodies have greater reach and legitimacy than self-regulatory efforts, which are many times restricted to certain corporations or narrow industries. Discussed bodies are also platforms for consensus and allow for resolving expert disagreements, which may be crucial for further development of AI technologies. Finally, international standards, due to the fact that they are disseminated through international trade rules, national policies or corporate strategies, have global reach and enforcement power.[394]

International standards themselves according to ISO are 'rules, guidelines or characteristics for activities or for their results, aimed at achieving the optimum degree of order in a given context. It can take many forms. Apart from product standards, other examples include test methods, codes of practice, guideline standards and management systems standards'.[395]

Currently there are works taking place within both ISO/IEC JTC 1 SC 42 and IEEE aimed at developing International AI standards dedicated to the following problems: AI—Concepts and terminology (SC42 CD 22989[396]); Framework for AI Systems Using Machine Learning (SC42 WD 23053[397]); Draft Model Process for Addressing Ethical Concerns During System Design (IEEE P7000[398])Transparency of Autonomous Systems (defining levels of transparency for measurement) (IEEE P7001[399]); Data Privacy Process (IEEE P7002[400]); Algorithmic Bias Considerations (IEEE P7003[401]); Standard for child and

---

393 See, https://standards.ieee.org/content/ieee-standards/en/about/index.html accessed 22 July 2020.

394 Peter Cihon, 'Standards for AI Governance: International Standards to Enable Global Coordination in AI Research and Development' (2019) 10–15 https://www.fhi.ox.ac.uk/wp-content/uploads/Standards_-FHI-Technical-Report.pdf accessed 22 July 2020.

395 ISO 'Deliverables' (2019) www.iso.org/deliverables-all.html accessed 22 July 2020.

396 See, https://www.iso.org/standard/74296.html accessed 22 July 2020.

397 See, https://www.iso.org/standard/74438.html accessed 22 July 2020.

398 See, https://standards.ieee.org/project/7000.html accessed 22 July 2020.

399 See, https://standards.ieee.org/project/7001.html accessed 22 July 2020.

400 See, https://standards.ieee.org/project/7002.html accessed 22 July 2020.

401 See, https://standards.ieee.org/project/7003.html accessed 22 July 2020.

student data governance (IEEEP7004[402]); Standard for Transparent employer data governance (IEEE P7005[403]); Personal Data AI agent (IEEE P7006[404]); Ontologies standard for Ethically Driven Robotics and Automation Systems (IEEE P7007[405]); Standard for Ethically Driven AI Nudging for Robotic, Intelligent and Autonomous Systems (IEEE P7008[406]); Standard for Fail-safe design of Autonomous and Semi-Autonomous Systems (IEEE P7009[407]); Wellbeing metrics for Autonomous and Intelligent Systems AI (IEEE P7010[408]); Standard for the Process of Identifying and Rating the Trustworthiness of News Sources (IEEE P7011[409]); Standard for Machine Readable Personal Privacy Terms (IEEE P7012[410]); Benchmarking Accuracy of Facial Recognition systems (IEEE P7013[411]); Standard for Ethical considerations in Emulated Empathy in Autonomous and Intelligent Systems (IEEE P7014[412]). When comparing the extent of works of both standardisation bodies, one can notice that IEEE works are much more extensive. Yet in terms of the impact, the ISO/IEC standards have more mechanisms for global reach, since states have a greater influence on the development of its standards and assurance of their enforcement.[413]

Apart from standard-setting, IEEE has launched The Ethics Certification Program for Autonomous and Intelligent Systems for products and services in transparency, accountability, and algorithmic bias in systems (IEEE ECPAIS[414]). The certification process is intended to raise transparency and visibility of sound and robust systems, thus is intended to improve trust to AI. Participation in the certification processes is open to corporate members of IEEE SA. The EPCAIS is divided into three sub-certifications related to transparency, accountability and algorithmic bias.

At European level, currently, there is a policy call for the development of a clear strategy in terms of key standardisation fora and adequate resources. A European input is needed for the main components of Trustworthy AI that may necessitate standards.[415] In the European Parliament's draft proposal for a regulation on a framework of ethical aspects of AI, robotics and related

---

402 See, https://standards.ieee.org/project/7004.html accessed 22 July 2020.
403 See, https://standards.ieee.org/project/7005.html accessed 22 July 2020.
404 See, https://standards.ieee.org/project/7006.html accessed 22 July 2020.
405 See, https://site.ieee.org/sagroups-7007/ accessed 22 July 2020.
406 See, https://standards.ieee.org/project/7008.html accessed 22 July 2020.
407 See, https://standards.ieee.org/project/7009.html accessed 22 July 2020.
408 See, https://sagroups.ieee.org/7010/ > accessed 22 July 2020.
409 See, https://sagroups.ieee.org/7011/ accessed 22 July 2020
410 See, https://standards.ieee.org/project/7012.html accessed 22 July 2020.
411 See, https://spectrum.ieee.org/the-institute/ieee-products-services/standards-working-group-takes-on-facial-recognition accessed 22 July 2020.
412 See, https://standards.ieee.org/project/7014.html accessed 22 July 2020.
413 Cihon (n 394) 20.
414 See, https://standards.ieee.org/industry-connections/ecpais.html accessed 22 July 2020.
415 HLEG AI 'Policy and Investment Recommendations for Trustworthy AI' (n 5) 43.

technologies, there is an expressed provision pointing at the tasks of new to-be-established European Agency for AI, whose one of the major tasks would be to develop common criteria and application process for granting of a European certificate of ethical compliance. Such a seal would be issued upon a request of any developer, deployer or user willing to certify the positive assessment of compliance carried out by the respective national supervisory authority.[416] Also, the European Commission, in its White Paper on AI, is proposing the voluntary labelling system for no-high risk AI applications. As such applications should be considered the ones, which are not used in particular sectors enlisted by future legislation (ex. healthcare, transport, energy, parts of public sectors like the judiciary, migration services) and do not produce legal effects or are not prone to pose a risk to human life. The economic operators of such no-high risk AI applications would be able to follow the adopted legislative requirements and scheme voluntarily and would be given the opportunity to be rewarded for such an effort with the quality label for their AI systems, which could help to communicate their trustworthy character.[417]

5.3 Inclusiveness

5.3.1 *Involving design teams*

Inclusiveness is a ground feature of the process building trust towards AI and its ethical dimension. It is closely linked to the requirement of diversity, non-discrimination and fairness. Inclusiveness may be achieved by building diverse research and developing teams.[418] By doing so, algorithmic bias may be mitigated. Nowadays, only 12% of leading AI researchers are female.[419] On average, there are four times more men with ICT-related studies than women in Europe. Also, the overall percentage of Europeans with ICT-related education is decreasing. In terms of employability—in 2015, only 5.8% of European workers were employed in digital jobs.[420]

Such a situation may be a significant hurdle in building an ethical and trustworthy environment around AI.[421] The most fundamental European values which are at the heart of the EU's regulatory approach, may not be fully

416 European Parliament (2020/2012(INL) (n 35) 7.
417 Commission COM(2020)65 final (n 168) 17, 24.
418 Floridi, *The 4th Revolution* (n 38) 38.
419 UNESCO Report, 'I'd blush if I could — Closing Gender Divides in Digital Skills through Education' (2019) https://2b37021f-0f4a-464083520a3c1b7c2aab.filesusr.com/ugd/04bfff_06ba0716e0604f51a40b4474d4829ba8.pdf accessed 22 July 2020.
420 Carlota Tarín Quirós et al., 'Women in the digital age' A study report prepared for the European Commission (2018) https://ec.europa.eu/digital-single-market/en/news/increase-gender-gap-digital-sector-study-women-digital-age accessed 22 July 2020.
421 More on the infosphere as a new environment see, L. Floridi, *The 4th Revolution* (n 38) 219.

respected when research and design teams have very little representation of European members. Also, the underrepresentation of women in tech and in particular, the AI industry brings serious threat to perpetuate gender bias into AI systems, which are mostly designed and developed by men. The vivid example of such a practice is the feminisation of AI assistants—their voices are mostly female; their reactions to sexual harassment are playful or apologetic when abused verbally. It is stressed that in order to avoid it, the design teams should be multi-ethnic, multicultural and multi-gendered.[422] Apart from fighting bias, assuring the diversity within AI research and design teams are believed to increase the relevance and quality of research and innovation for the economy and society as a whole. Problem-solving capabilities and decision quality, performance and in-novation of business are just a few aspects which benefit from diversity.[423]

At the EU level, there are particular policy directions, mainly intending to increase women presence in the AI industry. It shall be done through prior-itisation of gender equality in all AI policies, with the quantitative goal of reaching at least of 30% of female talents' presence in AI higher education, AI labour market and eco-systems by 2030. It entails the maintenance of dedicated and substantial funding opportunities and scholarships based on the inclusive approach. Also, using soft tools of networking, mentoring and coaching pro-grams for women in AI is stressed.[424] Worth mentioning is the project run at the European Institute of Innovation and Technology, which within the framework of the Commission's Digital Education Action Plan,[425] promotes digital and entrepreneurship skills among girls.[426]

5.3.2 AI literacy and education

The knowledge of AI and its understanding should be enhanced across all sectors and all entities using these technologies. It should be promoted in particular in government institutions, oversight bodies and agencies, judiciary and law en-forcement institutions and education system. The users should be aware of the very existence of AI-based systems that impact them and should know what influence on fundamental rights AI technologies may have. AI literacy is one step further from the digital literacy, which according to the UNESCO's Digital Literacy Global Framework 'is the ability to access, manage, understand, in-tegrate, communicate, evaluate and create information safely and appropriately through digital technologies for employment, decent jobs and entrepreneurship.

---

422 UNESCO Report, 'I'd blush if I could' (n 419) 124–125.
423 See, Rocío Lorenzo et al., 'The Mix That Matters. Innovation Through Diversity' (BCG 2017) https://www.bcg.com/publications/2017/people-organization-leadership-talent-innovation-through-diversity-mix-that-matters.aspx accessed 22 July 2020.
424 HLEG AI 'Policy and Investment Recommendations for Trustworthy AI' (n 5) 34–35.
425 Commission, COM(2018) 22 final (n 106).
426 See, https://eit.europa.eu/our-activities/education/doctoral-programmes/eit-and-digital-education-action-plan accessed 22 July 2020.

It includes competencies that are variously referred to as computer literacy, ICT literacy, information literacy and media literacy'.[427] At European level, there is the Digital Competence Framework for Citizens, which explains eight proficiency levels from the simplest and most basic, to highly specialised being able to resolve complex technical problems and propose new ideas.[428]

Once we discuss the question of AI literacy, we should bear in mind that this goal is really difficult to achieve. We can distinguish several dimensions of the analysed problem. First relates to the increase in the number of ICT professionals in Europe, who would be working in the AI industry and would be designing, coding and managing algorithmic systems. There is a demand for skills in AI since almost all Member States are facing shortages of ICT professionals. If Europe really wants to be a global driving force for the ethical AI, there should be more incentives on higher education programmes aimed at providing fully-fledged AI education of multidisciplinary character, combining not only technical knowledge but also elements of psychology, ethics and law. In response to this need, the Commission adopted the abovementioned Digital Education Action Plan (2018–2020) and currently is holding an open public consultation on its new edition for 2020 and beyond, which is mainly focusing on the impact of COVID-19 on teaching and learning.[429] The pandemic had disrupted education system in an unprecedented way in Europe's recent history, which prompts the reflection on the future of education systems of all levels and also possible use of algorithmic tools and systems in this sphere.

In terms of more AI-oriented educational initiatives, it is worth mentioning that the European Institute of Innovation and Technology is in the process of integrating AI across curricula in the education courses it supports, at Master and PhD level.[430]

The second aspect touching upon AI literacy and education is research. Europe in this field, apart from legislative and regulatory attempts, must demonstrate its intellectual and commercial leadership in AI, which reaches beyond European borders. Research shall have academic and industry-based dimension. Its results should help to achieve a better understanding of AI technologies. To do so, even more centres of excellence in AI should be established in order to promote cooperation between industry and academia and to develop ways of establishing human-centric AI. Research shall have interdisciplinary and multi-disciplinary character and should be taken into consideration by policymakers.[431]

---

427 See, http://uis.unesco.org/sites/default/files/documents/ip51-global-framework-reference-digital-literacy-skills-2018-en.pdf accessed 22 July 2020.

428 Stephanie Carretero, Riina Vuorikari, Yves Punie, 'The Digital Competence Framework for Citizens. With eight proficiency levels and examples of use' (Publications Office of the EU Luxembourg 2017).

429 See, https://ec.europa.eu/education/news/public-consultation-new-digital-education-action-plan_en accessed 22 July 2020.

430 Commission, COM(2018) 795 final (n 3) 11–12.

431 HLEG AI 'Policy and Investment Recommendations for Trustworthy AI' (n 5) 9–11.

Finally, AI literacy is a very general problem touching average end-users of AI-powered technologies. Poor technical knowledge and general low level of digital skills in the broader population may hinder the accessibility of AI-based solutions. Thus, there is a need to include the AI components to primary, secondary and tertiary educational levels, also by providing necessary training to teachers. Apart from basic knowledge on machine learning, there is a pressing need to raise awareness of data protection rights, also on how data can be used and how to prevent the data misuse, as well as it is crucial to mainstream ethical principles developed by the Union in the curricula of teaching programs of all levels. Once the level of AI literacy is increased, it is believed that the potential adverse impact of new technologies could be reduced and that members of society will be better prepared for the ongoing digital transformation.[432] The AI literacy for the individual, average users, are of particular importance once they are recipients of public governance services powered by AI. Altogether, AI literacy is closely linked to the requirement of explainable AI, which can be fully met when not only epistemic groups of ICT professionals are capable of grasping the idea of AI functionalities, but also when the general public, is able to achieve basic knowledge and awareness, necessary to use AI systems consciously and if necessary, challenge their outcomes.

5.3.3 *Participative democracy and social dialogue*

Participation is currently one of the key topics of discussion about democracy in Europe. When we approach this question from an AI perspective, we can distinguish two major angles. The first one concerns the regulatory processes leading towards the adoption of the EU AI legislation. The second aspect relates to the general, ethical use of AI technologies as a tool facilitating participative mechanisms applied for democratic processes at local, national or the EU level. These aspects, touching at first glance quite separate spheres, are nevertheless interrelated. Involvement of citizens and relevant stakeholders into AI regulatory and legislative processes can contribute to building trust and spread of the knowledge on the potential impact of AI systems on socio-economic structures. It may make people aware that they can take part in shaping societal development.[433] The participation of citizens and social dialogue at this stage, can, in consequence, contribute to better use of AI technologies in public governance and make political participation more effective.

Participatory democracy, in its essence, seeks to increase effectiveness and quality of policy and law making by involving citizens in decision processes. Participatory tools covered by the notion of democratic innovations[434] take

---

432 Ibid.
433 Floridi, *The 4th Revolution* (n 38) 176.
434 Graham Smith, *Democratic Innovations. Designing Institutions for Citizen Participation* (Cambridge University Press 2009).

diverse forms. They can be classified into three major categories: collaborative governance, deliberative procedures and direct democracy.[435] Their examples include participatory budgets, citizen juries, deliberative surveys, referenda, citizens' initiatives, town meeting, online citizen forums, e-democracy, popular assemblies, mini-publics.[436] They are mostly used at local government level; however, there are scholarly debates that the pattern of participative mechanisms should be moved to multi-level—national and supranational (EU) levels at present.[437] Within the European Union, the legal basis for such a participatory mechanism is art. 10.3 of the TEU states that every citizen shall have the right to participate in the democratic life of the Union.

The EU AI policy making is using participative mechanisms since it is believed that an open discussion and the involvement of social partners and stakeholders, including the general public is needed to build a sound ethical and legal framework around AI. A crucial issue which should be consulted with stakeholders is how to guarantee the legal certainty, the safeguard of the EU values (human right, the rule of law and democracy) and at the same time promote beneficial innovation. The European Commission is seeking participation and dialogue in this field mainly through the HLEG AI, European AI Alliance and AI4EU.[438] As discussed above in paragraph 3.3, the HLEG AI is an expert body, representing stakeholders' voice in shaping ethical approach towards AI in the EU. At the same time, it is also the steering group for the European AI Alliance, which is a multi-stakeholder forum for engaging in broader discussion and consultations on all aspects of the development of AI in the EU. In June 2019 a first European AI Alliance Assembly took place, where HLEG AI presented the Policy and Investment Recommendations on AI and launched the piloting process of the AI Ethics Guidelines. The latter aims to obtain structured feedback from stakeholders, which would concentrate on the assessment list, which the HLEG AI has drawn up for each of the key requirements of trustworthy AI. The feedback could have been given in three ways. Firstly, by completing the preceding surveys, secondly by sharing through European AI Alliance best practices on how to

---

435 Brigitte Geissel, 'Introduction: On the Evaluation of Participatory Innovations' in Brigitte Geissel, Marko Joas (eds.), *Participatory Democratic Innovations in Europe: Improving the Quality.of Democracy?* (Barbara Budrich Publishers 2013) 10.

436 See more on the typologies of democratic innovations, Stephen Elstub, Oliver Escobar, 'A Typology of Democratic Innovations', Paper for the Political Studies Association's Annual Conference, 10–12 April 2017, Glasgow, https://www.psa.ac.uk/sites/default/files/conference/papers/2017/A%20Typology%20of%20Democratic%20Innovations%20-%20Elstub%20and%20Escobar%202017.pdf > accessed 22 July 2020.

437 Adrian Bua, Oliver Escobar, 'Participatory-deliberative Processes and Public Agendas: Lessons for Policy and Practice' (2018) 1:2 Policy Design and Practice 126–127.

438 AI4EU was launched in January 2019 and it is a project that which by bringing together algorithms, tools, datasets and services helps organisations, in particular small and medium-sized enterprises, to implement AI solutions. It is equipped with the Platform intended to act as a 'one-stop-shop' for providing information about AI. See, https://www.ai4eu.eu/ai4eu-platform accessed 22 July 2020.

achieve trustworthy AI and thirdly by taking part in in-depth interviews organised by the Commission.[439] More than 450 stakeholders were registered for the
piloting phase and their feedback on the guidelines was supposed to be evaluated
by the end of 2019. It was estimated that in 2020, based on the feedback evaluation, HLEG AI will review and update the guidelines, taking due consideration of the opinions expressed by stakeholders.[440]

Apart from the participative mechanisms used in order to shape ethical approach
towards AI, the Commission is in the process of consulting stakeholders (namely
AI developers and deployers, companies and business organisations, SMEs, public
administration, civil society organisations, academics and citizens) on the White
Paper on AI. From 20 February 2020 until 14 June 2020, interested parties had a
chance to fill in the questionnaire. The Commission shall take the received
feedback before submitting proper legislative proposals of the regulations on AI.

The second aspect of relations between participatory democracy and AI is linked
to the usage of AI as a tool for empowering more effective, diffused forms of
political participation. Many of the abovementioned forms of citizens' participation can be done nowadays through digital solutions—for example—the public
consultations, participatory budgets or the EU citizen initiatives are governed by
online tools—website, platforms, mobile applications. Citizens taking part in such
initiatives can vote, support ideas, deliberate, track governmental activities. Many
marginalised groups may join in democratic processes with the sensation, that their
political representatives will hear their voices. Governments, on the other hand, are
using digital technologies to provide access to their activities, by establishing 'open
government' and 'open data' for the benefit of citizens, building their trust and
strengthening their participation.[441] These are the upsides of new technologies
used in the democratic process, many times driven by algorithms. Downsides may
cover issues related to citizens' data collection and processing, which may be used
to nudge and manipulate citizens during electoral and social campaigns, building
the illusory vision of enhanced citizens' legitimacy, built however on false
premises.[442] Thus, to this end, a strong ethical and legal dimension for AI used in
democratic (be it representative or participative) process is crucial for making them
reliable and trustworthy.

5.4 Achieving trustworthiness – a focal problem reviewed

Achieving trustworthiness is a complex, long-lasting process, composed of various elements of legal, ethical, social, economic and technical character. Despite

---

439 See, https://ec.europa.eu/futurium/en/ethics-guidelines-trustworthy-ai/register-piloting-
process-0 accessed 22 July 2020.
440 Commission, COM (2019) 168 final (n 6) 7–8.
441 See, Beever, McDaniel, Stamlick (n 13) 174.
442 See, Paulo Savaget, Tulio Chiarini, Steve Evans, 'Empowering Political Participation
Through Artificial Intelligence' (2018) Science and Public Policy, 2.

existing legal requirements, there are particularly critical applications of AI technologies, which deserve utmost attention in policy making and later enforcement of adopted rules. The most problematic uses of AI, despite their formal compliance with the existing legal framework, may still raise concerns of ethical character. This can happen in particular, because of the fast-progressing technological development and also evolving nature of the understanding of given ethical rules.

The first major concern relates to the invigilation of individuals by AI systems. AI allows for tracking effectively individual persons, both by private and public entities. The most notorious example of such AI usage is face recognition systems and other applications using biometric data. Such control techniques may serve to the benefit of the public good. Its desirable outcome may be beneficial in the area of criminal law and law enforcement-fraud detecting or terrorist financing are just two examples where desired outcomes are fully aligned with ethical principles.[443] Also, during COVID-19 pandemic, one may see positive sides of the application of such systems for the protection of public health. Yet in the latter case, the outcomes are not so obviously aligned with ethics, since COVID-19 tracking applications may undermine the principle of human dignity and privacy and result in a difficult ethical dilemma of balancing individual freedom against societal needs. As it is pointed, automatic identification may raise concerns of both legal and ethical nature. Thus, the regulatory approach should be particularly attentive, and it should promote a proportionate use of discussed techniques in AI in order to defend the autonomy of European citizens, prevent the privacy erosion and fight against discrimination. The intensity of facial recognition systems' regulation shall depend on the type of given application. Public surveillance facial recognition systems may be far more intrusive towards individuals' integrity, hence bringing more questions on its ethical character, than the facial recognition or biometric systems used by smartphones in order to identify its user. Another important issue related to the facial recognition systems is a quality of data fed into an algorithm. As it was pointed above, once training data is flawed, there is a high risk of bias and discriminatory output of the AI system. All these concerns shall be reflected in law.[444] At European level, GDPR right now provides some limitations on the use of facial recognition regulation and the use of data necessary to the functioning of given AI systems. The practical problem here is linked to the proper consent to use data, which shall be verified and meaningful and not just automatic and deprived of any deeper reflection of the possible consequences of decision allowing for the use of given data.

In terms of prospective EU regulation, we may notice an interesting switch of the EU policy approach towards facial recognition. In January 2020 the draft of

---

443 More on why so little has been done despite the capacities of technology see e.g. Pasquale
   (n 45) 195.
444 HLEG AI 'Ethics Guidelines for Trustworthy AI' (n 134) 33–34.

the Commission's white paper on AI was leaked.[445] According to the revealed document, the EU was considering including in the future regulatory framework a temporary (3–5-year long) ban on facial recognition. The idea was to use that time to develop a sound methodology for impact assessment and possible risk management of discussed technology. In the final version of a white paper on AI, there is no such limitation. The explicit ban was removed due to concerns that it would impede innovation and have a detrimental impact on national security.[446] The current version of the Commission stance on facial recognition is stressing the specific risk that such technology may have on fundamental rights. However, there is no outright prohibition and just a recall of existing legislative foundations (ex GDPR, the Law Enforcement Directive[447] and EU Charter of Fundamental Rights), according to which AI can only be used for remote biometric identification when such use is duly justified, proportionate and subject to adequate safeguards.[448]

The second group of ethical and regulatory concerns AI systems which are covert and their true nature may not be clearly determined. The legal and ethical requirement resembles the major rule of advertising law, introducing a general ban on covert (hidden, subliminal) forms of advertising. Like in the case of advertising, a consumer should be aware of the fact that he is an addressee of the advertising content, with AI, humans shall always know that they are interacting with the machine. In the case of advertising, logic is that humans are aware that this kind of communication may use excessive statements, which intend to work on human emotions and final decisions concerning the purchase. Once an individual knows that he is dealing with the advertising and not an objective informational content, he has greater distance and is more alert in terms of taking certain claims for granted. In case of AI, the assurance of the visibility of AI systems shall be in the hands of AI practitioners who should ensure that humans are made aware of— or able to request and validate the fact that—they interact with an AI system. One of the ways to do so is an introduction of the system of clear and transparent disclaimers.[449] However, it is worth noting that there are cases that escape clear distinctions, like the use of and AI-filtered voice spoken by

445 See, https://www.euractiv.com/section/digital/news/leak-commission-considers-facial-recognition-ban-in-ai-white-paper accessed 22 July 2020.

446 See, https://www.ft.com/content/ff798944-4cc6–11ea-95a0–43d18ec715f5 accessed 22 July 2020.

447 Directive (EU) 2016/680 of the European Parliament and of the Council of 27 April 2016 on the protection of natural persons with regard to the processing of personal data by competent authorities for the purposes of the prevention, investigation, detection or prosecution of criminal offences or the execution of criminal penalties, and on the free movement of such data (2016) OJ L 119/89.

448 European Commission, COM(2020)65 final (n 168) 21–22. See also, the European Parliament, 2020/2012(INL) (n 35) 6–7, 28.

449 HLEGoAI 'Ethics Guidelines for Trustworthy AI' (n 134) 33–34.

a human. The confusion between humans and machines may raise issues of attachment, influence, vulnerability or reduction of the value of being human.[450]

Another focal problem concerns AI-powered citizens' scoring. The very existence of social scoring is nothing new and nothing AI-specific. Such solutions already exist in various domains, like financial and insurance sector, school admissions or driver license monitoring systems. However, there are always concerns raised, and in the case of AI-powered scoring systems, it is particularly valid, to which extent it diminishes individual freedom and autonomy. Again, once some scoring systems serve the public goal (ex. road safety) they should be allowed, provided that they fulfil the condition of proportionality, fairness and that citizens are aware that they are being scored and accept this fact. However, as was raised in Ethics Guidelines for Trustworthy AI, any type of normative citizen scoring, evaluating his morals and ethical integrity done by public or private entities, brings a threat to individual freedom, privacy and autonomy.[451] While normative scoring shall be avoided, the purely descriptive, sector-specific scorings, which nowadays use algorithmic decision-making shall be regulated in a way that assures transparency, both in terms of the very fact of the scoring taking place, but also in terms of the methodology used and defined purpose to which it shall serve. Explainability of such scoring systems is thus crucial and shall allow the individual subject to it to take appropriate action, by which it can protect his autonomy and right. Hence, the challenging and correcting mechanisms shall be assured and if possible, the opting-out decisions should be allowed.

The European approach towards citizens' scoring shall be in stark opposition to Chinese social scoring system, which is of normative character and allows for surveillance and ranking of citizens based on their overall behaviour, which would 'commend sincerity and punish insincerity'.[452]

Another particularly important issue which touches upon the most crucial ethical dilemmas of AI application is related to access to trustworthy information and informed choices to be made by citizens in all spheres of their lives—poli-political, commercial, social, private. Since nowadays citizens access information mainly through on-line resources—social media, electronic press, communicators, digital platforms, which use algorithmic technologies—it is crucial for the stability of a political and socio-economic system that the information dissemination is fair, reliable and truthful. The Commission, together with major digital platforms and entities engaged in the initiative of self-regulation aiming at the fight with the disinformation and fake news. In October 2018, the Code of Practice was signed by Facebook, Google, Twitter, Mozilla and advertising

---

450 Ibid.
451 Ibid.
452 See, Chinese State Council Notice concerning Issuance of the Planning Outline for the Construction of a Social Credit System (2014–2020) https://chinacopyrightandmedia. wordpress.com/2014/06/14/planning-outline-for-the-construction-of-a-social-credit-system-2014–2020/ accessed 22 July 2020.

industry. Later, in May 2019 Microsoft and in June 2020 TikTok joined as signatories. One of the elements of signed Code is the commitment of the signatories to invest in products and technologies which can help to make informed decisions, verify false content, prioritise authentic and authoritative information, empower citizens with tools to obtain diverse perspectives.[453] Listed elements may be powered by algorithmic solutions. In order to deploy these systems, signatories should take due to account and comply with the legislative measures and ethical standards which are adopted at the EU level. They should cooperate with civil society, governments in order to meet the requirements of Trustworthy AI. The Code should be the way in which democratic processes are protected, consumer rights are given priority and European values, in general, are safeguarded. However, the COVID-19 crisis brought some critical opinions about the effectiveness of the adopted approach. In June 2020, a group of member states (Estonia, Lithuania, Latvia, Slovakia) have prepared a position paper in which they concluded that the Code, in the face of a pandemic, has proven to be insufficient and unsuitable to serve as the measure to address misinformation on social media.[454] These countries are opting for the EU regulation to be adopted, since soft-law, voluntary, deprived of sanction, self-regulatory code makes it difficult for the platforms to be truly held accountable for possible breaches of the code provisions.

453 Find the text of the Code at https://ec.europa.eu/digital-single-market/en/news/code-practice-disinformation accessed 22 July 2020.
454 See, https://www.euractiv.com/section/digital/news/eu-code-of-practice-on-disinformation-insufficient-and-unsuitable-member-states-say/ accessed 22 July 2020.

6 Horizontal Regulatory Approach

6.1 Preliminary remarks

The goal of the present chapter is to define the most important areas of regulation, which are of horizontal and universal nature and should be taken into consideration by all industries, public and private entities present in the EU, also the ones operating in the field of AI. The choice made reflects the most complex issues that the EU legislators have tackled with. Each of the discussed topics contains a load of ethical issues, which to some extent were signalised in previous chapters as a requirement for trustworthy AI (ex. non-discrimination and bias, privacy and data protection). This chapter will focus more on the lawfulness of ethical AI in the context of the existing and emerging legislative framework. First, we will analyse relevant measures which protect important rights and principles, which can be threatened by AI technologies. The second part of the chapter will be devoted to a thorough analysis of liability regimes.

6.2 What is under threat?

6.2.1 Non-discrimination and equality

In the previous chapter, we discussed the issue of algorithmic bias in the context of general requirements for the establishment of trustworthy AI. In the present paragraph, we will point at the particular fields in which AI may bring a risk of discrimination and will indicate existing European legal framework which may be used to fight it. In the public sector, the most problematic may be algorithms used by the police and justice system, which provide automated predictions about the likelihood of who, when and where may commit crimes.[455] Such predictive systems, may reproduce and petrify existing discrimination based on ethnic origin once algorithms are built upon biased historical data. In the private sector, the examples of discrimination are varied and may encompass employment and selection procedures, when wrongly trained algorithms give

---

455 Brownsword (n 185) 212.

preferences to male candidates; in online advertising, when depending on the gender of the user, the search engine displays content which may give more attractive job offers once a user declares himself as a man.[456] It was revealed that Facebook allows advertisers to target users based on their interest and background (age, gender, sexual orientation) and also to let advertisers exclude specific groups (usually based on race).[457] Also, there are some examples of gender bias in Google translator, when translating from gender-neutral languages (like Hungarian or Turkish) to English provides results which have strong male defaults.[458]

In terms of legislative measures, which can help to fight algorithmic discrimination, in the European Union already exists a strong legislative framework of equality and non-discrimination law. The EU Charter of fundamental rights provides the general legal basis for the fight against non-discrimination (art. 21 of the Charter). Non-discrimination is the general principle of the EU law, which, when expressed in the Treaty, provides directly effective protection against discrimination based on nationality (art. 18 TFEU). Other forms of discrimination based on gender, race, ethnic origin, disabilities, religion or belief, age and sexual orientation are subject to harmonisation measures resulting from secondary legislation. Currently, the most important non-discrimination directives are directive 2006/54/EC on equal treatment of men and women[459]; directive 2000/43/EC on race equality[460]; directive 2000/78/EC on the employment equality[461]; directive 2004/113/EC on gender-equal treatment in the access to supply of goods and services.[462] This set of harmonisation measures applies mostly to discrimination in the labour market, where the protection is the most extensive. At the consumption market (encompassing consumers and service providers), the protection covers mostly gender and race or ethnic origin cases, thus is more limited.[463]

The EU non-discrimination directives distinguish and prohibit two major forms of discrimination — direct and indirect. The former occurs 'where one

---

456 Borgesius (n 241) 14–15.
457 See, Julia Angwin, Terry Parris Jr, 'Facebook Lets Advertisers Exclude Users by Race' (2016) ProPublica https://www.propublica.org/article/facebook-lets-advertisers-exclude-users-by-raceaccessed 22 July 2020.
458 Borgesius (note 241) 17.
459 Directive 2006/54/EC of the European Parliament and of the Council of 5 July 2006 on the implementation of the principle of equal opportunities and equal treatment of men and women in matters of employment and occupation (recast) (2006) OJ L 294/23.
460 Council Directive 2000/43/EC of 29 June 2000 implementing the principle of equal treatment between persons irrespective of racial or ethnic origin (2000) OJ L 180/22.
461 Council Directive 2000/78/EC of 27 November 2000 establishing a general framework for equal treatment in employment and occupation (2000) OJ L 303/16.
462 Council Directive 2004/113/EC of 13 December 2004 implementing the principle of equal treatment between men and women in the access to and supply of goods and services (2004) OJ L 373/37.
463 Xenidis, Senden (n 332) 160.

person is treated less favourably than another is, has been or would be treated in a comparable situation on the grounds of membership in a protected class.[464] Discriminating measure must directly refer to the protected class or must be motivated by it. As Hacker indicates, this type of discrimination is relatively rare in cases of algorithmic discrimination, since it will only take place once the explicit or implicit bias of the decision maker informs the model. Accidental discrimination resulting from wrongful sampling or historic bias escapes the scope of direct discrimination.[465]

The second type is indirect discrimination, which occurs where apparently neutral provision, criterion or practice would put a person of one protected class (ex. sex, race, age) at a particular disadvantage compared with other persons unless that provision, criterion or practice is objectively justified by a legitimate aim and the means of achieving it are appropriate and necessary.[466] In case of indirect discrimination, there is a formal equal treatment; however, *de facto* there exists a particular disadvantage of protected groups. In practice, it can be determined by statistics, proving that regardless of the reason given for particular treatment, the result puts certain protected groups at a disadvantage.[467] Indirect discrimination is the most typical form of algorithmic discrimination. The algorithmic criteria that lead to a given decision are many times neutral ones, yet their outcomes may be discriminatory.

One shall bear in mind, that according to the EU law, discriminatory outcomes, may still be justified by overriding legitimate interests, yet with full respect of the principle of proportionality. It means that the discriminatory measure shall pursue a legitimate aim, appropriately pursued by the questionable criterion, must be necessary and proportional in the strict sense — meaning that there should not be any less-discriminatory mean allowing for the attainment of the same goal.

The biggest problem with enforcement of non-discriminatory rules towards AI is the determination of such algorithmic discrimination. The transparency of AI systems, as was discussed above, many times is not assured and brings the most serious threats to the ethical operations of given systems.[468] Thus, right now, the most important challenge is firstly to find the way in which the explicit obligations will be imposed on AI developers to check the absence of bias in the AI decision making processes. And secondly, establish proper auditing mechanisms allowing public enforcement entities or regulators to determine illegal AI outcomes that cause unfair bias and discrimination.[469] As Hildebrandt indicates, there are already

---

464 See art. 2.2(a) of directive 2000/43/EC, art. 2.1(a) of directive 2006/54/EC, art. 2.2(a) of directive 2000/78/EC, art. 2(a) of directive 2004/113/EC.
465 Hacker (n 334) 1151–1152.
466 See art. 2.2(b) of directive 2000/43/EC, art. 2.1(b) of directive 2006/54/EC, art. 2.2(b) of directive 2000/78/EC, art. 2(b) of directive 2004/113/EC.
467 Hacker (n 334) 1153; Mireille Hildebrandt, *Smart Technologies and the End(s) of Law* (Edward Elgar 2015) 96.
468 Hildebrandt (n 467) 96–97, 192–193.
469 HLEG AI, 'Policy and Investment Recommendations for Trustworthy AI' (n 5) 39,41.

some techniques of 'discrimination-aware data mining' which may enhance the process of compliance with the major ethical and legal requirements. As the author rightly points, the application of such techniques does not provide effective protection.[470] Yet within time, once developed better, we shall learn to use them in order to eliminate other perilous technological solutions.

6.2.2 Consumer protection

The consumer in the AI-driven world deserves particular attention. Even if the benefits of algorithmic technologies may relate to the speeding up of consumer's decision-making, raising the analytical sophistication which goes beyond human capacities, reducing information and transaction costs or avoidance of consumer bias, new harms and risks are being generated.[471] The reduced level of autonomy, increased vulnerability to certain harms (like biased decisions' outcomes, infringement of privacy), exposure to deception, exploitation, manipulation—are just a few examples of the concerns related to the consumer's position in the algorithmic environment, which should be addressed by law.[472]

The consumer protection is the area of the EU law, mostly rooted in the Internal market logic, however reaching for empowering consumers in the market in terms of their safety, equality, right to informed choice, education and associations aiming at protecting their interests.[473] The EU existing legislative framework for consumer protection is developing since 1980 when the European Economic Community was attributed with the competence in this field. Current regulation is complex and in many ways sector-specific (ex. there are harmonisation measures on consumer protection in tourism, air transport, banking or financial institutions). However, there are also measures on more general and horizontal character, which shall be applied to all AI-enabled systems used in B2C transactions, regardless of their specificity. Among those we shall name directive 2005/29/EC on unfair commercial practices (UCPD),[474] directive 2011/83/EU on consumer rights,[475] directive 2000/31/CE on e-commerce,[476] directive 98/6/EC on the prices'

---

470 Hildebrandt (n 467) 193.

471 Michal S. Gal, Niva Elkin-Koren, 'Algorithmic Consumers' (2017) 30 Harvard Journal of Law and Technology 318–322.

472 Ibid 322–3325.

473 See, art. 169 TFEU.

474 Directive 2005/29/EC of the European Parliament and of the Council of 11 May 2005 concerning unfair business-to-consumer commercial practices in the internal market (2005) OJ L 149/22.

475 Directive 2011/83/EU of the European Parliament and of the Council of 25 October 2011 on consumer rights (2011) OJ L 304/64.

476 Directive 2000/31/EC of the European Parliament and of the Council of 8 June 2000 on certain legal aspects of information society services, in particular electronic commerce in the Internal Market (2000) OJ L 178/1.

indications[477] or directive 2019/216/EU on better enforcement of consumer protection.[478] Apart from the approximation of national laws through listed directives, the EU unifies rules on consumer protection at the intersection with new technologies. Among them, it is worth mentioning the regulation (EU) 2018/302 on geo-blocking[479] or the recently adopted regulation (EU) 2019/1150 on promoting fairness and transparency for business users of online intermediation services.[480]

Our aim is not to analyse these legal acts in detail, but rather to identify the relevant issues from the point of view of consumer-user of AI-based services or products and put them in the context of the existing legal framework, which is supposed to provide some guidance on the legal and ethical use of algorithmic systems. EU AI consumers should benefit from some general principles of EU consumer law, which are: protection of the weaker party, regulated autonomy, non-discrimination (equal treatment) and privacy.[481] The non-discrimination has been discussed above and the privacy and data protection will be analysed in the following paragraph. In this place, we would like to focus more on the principles of the protection of the weaker party and regulated autonomy. The protection of the weaker party principle over the years in the EU law has been instrumentalised in order to push the internal market further, at the same time bringing some limitations to the position of the consumer as a weaker party. The most prominent example is the notion of an average consumer, that has been firstly interpreted by the CJEU[482] and later codified in the UCPD. The average EU consumer is 'reasonably well-informed, reasonably observant and circumspect, taking into account social, cultural and linguistic factors'.[483] Such a normative notion lowers in practice the protection level in case of misleading practices. Since an average consumer is supposed to be well aware and informed, he shall approach commercial communication addressed to him with natural reservation. Yet, recently the notion of consumer

---

477 Directive 98/6/EC of the European Parliament and of the Council of 16 February 1998 on consumer protection in the indication of the prices of products offered to consumers (1998) OJ L 80/27.

478 Directive (EU) 2019/2161 of the European Parliament and of the Council of 27 November 2019 amending Council Directive 93/13/EEC and Directives 98/6/EC, 2005/29/EC and 2011/83/EU of the European Parliament and of the Council as regards the better enforcement and modernisation of Union consumer protection rules (2019) OJ L328/7.

479 Regulation (EU) 2018/302 on geo-blocking of the European Parliament and of the Council of 28 February 2018 on addressing unjustified geo-blocking and other forms of discrimination based on customers' nationality, place of residence or place of establishment within the internal market (2018) OJ L60/ 1.

480 Regulation (EU) 2019/1150 of the European Parliament and of the Council of 20 June 2019 on promoting fairness and transparency for business users of online intermediation services (2019) OJ L 186/57.

481 Jabłonowska et al. (n 24) 8.

482 For the notion of an average consumer, see Case C-210/96 Gut Springenheide, ECLI:EU:C:1998:369 and C-470/93 Mars GmbH, ECLI:EU:C:1995:224

483 See, recital 18 of directive 2005/29/CE.

vulnerability is becoming more visible in the consumer policy. The European Commission in 2016 presented the results of the research on consumer vulnerability.[484] Main drivers for vulnerability were defined, which relate to consumers' personal characteristics (age, gender, level of education, nationality), to their behaviour, difficulties with access (digital illiteracy), market-related issues or some situations leading to vulnerability (like financial situation).[485] Recognising vulnerability may nuance the level of consumer protection and brings back the concept of the consumer as the weaker party.[486] However, the question, to which extent this concept may be effectively applied towards AI-consumers is still debatable.[487] Yet, one may notice vulnerability through the fact that AI systems shake the balance of information ownership, giving advantages to AI designers, deployers and owners versus consumers, who may not be aware of the very existence of algorithmic influence or nudging they are subject to and may be unable to make well-informed choices.[488]

Regulated autonomy principle goes beyond the realm of consumer law and refers to the most basic ethical concepts which were discussed in our previous chapters. Sax et al. provide a comprehensive ethical analysis of the notion of autonomy which may inform legal understanding of the concept.[489] The autonomous consumer is the one who is independent in consideration of all information and options in order to decide what shall be desirable for his choices. In the case of AI-enabled products, consumers should, as in any kind of transaction, receive clear information on the use, features and properties of purchased products.[490] Also, when AI systems enable advertising itself, the consumer shall have the right to know that he is subject to algorithmically designed content, which is based on the data provided by the consumer. Such a data provision for marketing purposes shall be conditional to consumers' consents expressed in an explicit way (by allowing cookies or through GDPR-based marketing clauses). The problem here is linked to the fact that nowadays, many consumers do not make conscious decisions while giving consents. Many times, they do it automatically, because they do not want to lose functionalities of internet webpages (in case of cookies) or simply because they are not capable of reading all lengthy disclaimers and grey-printed clauses.

---

484 Consumer *vulnera*bility across key markets in the EU. Final report (2016) https://ec.europa.eu/info/sites/info/files/consumers-approved-report_en.pdf accessed 22 July 2020.

485 Ibid.

486 Jabłonowska et al. (n 24) 11.

487 Ibid.

488 More on humans' vulnerability and the relations between their defenceless exposures and new technologies' capabilities see, Brownsword (n 185) 79.

489 Marijn Sax, Natali Helberger, Nadine Bol, 'Health as Means Towards Profitable Ends: mHealth Apps, User Autonomy, and Unfair Commercial Practices' (2018) 41 Journal of Consumer Policy 105.

490 Brownsword (n 185) 273.

Another feature shaping autonomy is authenticity in the sense that the decision taken by a consumer is truly personal and free from excessive persuasion from the side of the trader. Any form of commercial practice contains some level of persuasiveness, yet it is important that it does not impair the consumer's freedom of conduct. Also, the options offered to consumers are an element of their autonomy.[491] In the market economy, the variety of choice is something inherent to it. The autonomy of consumer may be particularly put at stake by AI technologies which may address consumers with different forms of hidden, deceptive, misleading advertising or other aggressive commercial communication techniques. Nowadays, the major legal act addressing these challenges is UCPD, which provides a general framework for assuring fairness in B2C transactions forbidding unfair commercial practices, englobing mostly misleading and aggressive ones. The problem with the UCPD is its enforcement, whose efficiency differs depending on the member states adopted and existing mechanism of consumer protection.

6.2.3 Data protection

'Data is the lifeline of AI'.[492] This statement is the most accurate way that depicts the importance of data in the AI industry. All algorithmic technologies, and in particular machine learning is data-driven and require well-functioning data ecosystem, supported by a sound regulatory framework which enhances trust and data availability, at the same time safeguarding privacy rights. European Union, by adopting GDPR,[493] has taken an essential role, not only in Europe but globally in shaping the desirable approach towards data privacy as a fundamental human right.[494] It has established a new universal standard with a strong emphasis on the rights of individuals, European values, and trust.

The GDPR, which has entered into force on 25 May 2018 contains detailed regulation on the personal data collection, processing, privacy impact assessment, consents for data use and corroborates the crucial rights of access to data, right to object, to be informed and to be forgotten.[495] The rules stipulated in the GDPR are enforced through the rights to an effective judicial remedy against a controller or processor. Also, the supervisory authority's (every member state shall establish one) decision is subject to a judicial remedy. In order to assure the effective

---

491 Sax et al. (n 489) 108–109.
492 Max Craglia et al. (ed.), 'Artificial Intelligence: a European Perspective' (Publications Office of the EU Luxembourg 2018) 103.
493 See (n 125).
494 Schwartz (n 313) 773.
495 More on the right to be forgotten in the context of AI, Eduard Fosch Villaronga, Peter Kieseberg, Tiffany Li, 'Humans Forget, Machines Remember: Artificial Intelligence and the Right to be Forgotten' (2017) Computer Security and Law Review (forthcoming) https://ssrn.com/abstract=3018186 accessed 22 July 2020.

compliance with the GDPR, the system of fines was established, which for undertakings may reach up to 4% of the total worldwide annual turnover.

The GDPR regulation is built around 6 major principles, which are enumerated in art. 5.1 (a-f). Firstly, personal data shall be processed lawfully, fairly and transparently.[496] It shall be collected for specific, explicit and legitimate purposes. Personal data shall be subject to 'data minimisation', which means that is shall be adequate, relevant and limited to what is necessary for the processing purpose. Personal data shall be accurate and kept up to date. It shall be stored for the limited period — in principle, no longer than is necessary. However, there is an exception allowing for data storage for achieving public, scientific, historical research or statistical purposes. Finally, personal data should be processed with full respect for integrity and confidentiality, allowing for the appropriate measure of security and protection against unauthorised or unlawful processing. This principle needs to be enforced through relevant technical and organisational measures.[497]

The impact of GDPR on algorithmic systems is first of all of the general character since AI and machine learning, in particular, require big data volumes in training data sets, among which personal data take an important part.[498] All the above-mentioned principles shall be respected by the AI industry. However, meeting the requirements of some of them may be particularly difficult. Firstly, fairness and discrimination, as was stated in our previous chapters and paragraphs, may be challenged due to the use of biased data. It shall be stressed that AI development shall be a multidisciplinary endeavour. Designers need to closely cooperate with committees composed of experts representing various disciplines (law, ethics, psychology) in order to mitigate the negative consequences of AI technologies. Such an approach would help to run participatory forms of risk assessment of data quality.[499] Another challenge may be related to a data purpose limitation. AI systems many times use information which is collected on the side of the main purpose. In this case, in order to comply with GDPR rules, the data collector should get additional consent from the data subject. This principle is linked to data minimisation rule, which in case of AI should be followed by developers who continuously need to review the type and quantity of training

---

496 Chrispher Kuner et al., 'Machine Learning with Personal Data: Is Data Protection Law Smart Enough to Meet the Challenge' (2017) 7 International Data Privacy Law 1–2.

497 Paul Voigt, Axel von dem Bussche, *The EU General Data Protection Regulation (GDPR). A Practical Guide* (2017 Springer) 87–92

498 Pasquale (n 45) 34.

499 Consultative Committee of the Convention for the Protection of Individuals with Regard to Automatic Processing of Personal Data (Convention 108). Guidelines on Artificial Intelligence and Data Protection, T-PD(2019)01 (Council of Europe 2019). See also, Alessandro Mantelero, 'Consultative Committee of the Convention for the Protection of Individuals with Regard to Automatic Processing of Personal Data (Convention 108). Report on AI. AI and Data Protection: Challenges and Possible Remedies (Council of Europe 2019) 9.

data required.[500] Finally, the biggest problem of compliance with GDPR is related to transparency and the right to information. Transparency includes prospective and retrospective elements. The former shall be understood in a way that gives individuals right to be informed about the ongoing data processing *ex-ante* — data controllers shall inform the data subject in a concise, easily accessible and easy-to-understand way about the controllers themselves, about the way data, is being processed, about its purpose and reason, together with a timeframe.[501] Retrospective (*ex-post*) transparency refers to the determination on how the decision has been made. In the world of ethical AI, this principle may be understood in the context of the requirement of explainability. As Felzman et al. point, among legal scholars, there is a debate taking place about the very existence of a right to an explanation of automated decisions under the GDPR.[502] The question is if the right of explanation may be drawn from the provisions of art. 13(2)(f) and 15 (1)(h) of the GDPR read in conjunction with the art. 22, which provides explicit regulation on solely automated individual decision-making, including profiling. Art. 22 GDPR states the right of an individual person not to be subject of such decisions if they produce legal effects concerning him or her or significantly affect them. The above-mentioned provisions, once there exists automated decision-making, including profiling, state that controller of data should, at the time when personal data are obtained, provide the data subject with 'meaningful information about the logic involved, as well as the significance and the envisaged consequences of such processing for the data subject'. The data subject should have the right of access to his personal data. As Wachter et al. indicate, there are several doubts if the GDPR provides a proper right to an explanation at all. Right to explanation, in theory, may concern the system functionalities or specific decisions, may also relate to ex-ante explanation (concerning system functionality) or ex-post (concerning both system functionalities and specific decisions). In the case of the GDPR and wording of the provisions of art. 13(2)(f), 15(1)(h) and 22, there is no direct mention on the right to obtain an explanation. Such a reference is made however in recital 71 of the GDPR, yet even if it is intended to provide interpretative guidance to the core provisions of the legal act, recitals themselves are not binding.[503] Leaving,

---

500 See, 'How to Train an AI with GDPR Limitations', 13 September 2019 https://www.intellias.com/how-to-train-an-ai-with-gdpr-limitations/ accessed 22 July 2020.

501 Heike Felzman et al., 'Transparency You Can Trust: Transparency Requirements for Artificial Intelligence Between Legal Norms and Contextual Concerns' (2019) Big Data & Society 3.

502 Ibid. See also, Sandra Wachter, Brent Mittelstadt, Luciano Floridi, 'Why a Right to Explanation of Automated Decision-Making Does Not Exist in the General Data Protection Regulation' (2017) International Data Privacy Law https://ssrn.com/abstract=2903469 accessed 22 July 2020; Bryce Goodman, Seth Flaxman, 'European Union Regulations on Algorithmic Decision-Making and a "Right to Explanation' (2016) arXiv:1606.08813 accessed 22 July 2020.

503 Wachter et al. (n 502) 8–11.

theoretical debates aside, we may reflect on the major problem concerning the scope of 'meaningful' information about the logic involved. Meaningful, being vague notion and rather subjective in its essence, should be assessed from the perspective of the individual demanding given information. All in all, it should, as much as it is possible to allow the data subject to determine the main factors that lead or altered given decision.[504]

The art. 22 of the GDPR provides a general safeguard of data protection in case of decisions taken solely by automated processing, including profiling, which is 'any form of automated processing of personal data consisting of the use of personal data to evaluate certain aspects relating to a natural person' (art. 4 (4) GDPR). Apart from profiling, such decision-making may cover several decision types—recommendation systems, displaying search engines results, automated credit decisions, insurance risk assessments, behavioural advertising or administrative or judicial decisions. Automated decisions will fall under the scope of art. 22 GDPR only when they involve the processing of personal data.[505] The protection granted by this provision consists in the right to oppose to be subject of such decisions and is intending to strengthen the human autonomy versus algorithmic decisions. However, it also regulates exceptions from this general rule. Firstly, this right does not apply to contractual situations between the data subject and the data controller. It also is not applied to the automated decisions which are authorised by Union or member state law to which the controller is subject. Finally, this right does not cover automated decisions which are based on the data subject's explicit consent. Whenever exceptions are in place, the data controller shall implement appropriate measure to protect the data subject's right, with the minimum standard of assuring the right to obtain human intervention on the part of the controller and the possibility for the data subject to express his or her opinion and challenge the decision. The scope of these exceptions is quite broad and brings the threat that actually they can become rules. In particular the exception concerning contractual situations, due to its potential widespread use, may put in doubts the effectiveness of the basic right expressed in art. 22 (1) GDPR.[506]

Apart from the regulation on personal data protection, new rules on the free flow of non-personal data were adopted. The application of Regulation 2018/1807[507] started in the mid-2019. The examples of non-personal data are 'aggregate and anonymised data used for big data analytics, data on precision farming that can help to monitor and optimise the use of pesticides and water, or data on maintenance needs for industrial machines'.[508] The major goal of this

504 Felzman et al. (n 501) 3.
505 Maja Brkan, 'Do Algorithms Rule the World? Algorithmic Decision-making and Data Protection in the Framework of the GDPR and Beyond' (2019) 27 International Journal of Law and Information Technology 97. See as well, Goodman, Flaxman (n 502) 1.
506 Brkan (n 505) 120–121.
507 See (n 128).
508 Regulation 2018/1807, 9 recital.

regulation is to help unlock data and facilitate the cross-border operation of businesses based on the processing of other than personal data in the Union. Non-personal data regulation provides rules relating to data localisation requirements, the availability of data to competent authorities and the porting of data for professional users. The data localisation requirements introduced by the member state, which hindered cross border data storage, right now, under new rules should be prohibited, unless justified on the grounds of public security, with due respect of the principle of proportionality. Thus, member states are banned from imposing any requirement to localise or process data domestically. It means that more efficient and centralised data storage systems may emerge.

From the policy goals perspective, there is a need to facilitate sharing of data between public and private sectors, which shall lead to the creation of common European Data Space,[509] which would be a unified digital area with the scale that would enable the development of new, high-quality products and services based on data.

6.2.4 *Intellectual property rules*

Intellectual property law and AI are strongly linked in several ways. Like in many areas nowadays, AI technologies may be a tool which facilitates the management of intellectual property rights. In Europe and in particular in the European Union, two major IP Offices—European Patent Office and European Intellectual Property Office- are implementing AI systems *inter alia* to facilitate patent or trademark and design searches or they are using machine translating systems which help their internal examiners in their day to day work.[510] Apart from the utilitarian aspect of the intersection between AI and IP, by far the most interesting and at the same time complex, are the issues touching upon the problems of protecting AI through the IP rights. In this field, the major scholar reflection is circulating around two major points. Firstly, the use of patent and copyright rules to protect AI systems (embodied or non-embodied) and secondly the problem of IP protection for assets (works, patents) generated by AI.[511]

IP law in European Union is quite extensively regulated with the strongest legislative framework covering trademark and design protection, under either national harmonised rules being result of the transposition of EU directives[512] or

---

509 Commission, 'Towards a Common European Data Space' (Communication) COM(2018) 232 final.

510 See, WIPO, 'Index of AI Initiatives in IP Offices' https://www.wipo.int/about-ip/en/artificial_intelligence/search.jsp. accessed 22 July 2020.

511 Celine Castets-Renard, 'The Intersection Between AI and IP: Conflict or Complementarity' (2020) 51 ICC-International Review of Intellectual Property and Competition Law 142–143.

512 Directive (EU) 2015/2436 of the European Parliament and of the Council of 16 December 2015 to approximate the laws of the Member States relating to trademarks (2015) OJ L336/1.

by a unified system of EU Trademark and EU Design which are registered at the European Intellectual Property Office in Alicante.[513]

In terms of AI technologies and their IP related issues, one should indicate four major areas. This is copyright law,[514] patent law, databases protection[515] and finally the trade secrets regulation,[516] which belongs to the area of unfair competition law. When we take a closer look at the system of IP law in the EU and its possible applicability to the AI technologies, we need to sum up the actual state of legal possibilities for the protection of AI systems and results/product of their operation.

AI technologies, as we know, may take different forms; however, they have a common feature — they are based on algorithms accompanied with the datasets to train them. Thus, when we approach these technologies from the patent law point of view, we should determine that AI systems are regarded as mathematical methods. This is a commonly accepted rule, present in the European systems of patent law, which at the moment is not unified yet under EU law. According to the European Patent Convention[517] patentability of mathematical methods is explicitly excluded (art. 52 (3) of European Patent Convention). Patents, however, may be granted when trained algorithms are embodied into some physical structure, like computation unit circuit or simply some device operating based on them.[518] In such a case, general rules of patentability apply, which include the novelty and the lack of self-evident character of the invention, involving an inventive step and its susceptibility of industrial application. When assessing the inventive step, all features which contribute to the technical character need to be scrutinised. In the case of the mathematical method like AI algorithm, it must be checked if such a method contributes to the technical

513 Regulation (EU) 2017/1001 of the European Parliament and of the Council of 14 June 2017 on the European Union trademark (2017) OJ L 154/1; Council Regulation (EC) No 6/2002 of 12 December 2001 on Community designs (2001) OJ L 3/1.

514 At EU level copyright law within information society is harmonised mostly through: directive 2001/29/EC of the European Parliament and of the Council of 22 May 2001 on the harmonisation of certain aspects of copyright and related rights in the information society (2001) OJ L 167/10; Directive (EU) 2019/790 of the European Parliament and of the Council of 17 April 2019 on copyright and related rights in the Digital Single Market and amending Directives 96/9/EC and 2001/29/EC (2019) OJ L130/92; Directive 2009/24/EC of the European Parliament and of the Council of 23 April 2009 on the legal protection of computer programs (2009), OJ L 111/16.

515 Directive 96/9/EC of the European Parliament and of the Council of 11 March 1996 on the legal protection of databases (1996) OJ L77/20.

516 Directive (EU) 2016/943 of the European Parliament and of the Council of 8 June 2016 on the protection of undisclosed know-how and business information (trade secrets) against their unlawful acquisition, use and disclosure (2016) OJ L 157/1.

517 European Patent Office (EPO), under the European Patent Convention, provides a single patent grant procedure, based on which bundle of national patents are granted and as such they constitute a European patent See, https://www.epo.org/law-practice/legal-texts/html/epc/2016/e/index.html accessed 10 July 2020.

518 Cubert, Bone (n 86) 421.

character of the invention.[519] The practical problem with the patentability of AI-based inventions is connected with the registration procedure, which necessitates a comprehensive description of the underlying technology. A patent application shall disclose the invention in a sufficiently clear and complete manner. In the case of AI innovations, there is a stressed need for a proper disclosure to avoid algorithmic opacity and decisions being taken by 'black boxes'.[520] Such a description may be problematic in case of AI, due to the complexity of the reasoning involved with a given invention or solution. The innovation needs to be described both in terms of its structure and function. For example, for the neural networks, the description shall include neural topology and how the weights are set.[521] Strict disclosure requirements may be a discouraging factor for the companies, which instead of pursuing patent applications may turn to use trade secret protection. Directive 2016/943 harmonises trades secrets[522] protection in the EU. According to its rules, an owner of a trade secret is protected against unlawful acquisition and use of it and is entitled to civil remedies. The trade secret protection is comprehensive. In order to rely on it, an owner shall implement internal trade secret policies and keep appropriate documentation in order to prove the possession of the relevant trade secrets (know-how which may relate to algorithmic solutions and systems) in case of legal disputes resulting in unlawful acquisition and use.

Another legal option for protecting AI systems is copyright. AI software, like computer programmes, may be granted copyright protection when such software is original. However, according to art. 1(2) of the directive 2009/24/EC, protection may be granted only to the expression in any form of the computer program. Ideas and principles which underlie it are not protected. In the case of AI, it may mean that the original code of an algorithm may be protected, but ideas and concept behind it not.

AI systems, since they are based and dependent on data used for training of algorithms, may deserve protection based on the database's sui generis right. When datasets are being processed and annotated, they may become a particularly valuable asset. If such annotated data takes the form of a database, which is a collection of independent works or data arranged in the systemic or

---

519 See, EPO Guidelines for Examination, part G 3.3.1.

520 Maria Iglesias, Sharon Shamuilia, Amanda Anderberg, 'Intellectual Property and Artificial Intelligence. A Literature Review', EUR 30017 EN (Publications Office of the EU Luxembourg 2019) 7.

521 Ibid, 8.

522 According to art. 2 (1) of the directive 2016/943, a 'trade secret' means information which meets all of the following requirements: (a) it is secret in the sense that it is not, as a body or in the precise configuration and assembly of its components, generally known among or readily accessible to persons within the circles that normally deal with the kind of information in question; (b) it has commercial value because it is secret; (c) it has been subject to reasonable steps under the circumstances, by the person lawfully in control of the information, to keep it secret.

methodological way and accessed individually by electronic or other means,[523] it may deserve a *sui generis* right protection. Condition is that making of such a database entailed substantial investment in obtaining, verifying or presenting the contents of the database.

A separate issue, which is currently attracting the public eye, is the protection of the works and assets generated by AI. AI systems are capable nowadays of producing artistic works and inventions. The application of the currently existing legislative framework in order to grant IP right to such assets is problematic. The biggest problem is whether an AI system may be considered an author or an inventor of a given work or invention. The human centricity of both copyright systems and approach towards AI in EU, speaks against granting copyright ownership to an AI system. Works created by the machines lack the most important element of originality because it lacks human attributes required by law. In terms of patentability, in a similar vein and according to recent decisions of EPO or USPTO (United States Patent and Trademark Office), only named persons and not AI systems can be listed as the inventors.[524] In the recently published draft report of the European Parliament on intellectual property right for the development of artificial intelligence technologies[525] there is an expressed view to consider the way technical and artistic creations generated by AI may be protected with the goal to encourage these forms of creations. The European Parliament proposes that AI-generated works may be protected by copyright, yet the ownership of the rights shall be assigned to the persona who prepares and publishes work lawfully.

6.2.5 *Cyber security*

Cyber security is one of the biggest challenges of contemporary times. Information and communications technology bring digitisation and connectivity to the products and services widely used by citizens. Many of them use algorithmic solutions and are connected to the internet. At the same time, the level of security and resilience of used devices is not sufficiently built-in, leading to serious gaps and risks to cybersecurity. Cyber-crime industry is exploiting technical shortages and brings serious threats to both individual citizens and society as a whole together with governmental structures. When we add AI dimension to it, we can distinguish three major areas where AI impact on security is particularly visible. First of all, AI could enhance the goals of the security sector with the use of predictive algorithms helping to prevent cybercrimes. Secondly, AI systems may be a target of cyberattacks and there should be a reflection on how it can be protected from attacks. Finally, AI may be a tool of cyber threats and as such,

---

523 See, art. 1 of a directive 96/9.
524 See, https://www.jdsupra.com/legalnews/can-ai-be-an-inventor-not-at-the-74975/ accessed 22 July 2020).
525 European Parliament, 2020/2015(INI).

may be abused for achieving malicious purposes. Policy making processes shall address all these aspects in a way that promotes a user-centric, systemic and pluralistic approach to the problem of cybersecurity and AI-related issues.[526]

The EU law is addressing the cybersecurity with the regulation on the EU Cybersecurity Act.[527] First and major goal of this legal act is to strengthen the position of ENISA (the EU Agency for Network and Information Security), by granting a permanent mandate and empowering it with operational and regulatory competences. ENISA is supposed to increase the cooperation at the EU level, by helping member states with handling cybersecurity incidents. ENISA, in particular, should support member states in developing AI techniques which would help in defence against cyberattacks. From the viewpoint of industry, an important aspect of ENISA's work is the one related to the cybersecurity certification mechanisms. Introduction of European cybersecurity certification scheme is intended to support trust and security of products and services present at the Digital Single Market. For the AI industry, obtaining such a certification would be just another expression and proof of reliability and trustworthiness, which is multidimensional in its essence, encompassing not only the ethical dimension but also more utilitarian one. The European cybersecurity certification framework will refer to three assurance levels — basic, substantial and high. Appropriate assurance level will respond to the level of risk associated with the use of the product. Basic level assurance means that products for which such a certificate was issued meet the security requirements evaluated at a level to minimise the known basic risks of cyberattacks and incidents. Once the product obtains the 'substantial' assurance, it would mean that it passed highest security tests at a level to minimise the known cybersecurity risks and cyberattacks carried out by actors with limited skills and resources. The 'high level' confirms the conformity with security requirements at a level intended to minimise the risk of state-of-the-art cyberattacks carried out by entities with significant skills and resources.[528] Introduction of such a uniform certification system would prevent from so-called 'certification shopping' which exists when there are different levels of requirements' strictness applied in different member states and undertakings are choosing for certification processes the ones with the softest approach.

6.3 Whose liability?

6.3.1 Investor/producer

One of the key questions that should be asked in the process of analysing the legal framework of the AI technologies is the liability of those persons that were engaged in setting up that technology. Among the roles which are crucial in this

---

526 HLEG AI, 'Policy and Investment Recommendations' (n 5) 30–31.
527 See (n 130).
528 See, art. 53 of the regulation 2019/881.

process, firstly there is an investor. There is a feeling that investor — or more broadly also a producer who acts in the investor's capacity — should be strictly liable for defects in digital technologies. That should also be understood as liability put on them even if the defects emerge after the product was put into use, provided they were in control of updates to the technology.[529] In that case, the argument of development risk defence should not apply. Moreover, their strict liability should be there in indemnifying damage caused by defective products and also the components and that all irrespective of which form they take — tangible or digital.[530] That means that if it is proven that a given digital technology has caused harm, the burden of prove of the defect should be reversed in case there might be disproportionate difficulties or costs pertaining to establishing the relevant level of safety or that the expected level of safety has not been met.[531]

The general principle of investor responsibility related to traditional products should also apply to digital technologies. The rationale behind it is that eventually even if the product or just one of its components is in digital form, it remains a product and that liability related to its deficiencies stays unchanged regardless of its essential or operational characteristics. Therefore, general principles related to product liability like a fair distribution of risks and benefits resulting from commercial production, a spreading of the costs of individual harm to all buyers of a given type of product, and an attributable responsibility for the prevention of harm are fully valid also in case of digital products.

It is in line with the principle of functional equivalence that damage caused by defective digital content should trigger the investor's liability since digital content fulfils many of the tangible movable items functions as in the directive on liability for defective products (PLD).[532] The same refers to defective digital elements of products when they come separately from the tangible item as well as its updates after the product has been put into circulation. It is also no different to digital services provided on a continuous basis during the product lifetime.

The investor has become liable if the defect had happened as a result of the producer's interference with the product already put into circulation or the producer's failure to act which itself should be regarded as a defect in the product. The time when a digital product is placed on the market does not set a strict limit on the investor's liability for defects if then the producer or a third party acting on behalf of them remain in charge of providing needed updates or digital services. The investor remains liable where the defect has its origin in a defective digital component or digital ancillary part or in other digital content or services provided for the product, or in the absence of an update of digital

---

529 Borghetti (n 22) 71.
530 Zech (n 32) 197.
531 Amato (n 75) 79.
532 See (n 162).

content, or of the provision of a digital service required to maintain the needed level of safety.[533]

Digital technologies might be characterised by limited predictability. The interconnectedness of appliances combined with cyber security issues contributes to difficulties in predicting the product's performance. A defect in digital content or in a product with digital elements may therefore result from the impact of the environment in which the product operates or from the product's evolution, for which the manufacturer only created a general framework but which they did not design in detail. In view of the need to share benefits and risks efficiently and fairly, the development risk defence, which allows the producer to avoid liability for unforeseeable defects, should not be available in cases where it was predictable that unforeseen developments might occur.

Such characteristics of digital technologies as opacity, openness, autonomy and limited predictability may result in difficulties to establish what should be a level of safety a user is entitled to expect. The same refers to establishing what might be categorised as a failure in achieving the expected level of safety. These characteristics may result in a situation when it is easier for the producer to prove relevant facts. This asymmetry between the investor and acting in his capacity producer and the user justifies the reversal of the burden of proof. Moreover, their liability for defective digital products refers directly to the failure in their monitoring duties.[534]

Together with the growing complexity of technologies, it is becoming more difficult to develop proper skills and instruments to discharge all duties. This is equally the responsibility of operators as much as producers and investors. Therefore, producers have to make sure their design, description and marketing of digital products should enable operators to discharge their duties. In many jurisdictions, the rules of product monitoring duties on the part of producers have been introduced for the purposes of tort law.[535] In the light of the described characteristics, which is their openness and dependency on other factors of the digital environment, this monitoring duty should be clearly put investors.[536]

---

533 Only recently, the EU has confirmed in the directive (EU) 2019/771 of the European Parliament and of the Council of 20 May 2019 on certain aspects concerning contracts for the sale of goods, amending Regulation (EU) 2017/2394 and Directive 2009/22/EC, and repealing Directive 1999/44/EC (2019) OJ L 136/28, that a seller is also liable for conformity with the contract of digital elements, including for updates provided for as long a period as the consumer may reasonably expect. Also, the directive (EU) 2019/770 of the European Parliament and of the Council of 20 May 2019 on certain aspects concerning contracts for the supply of digital content and digital services [2–19] OJ L 136/1, established a resembling model for digital content and digital services. The features of an investor's strict liability are the same, though constructed on different grounds.

534 Expert Group on Liability and New Technologies – New Technologies Formation, 'Liability for Artificial Intelligence and other emerging digital technologies' (n 7) 42–44.

535 Brownsword (n 185) 234.

536 Expert Group on Liability and New Technologies – New Technologies Formation, 'Liability for Artificial Intelligence and Other Emerging Digital Technologies' (n 7) 45.

6.3.2 Developer

All technology-related products and services require constant development. The challenge for the legal and regulatory provisions will be to create appropriate conditions for developments of digital technology, including the AI that promotes innovation while ensuring the adequate level of protection and safety for users. This is on the EU to assess if current member states' safety and liability frameworks are rightly adjusted, taking into account these challenges or if there is still a room for the improvements in this sphere.[537] Developers, similarly to producers of digital technology products and services should be liable for damage caused by defects in their products, also in the case when the deficiencies were caused by changes made after they had been placed on the market. There are certain elements of this environment that should be considered for implementation. Firstly, in cases when there is a risk that the third parties might be exposed to an increased risk of harm there should be compulsory liability insurance that on the one hand could facilitate victims' access to compensation and on the other could protect potential tortfeasors against the risk of liability. Secondly, victims should be entitled to the facilitation of proof in cases when particular features of technology increase the difficulties of proving the existence of an element of liability. Thirdly, there should be a reversal of the burden of proof in cases when digital technologies have not come with logging features and resulted in logging failures or limited access to logged data to the detriment of the victim.

Fourthly, in addition to all above, any destruction of the users constitutes compensable damage. Fifthly, there is no need to contemplate devices or autonomous systems a legal personality, because the damage they cause is attributable to existing persons including, in particular, a developer.[538] And sixthly, looking at the developer's liability, it should not be analysed separately from the entirety of all circumstances. This refers in particular to the software updates, which might be necessary to protect from unwanted deficiencies or to tackle the problem of unadjusted or outdated data.

There emerges a question referring to the case when a developer using a most actual knowledge at the time the system was launched and then subsequently, choices made by the AI technology independently caused damage. In that situation, a difficulty is that the liability may not be automatically attributable to the developer. The question is to what extent the liability arises and a breach of duties of care is applicable to the developer if the level of information passed to the users that AI system might be a cause of harmful choices might be assessed as insufficient.

In other words, digitalisation and bringing AI technologies into the play is a cause of key changes within the surrounding environment. Many of them have an impact on liability law. In evaluating it, the features like the lack of transparency,

---

537 Commission, COM(2018) 795 final (n 3) 8.
538 Karner (n 375) 123.

controllability, complexity, predictability, openness, autonomy and vulnerability have to be taken into account.

Even though each of these changes may happen relatively slowly but their combination of gradual progress and frequency may eventually cause a disruption. Existing well-understood rules on liability offer solutions to the risks caused by digital technologies. However, their outcomes might not be sufficient as a fair and efficient allocation of loss is not achieved. The reasons for that might be multiple like for example, it might not be clear whose caused the damage, who benefitted from the caused damage, who was in charge of controlling the risks and to what extent they indeed were properly controlled and who might have decided to elect cheaper rather than the most appropriate solution, including a wrong choice of indemnifying insurance.

Regardless the above complications or rather because of their existence, a well though, the appropriate and just response of law and regulatory requirements to the liability questions should be worked out to avoid situations when victims of harm caused by digital technologies cannot be certain of compensation unlike the victims in equivalent situations caused by human or conventional technology factors. This is why necessary adaptations and amendments to existing liability regimes should be looked for. Taking into account a multitude of complexities deriving from digital technologies and a wide range of risks associated with them it might be needed to come up with a variety of solution instead of a single and universal one. On the other hand, despite this variety of solutions, comparable risks should be governed by similar liability regimes. Eventually, these regimes should clearly determine to what extent which losses are recoverable. As with other defective products, both fault and strict liabilities should continue to coexist.[539] That should allow a victim to seek compensation against more than one person on more than one basis. Thus, rules on multiple tortfeasors should govern. When assessing the legal and regulatory regimes should be noted that contractual liability or other compensation regimes might apply alongside or instead of tortious liability which has to be accounted when determining to what extent they have to be amended.[540]

Strict liability as a response to risks created by digital technologies if they are emerging in conditions that may typically cause significant harm. In principle, they should lie with the person who is in control or in charge of the risk connected with the assuring and appropriate functioning of operation of these technologies (developer) or who benefits from their operation (deployer). If there is a collusion of these two persons' liabilities, then in the first instance there should be a liability of the person primarily deciding on and benefitting from the development or use of the relevant technology frontend developer or deployer. Otherwise, the liability passes to a person continuously defining the features of the relevant technology and providing essential and ongoing maintenance

---

539 Ibid 118.
540 Spindler (n 287) 132.

(backend developer of deployer). I any case, strict liability should lie with the one who has more control over the risks and solely for the purposes of liability, it does not seem necessary to contemplate autonomous systems a legal personality at this stage.[541]

6.3.3 Deployer

Apart from the investor and the developer, there is also a deployer liability for the use of technology-driven products and services. This derives from the assumption that strict liability lies with that who is in control of the risk connected with the operation of technologies and who benefits from them. Even though there is a legitimate argument that existing defences and statutory exceptions from strict liability may be reconsidered in the contests of autonomous and AI-driven technologies as they have been conceived primarily to traditional notions of control by humans, prior to doing so current legal constructs should be used. Therefore, the well-known strict liability rules should apply to new digital technologies.

The European specificity is that in part of jurisdictions there are either general clauses or they allow analogy to statutory regimes and at the same time the others do without the fault requirement in very rare and limited situations. Instead, they broaden the notion of fault. Often strict liability is more applicable to cases of physical harm whereas less to pure economic loss. The entire picture complicates even more given the fact that in some jurisdiction, there is more than one strict liability regime. That manifest in a multitude of available defences that liable persons have at their disposal. Simply, the novelty factor of technology is not a sufficient justification for introducing strict liability. It is more the fact that the harm caused by digital technologies might be equally great comparable to the risks being already subject to strict liability referring to conventional non-technological products. Therefore, according to this criterion, both should be subject to strict liability. The most convincing argument for this is that victims should be treated alike if they are impacted by a similar harm.[542]

This applies primarily to technologies related to the movement of vehicles or appliances in public spaces. Other products like home appliances more rarely would be appropriate for strict liability. Strict liability is also less likely appropriate for stationary robots even though they are AI-driven. They are usually deployed in a confined environment. The deciding factor might be that there is a limited range of people exposed to risk associated with their operations. Apart from that, it is worth mentioning that they are protected by a different contractual regime.

In case it seems appropriate to make the operation of this technology subject

---

541 van den Hoven van Genderen, 'Legal Personhood in the Age of Artificially Intelligent Robots' (n 11) 218.

542 The significance being determined by the interplay of the potential frequency and the severity of possible harm.

to a strict liability regime, the same features should characterise this as other no-fault liabilities for comparable risks. This applies to losses that are recoverable regardless of the caps that could be introduced or whether non-pecuniary damage is recoverable. The strict liability offers victims easier access to compensation, without excluding a parallel fault liability claim. Furthermore, while strict liability will typically channel liability onto the liable deployer of the technology, this person will retain the right to seek recourse from others contributing to the risk like investor, producer, developer or operator.

There have been discussions who strict liability for digital technologies should firstly refer to. It has been pointed out that based on the examples of autonomous vehicles as earlier, the majority of accidents have been caused by humans, in the future, most accidents will be caused by technology. This could mean that it would not be appropriate to hold the deployer strictly liable in the first place because it is the producer who for example for the cost's avoidance reasons might be in a position to limit the risk of accidents. However, it is still the deployer who decides how the technology is used and who benefits from it. If strict liability for operating the technology were on the producer, the cost of insurance might be transferred on to the deployers or even the owners anyway.

A neutral and flexible concept of a person who is in control of the risk connected with the deployment, maintenance and functioning of digital technologies and who benefits from such operation, in other words, is in control of it is a variable concept. A variety of accountable activities that could expose third parties to potential risks and that can be attributed to that person ranges from activating the technology, through steps in between, to determine the output of the technology use. That is regardless of the fact the more sophisticated and more autonomous systems mean less control over the details of the operations. Therefore, the way the systems are deployed, and the algorithms are defined influenced by continuous updates have a direct impact on the deployer's liability. Any such a deployer who might in fact be a backend operator may have a certain degree of control over the risk's others are exposed to. From an economic point of view that a person might benefit from the operation as they can, for example, profit from data generated or collected by the operation of a deployed system. They can also economically benefit as they remuneration might be commissioned on the basis of the duration, continuous nature or intensity of the operation.

In cases when there is more than one deployer that strict liability should be on the one who has more control over the risks posed by the deployed system. It would be missing needed transparency if an assessment of liabilities relied only on benefit as the decisive factor for deciding who should be liable. Equally control and benefit should be decisive for qualifying a person who should be put under the liability in that a case. In theory, the deployer of the frontend would have more control, but where digital technologies become more backend-focused, there are cases where control over the technology remains with the backend deployer. It makes a lot of sense to hold the backend deployer liable as the person primarily in a position to control, reduce and ensure the risks connected with the use of the technology.

Eventually, the legislators should define who should be liable under which circumstances, and all other matters that need to be regulated. For instance, the deployer should take out insurance and reduce their own costs could pass on the premiums through the fees paid for its services. In case several deployers fulfil the function of backend operators, one of them would have to be designated as a responsible operator.

In most of the EU member states, all elements could be implemented by way of a simple enlargement of existing strict liability models. Many of these schemes include a variety of exceptions and exclusions that a deployer may use for its defence. However, not all of them may be appropriate for digital technologies as they reflect a focus on a human control.[543]

Deployers should have to comply with a range of duties of care, including those referring to choosing the right system for the right task, monitoring the system or maintaining the system. Provided that producers designed, described and marketed products in a way effectively enabled operators to comply with their duties, the deployers should be liable for damages connected with adequate monitoring the product deployment after putting it into circulation.

The well-established model referring to traditional technologies recognises that the operators have to discharge a range of duties of care and this is related to the choice of technology. The factors determining this are the tasks to be performed, the operator's abilities, the organisational framework, appropriate monitoring, maintenance, safety checks and repairs. In the absence of the right performance of these duties, the fault liability would apply regardless of the operator's strict liabilities for the risk created by the technology-related products. The duty of care is usually raised to a point where it is less obvious to differentiate between a fault and strict liabilities. In regard to digital technologies related products and services, the duties of care principle become even more needed.[544]

6.4 What liability?

6.4.1 Civil liability and accountability

In the areas referring to individuals' safety and fundamental rights affecting applications, it is necessary to introduce traceability and reporting requirements to facilitate their auditability. In practice, the ex-ante oversight approach could be useful. Also, before AI systems are deployed systematic monitoring on an ongoing basis could be introduced. That could include an obligation for human intervention and oversight in situations when AI decisioning is deployed in specific sectors. Civil strict or tort liability rules must ensure adequate compensation in case of harm or violations of rights. Separately they may need to be

543 Expert Group on Liability and New Technologies – New Technologies Formation, 'Liability for Artificial Intelligence and Other Emerging Digital Technologies' (n 7) 39–42.
544 Ibid 44–45.

complemented with mandatory insurance obligations. Applying well-known liability schemes to new challenges relating to digital technologies is natural but given the number of novelty factors in digital technologies and limitations of existing regimes may leave risks of victims' damages uncovered. There is a threat that adequacy of existing liability rules considering they were formulated based on old concepts of monocausal models of inflicting harm may be questionable. The main purpose of tort law as indemnifying victims for losses they should not have on the basis of an assessment of all the interests involved but this refers solely to indemnifiable harm that is compensable. That all refers to damages to interests that legally are worthy of protection.

Generally, there is a universal consent that physical harm to a person or to a property triggers tortious liability; however, there is no similar consent to accept a purely economic loss. For example, damages being a result of applications based on self-learning algorithms operating on financial markets might remain uncompensated. This is due to the fact that some legal systems do not provide tort law protection of this type of interests or provide it only on a limited ground only if additional requirements are fulfilled. There might be contractual relationships between the parties.[545] Nor is it accorded that damage to or the destruction of data is a property loss. Namely, in some jurisdictions, the notion of property refers only to tangible corporeal objects. Other differences refer, for example, to the recognition of personality rights. They might be affected by digital technologies applications, in cases when certain data is released causing infringements on the privacy rights.[546]

It does not mean that digital technologies question the existing concepts of compensable harm. It is rather that some of the already recognised categories of losses might be less relevant in traditional tort scenarios. Damages and in particular their size and impact being prerequisite for liability is also a flexible concept and might vary, which effectively impacts the overall assessment and validity of justification of tort claims.[547]

An essential requirement for establishing civil liability is a causal link between the victim's damage and the defendant's sphere. The victim has to be able to prove that harm originated from conduct or risk attributable to the defendant. Usually, it is the victim that has to produce evidence supporting their position. However, in less evident, the sequence of events more complex dependencies of various factors might contribute to the damage. Therefore, it might become very

---

545 See Willem van Boom, Helmut Koziol, Christian Witting (eds.), *Pure Economic Loss* (Springer 2004) and Mauro Bussani, Vernon Valentine Palmer, 'The Liability Regimes of Europe – Their Façades and Interiors' in Mauro Bussani, Vernon Vaalentine Palmer (eds.), *Pure Economic Loss in Europe* (Cambridge University Press 2011 reprint) 120.

546 See Article 82 of the GDPR for a harmonised claim for compensation in cases of data breach.

547 See Article 2:102 paragraph 1 of Principles of European Tort Law (PETL): 'The scope of protection of an interest depends on its nature; the higher its value, the precision of its definition and its obviousness, the more extensive is its protection.'

difficult for the victim to establish causation without the circumstances when crucial links in the chain of events are within the defendant's control. In some jurisdictions, if the victim is not successful in persuading the court that something for which the defendant has to be accounted for caused the harm, they might lose their case. This is the risk regardless of how strong the victim's evidence would have been otherwise.

The tort laws in Europe are mainly based on a fault principle and allow for compensation if the defendant could be blamed for the damage.[548] The blame is linked to some misconduct by the tortfeasor. Regardless of the differentiation between objective or subjective wrongdoing and wrongfulness and fault, the basis of liability for misconduct remains crucial. It requires identification of the duties of care on the side of the perpetrator and to prove that the conduct of the perpetrator of the damage did not discharge those duties.[549] These duties are determined by multiple factors. They might be defined by the statutory language of norms requiring or prohibiting certain behaviour. Sometimes they have to be reconstructed on the basis of social beliefs about the prudent and reasonable course of action in given circumstances.[550]

The novelty of digital technologies complicates applying liability rules based on the fault principle. It is due to the lack of track record of right functioning of these technologies and the possibility of their development without direct human control through the self-learning capabilities.[551]

The AI-based systems cannot be assessed according to human conduct-based duties of care concept.[552] At least not without necessary adjustments requiring further justification. Given the variety of legal liability models in the EU and the fact that they are more advanced in regulating product and safety requirements, it might be the case that some necessary rules should be introduced to facilitate unifying the duties of care relevant for tort law in the technology-related cases.[553] The first and most probable unification attempt would refer to introducing legal or regulatory requirements which would trigger liability by shifting the burden of proof.

In the case of damage caused by digital technology, there might be difficulties with determining what constitutes a fault. Generally, it is the victim that must

---

548 See also the Commission Staff Working Document on Liability (SWD (2018) 137) 7, accompanying Commission Communication, COM(2018) 237 final (n 2).

549 See Helmut Koziol, 'Comparative Conclusions' in Helmut Koziol (ed.), *Basic Questions of Tort Law from a Comparative Perspective* (Jan Sramek Verlag 2015) 685, 782.

550 See Benedikt Winiger, Ernst Karner, Ken Oliphant (eds.), *Digest of European Tort Law III: Essential Cases on Misconduct* (De Gruyter 2018) 696.

551 Geslevich Packin, Lev-Aretz (n 31) 88.

552 See Commission, COM(2020) 64 (n 138) where it is confirmed that "The overall objective of the safety and liability legal frameworks is to ensure that all products and services, including those integrating emerging digital technologies, operate safely, reliably and consistently and that damage having occurred is remedied efficiently."

553 See Urlich Magnus, 'Why Is US Tort Law so Different?'(2010) 1 Journal of European Tort Law 102–124.

prove that those whose conduct is attributable to the defendant was at fault. The victim has to both identify which duties of care the defendant should have discharged and to prove that these duties were not observed and caused harm. To prove the defendant's fault entails providing evidence that proves what the applicable standards of care were and that they have not been met. Another difficulty is to prove how the event resulted in the damage. The complexity of the circumstances leads to complicating identification in providing relevant evidence. Usually, it could be very much complicated or even impossible to identify a bug in a long software code. Similarly, in the case of AI-related applications to examine the process leading to a specific result might be lengthy, difficult and costly.

European tort legislation differs substantially in their approach to holding someone liable for the conduct of another.[554] For example in some of them it is possible to attribute an auxiliary's conduct to the principal without additional requirements apart from that the auxiliary acted under the control of the principal and for the principal's benefit. In the others, it is possible to hold the principal liable in tort law only exceptionally. Those exceptions refer to situations like known dangerousness of the auxiliary, their unsuitability for the assigned task or a fault in selecting or supervising the auxiliary. There are also jurisdictions with mixed models where both approaches can be applied.

Jurisdictions where there is a neutral, broader definition of strict liability as liability without fault in general regard vicarious liability as a mere variant of strict liability. The strict liability is usually relating to some specific risk, whereas a vicarious liability is rather linked with fault liability. It is about the principal's liability without their own personal fault but for the passed-on fault of their auxiliary. This applies even if the auxiliary's conduct is not evaluated according to the benchmarks applicable to themselves, but to the ones of the principal.[555]

Regardless of existing differences, the vicarious liability concept is considered as a possible catalyst for arguing that operators of machines, computers, robots or similar technology-related deployments should be strictly liable for their operations. The arguments to this concept are built around the thinking that if someone can be liable for the wrongdoing of a human helper, the same principle should apply to the beneficiary of such support of a non-human helper. This is provided that they equally benefit from that delegation.[556] The so-called principle of functional equivalence means that using the assistance of an autonomous digitalised system should be treated similarly to employing a human auxiliary in cases when it leads to harm of a third party. However, the complication emerges

---

554 See the overview by Koziol (n 549) 795.

555 Suzanne Galand-Carval, 'Comparative Report on Liability for Damage Caused by Others', in Jaap Spier (ed.), *Unification of Tort Law: Liability for Damage Caused by Others* (Kluwer Law International 2003), 289.

556 See AJB Sirks, 'Delicts' in David Johnston (ed.), *The Cambridge Companion to Roman Law* (Cambridge University Press 2015) 246, 265.

in those jurisdictions which consider vicarious liability a variant of fault liability.[557] There holding the principal liable for the wrongdoing of another may be difficult as it needs identifying the benchmark against which the operations of non-human helpers will be assessed. This is given that fact they should mirror the misconduct of human auxiliaries. The argument is that the potential benchmark should take into account that application non-human auxiliaries might be safer and that it is less likely to cause damage by them than by human actors.[558]

6.4.2 Criminal liability

Although AI and other digital technologies, such as the Internet of Things or distributed ledger technologies, have the potential to transform the societies for the better, however, the application should have adequate safeguards built in to minimise the risk of bodily injury or other harm they might cause.[559] In the EU, this is the role of product safety regulations but these regulations cannot completely exclude the possibility of damage resulting from the operation of these technologies or humans accountable for them. In cases that would happen, the victims might seek appropriate redress. Typically, they would do so on the basis of various liability regimes available to them within the private civil law possibly in combination with insurance or the criminal law.[560] It is key to underline that only the strict liability of producers for defective products is harmonised at EU level. At the same time, all other regimes are regulated separately and differently by the member states. The exception here is only some specific sectors where certain regulations have been introduced.

In the cases when there is a necessity to ensure that criminal responsibility and liability, they should always be attributed in strict accordance with the fundamental principles of criminal law.[561] The emergence of AI, the complex digital ecosystems and the autonomous decision-making requires a reflection about the suitability of some established rules on safety and criminal law questions on liability.[562] The evolutionary enhancements of AI-empowered products like robots and the Internet of Things may act in ways not envisaged at the time when they were first put into operation. As AI use spreads out horizontal as well as sectoral rules should be reviewed, reassessed and adjusted.[563]

---

557 See, European Parliament, 'Draft Report with recommendations to the Commission on a Civil liability regime for artificial intelligence' 2020/2014(INL) https://www.europarl.europa.eu/doceo/document/JURI-PR-650556_EN.pdf accessed 22 July 2020.
558 Ryan Abbott, 'The Reasonable Computer: Disrupting the Paradigm of Tort Liability' (2018) 86 George Washington Law Review 1–45.
559 Commission, COM(2018)237 final (n 2) 14–17.
560 Brownsword (n 185) 212.
561 HLEG AI, 'Policy and Investment Recommendations' (n 5) 39.
562 Pagallo, Quattrocolo (n 61) 403.
563 For any new regulatory proposals that shall be needed to address emerging issues resulting from AI and related technologies, the Commission applies the Innovation Principle, a set of tools and guidelines that was developed to ensure that all Commission initiatives are

As the EU safety framework addresses the intended use of products when placed on the market, this triggers the development of standards in the area of AI-enabled devices continuously adapted together with technological progress.[564] The development of safety standards and support of the international standardisation organisations should enable businesses to benefit from a competitive advantage and increase consumer trust.[565] It is being assessed if the safety and liability frameworks are fit for purpose for these new challenges and whether any gaps should be addressed. It is believed that a high level of safety and efficient damages redress mechanisms should help to build wide societal acceptance of the new technologies.

In the EU, the assessments of the Product Liability Directive from the point of view of criminal liability have already been conducted.[566] The same refers to the Machinery Directive assessments.[567] From the beginning the AI-related technologies assessments have been carried out from the perspective of the existing liability frameworks.[568]

In its assessment of existing criminal liability regimes that might refer to digital technologies, it has been concluded that the liability regimes in the member states ensure some basic protection of victims whose damage is caused by the operation of such new technologies.[569] However, the specific characteristics of these technologies namely their complexity, constant changes due to their updating modifications, self-learning capabilities, limited predictability and openness to malpractices compromising cybersecurity cause the effect that it is difficult for the victims to seek redress even in justified cases. The difficulty in the allocation of criminal liability creates a risk that the currently unclear rules might

---

innovation friendly: https://ec.europa.eu/epsc/publications/strategic-notes/towards-innovation-principle-endorsed-better-regulation_en accessed 22 July 2020.

564 For example, the Machinery Directive (n 161), the directive 2014/53/EU of the European Parliament and of the Council of 16 April 2014 on the harmonisation of the laws of the Member States relating to the making available on the market of radio equipment and repealing Directive 1999/5/EC (2014) OJ L 153/62, the Directive 2001/95/EC of the European Parliament and of the Council of 3 December 2001 on general product safety (2001) OJ L 11/4, as well as specific safety rules for example for medical devices or toys.

565 Standards should also cover interoperability, which is crucial for offering consumers greater choices and ensuring fair competition.

566 The Product Liability Directive (n 162) states that if a defective product causes any damage to consumers or their property, the producer has to provide compensation irrespectively of whether there is negligence or fault on their part.

567 The evaluation of the Machinery Directive (n 161) indicates that some provisions do not explicitly address certain aspects of emerging digital technologies, and the Commission will examine whether this requires legislative changes. On the evaluation of the Product Liability Directive (n 162), the Commission will issue an interpretative guidance document, clarifying important concepts in the Directive.

568 See Commission SWD (2018)137 (n 548).

569 Spindler (n 287) 129.

make it unfair or inefficient.[570] To help this, the appropriate adjustments have to be introduced to EU and member states criminal liability regimes.

These adjustments should be based on certain principles according to which the liability regimes should be designed and in case it is needed also changed. Firstly, a human operating a technology that carries an increased risk of harm to others should be subject to criminal liability for damage resulting from its operation providing that all other indispensable conditions triggering the criminal liabilities are met. Secondly, when an AI-based product or service provider who ensures the necessary technical framework has a stronger control than the owner or user of the product or service equipped with AI, this should be taken into account in determining who primarily should be deemed liable for the technology.[571] Thirdly, a person using a technology that poses an increased risk of harm to others should be required to obey duties to properly select, operate, control, monitor and maintain the technology in use and eventually could be judged liable for breach of such duties if at fault. Fourthly, using a technology which has a degree of autonomy should not mean less criminal liability for harm than if a human would have caused harm. Fifthly, as in some other cases when the criminal liability might be accounted the victim should benefit from the alleviation of their own evidentiary burden with regard to the causal relationship between a defect of the deployed system and the harm.[572]

6.5 Upsides of the horizontal regulatory approach

As was discussed above, the extensive body of binding the EU legislative measures is applicable to various aspects related to the AI technology. The horizontal approach guarantees the sound level of legal certainty and equality before the law. From the viewpoint of the functioning the Internal market and in particular Digital Single Market, the EU legislative framework fights with the fragmentation of rules. Based on the analysed regulatory system, one shall conclude that in general terms, the EU law is addressing the first condition of the trustworthy AI—legality—in quite a comprehensive way. However, there are some areas in which existing horizontal framework would need some amendments. First of all,

---

570 Pedro M. Freitas, Francisco Andrale, Paulo Novais, 'Criminal Liability of Autonomous Agents: From the Unthinkable to the Plausible' in Pompeu Casanovas et al. (eds.), *AI Approaches to the Complexity of Legal Systems* (Springer 2014) 150.

571 Amato (n 75) 83.

572 To impose criminal liability upon a person at least two necessary elements must happen. The first (*actus reus*) is the external or factual element referring to criminal conduct. The second o (*mens rea*) is the internal or mental element referring to knowledge, understanding and will towards the conduct element. Both jointly are necessary for criminal liability to be imposed. See more on criminal liability for AI, Gabriel Hallevy, 'The Criminal Liability of Artificial Intelligence Entities' (2010) Ono Academic College, Faculty of Law https://papers.ssrn.com/sol3/papers.cfm?abstract_id=1564096 accessed 22 July 2020.

as the European Commission has indicated in its White Paper, the effective application and enforcement of existing the EU and national law should be improved. This is postulated chiefly due to the problems with the lack of transparency of AI, which makes it difficult to identify possible breaches of fundamental rights or liability rules.[573]

It is worth mentioning that apart from existing horizontal rules which are not AI-specific, currently at the EU level, there is legislative reflection taking place in order to create horizontal regulation, specifically for the AI industry. The Commission's White Paper, followed by subsequent public consultation and the European Parliament's motion based on the art. 225 TFEU[574] indicate the direction of the future regulation on ethical principles for the development, deployment and use of AI, robotics and related technologies. As we already stressed, the framework of proposed provisions concerns the implementation of AI Ethics Guidelines into the properly binding, directly applicable legal act. The logic of the European Parliament's proposal evolves around human-centricity, properly conducted a risk assessment, outlining the safety features, transparency and accountability, non-discrimination, non-bias, equality, social responsibility and gender balance, environmental protection and sustainability, privacy (including biometric recognition). The proposal also stresses the pertinence of sound governance rules, which at the national and supranational levels should take the form of the establishment of AI supervisory (regulatory) authorities. The draft proposed by the European Parliament can be described through the lens of regulatory flexibility. The horizontal regulation shall be as flexible and future oriented as it is only possible. Only such an approach can guarantee that regulation will be a constant point of reference, bringing sound legal foundations for fast-developing technologies.

---

573 Borghetti (n 22) 63.

574 Art. 225 TFEU states that 'the European Parliament may, acting by a majority of its component Members, request the Commission to submit any appropriate proposal on matters on which it considers that a Union act is required for the purpose of implementing the Treaties. If the Commission does not submit a proposal, it shall inform the European Parliament of the reasons'. See also, European Parliament, 2020/2012 (INL) (n 35).

7 Sectoral Regulatory Approach

7.1 Opening remarks

Apart from horizontal rules of the EU law, which are either already in place or will be adopted in order to regulate ethical foundations of Artificial Intelligence industry, we shall notice a growing number of sectoral initiatives aimed at regulation of particular industries and sectors of society. The sectoral approach is characterised by the mix of binding, traditional laws and measures adopted at the EU level and new forms and methods of regulation. Altogether those old and new methods contribute to the ethical governance of AI. This notion covers a set of processes, procedures, cultures, values designed to the highest standards of behaviours, which go beyond the black letter of the law.[575] In general terms, the problems with regulating digital transformations, in which AI plays a significant role, is faced with the 'pacing problem',[576] which describes the gap between technological development and measures and mechanism adopted to regulate it. The problem with sectoral regulation of AI industry in Europe and globally is connected with the fact that the policy cycle usually takes time. We may see it with the EU example already—the regulatory works in the AI field, even if they have a rather horizontal character, at the Commission's level are already taking more than two years. On the industry side—digital products, services, solutions are developed very fast and many times also become largely present on the market at a similar pace. Thus, there is a need for a more adaptive regulatory approach. Regulators, which are present also at the EU level, nowadays have in their hands a bunch of tools which allow for fast and responsive reaction to the rapid industrial changes.

---

575 Alan F.T. Winfield, Marina Jirotka, 'Ethical Governance Is Essential to Build Trust in Robotics and Artificial Intelligence Systems' (2018) 36 Philosophical Transactions Royal Society A 2.

576 Gary E. Marchant, 'The Growing Gap Between Emerging Technologies and the Law' in Gary E. Marchant, Braden R. Allenby, Joseph R. Herkert (eds.), *The Growing Gap Between Emerging Technologies and Legal-Ethical Oversight. The Pacing Problem* (Springer 2011) 19; William D. Eggers, Mike Turley, Pankaj Kishnani, 'The Future of Regulation', https://www2.deloitte.com/us/en/insights/industry/public-sector/future-of-regulation/regulating-emerging-technology.html#endnote-sup-49 accessed 22 July 2020.

The Commission stresses new methods which are present at the EU level and their usage in policymaking include regulatory sandboxes, self-regulatory measures and innovation deals. In general, in this area there is a growing number of soft law instruments, which are not directly enforceable and binding; however, they can include some guidance towards self-regulation, codes of best-practice or codes of conduct. The risk with self-regulatory practices is however related to favouring of the goals of industry, rather than of other stakeholders.[577]

7.1.1 Regulatory sandboxes

As cyber reality is new, it also requires a new approach to regulatory measures. It is becoming increasingly popular among the regulators to test the new methods that allow for more efficient reference to new areas of activities that need a closed-up oversight. Regulatory reactions should and indeed very often are faster, smarter, better adjusted and more agile than law requirements. They have to be distinguished from both industry standards which represent the interests of the business and the legal norms that tend to be late. It is not unusual that what has been formulated within the regulatory requirements has not been recognised by the lawmaker yet. On the other side, they play a different role. For example, their relevance in a tort action where the liability is searched from the wrongdoer is weaker. It is so even if the courts may look at such requirements and take them into account in assessing whether a given conduct complied with the duties that needed to be discharged.

Among several new methods of regulatory approaches, the ones that may particularly fit the technology and especially AI-related products and services are the regulatory sandboxes. The concept is about testing new, rather friendly and non-intrusive regulations before they are broadly and bindingly introduced. These new regulations are introduced in parallel to new technologies. As much as bringing technology to market relates firstly to experimenting and testing emerging technology in real-world environments, the new regulations putting supervisory requirements on them are introduced at the same time.[578] Basically, the regulatory effort is not to let technology develop unattended but rather accompany it already at the testing phase long before it is widely launched for the production. For example, in view of avoiding unnecessary duplications or competing efforts, a limited number of large-scale reference sites are being developed and the results of these testing facilities stay open to other interested entities. Examples of such testing facilities include the testing of connected and autonomous driving, shipping and creation of data spaces.[579] The need to

---

577 Cath et al. (n 188).
578 A Reference Testing and Experimentation Facility is a technology infrastructure that has specific expertise and experience of testing mature technology in a given sector, under real or close to real conditions (smart hospital, clean rooms, smart city, experimental farm, corridor for connected and automated driving, etc.).
579 von Ungern-Sternberg (n 15) 253.

identify the new testing facilities for the latest AI technologies in key areas as mobility, healthcare, manufacturing, food production and processing or security is constantly growing. The regulatory sandboxes where regulation is limited or favourable to testing new products and services in selected areas provide authorities with sufficient requirements to control their suitability and allow for needed adjustments.[580]

The adjusted supervisory monitoring that includes regulatory sandboxes and other methods for policies and governance experimentation can help encourage the development of AI-based innovation where the law provides regulatory authorities with a sufficient margin of manoeuvre.[581] At present much of the focus is put on assessing if the regulatory framework in Europe is suitably adjusted to digital technologies and in particular for connected and automated AI-related driving.[582] It is assessed to what extent the creation of environments that are conducive to innovation such as regulatory sandboxes, and public testing are valuable and worth larger scaling initiatives.[583] If they prove efficient, the EU member states would be encouraged to replicate such environments and solutions on a larger scale. They would be expected to create one-stop-shop for companies developing AI applications. It would allow for identifying specific regulatory needs in the future.[584]

The creation of agile policy-making solutions such as regulatory sandboxes should involve multiple public and private stakeholders to help innovators and allow fast assessments for new innovations without hampering the public or private interests and at the same time help stimulating innovation without creating unacceptable risks. However, the limitations of that a method of regulation should be thoroughly assessed and their cohesion and usefulness should be ensured. Especially, regulatory sandboxes could help developing fundamental rights impact assessment relating experimental AI implementations.[585]

7.1.2 Self-regulation incentives

Self-regulation, as opposed to legal regulation characterised by the top-down approach, is an expression of a bottom-up approach. This is a type of regulation characterised by the voluntary initiatives, taken by the economic actors, social partners, NGOs, industry associations, taken in order to adopt certain guidelines, set of rules that will be applied by them. Many times, self-regulation is a starting point for the co-regulatory measures, which go in between legal regulation and self- regulation, shaping the mutual interaction between the two.[586] Ideally there

580 Commission, COM(2018) 795 final (n 3) 8.
581 While regulatory sandboxing is needed tool, innovation can be supported with softer approaches such as innovation centres and policy labs.
582 Commission, COM(2018) 795 final (n 3) 18.
583 Ibid.
584 Ibid.
585 HLEG AI, 'Policy and Investment Recommendations' (n 5) 41.
586 Pagallo et al. (n 371) 10–11.

should be very little discrepancies between industry- or company-specific self-regulation and the general regulatory requirements. This is not for any other reason than just for the fact that early business self-regulating allows preceding potentially more difficult to implement supervisory requirements. Self-regulation, at least in the ideal theory, should be more convenient for the businesses themselves. On the flip side, self-regulation is also convenient for the market regulators as the self-regulated entities tend to be more easily compliant due to their buy-ins to their own norms and obligations that they came up with. Specifically, self-regulation provides first benchmarks that could help the assessment of technology-based applications. When the outcomes of such self-regulations are assessed, supervisors could ensure that the regulatory frameworks for AI technologies are in line with these values, fundamental rights, expected conduct and the desired shape of the market practices.[587] The existing regulatory frameworks should, therefore, be monitored from the viewpoint of their suitability to the developments of the technology-based practices and reviewed to adapt them to constant challenges better.[588]

The available technology and using new approaches like design thinking processes boost agile policymaking. It expands the range of stakeholders involved in the consultation process regarding the development of policies. Gathering stakeholders whose real needs are to be tackled by projected policies could help to respond to the actual problems and not assumed ones. It fosters planning, controlling, testing, implementing and monitoring policies which could then get immediate feedbacks and needed amendments. It also allows for a dynamic evaluation for regulations as all stakeholders can share their views and changing expectations as well as their values. Although public authorities are central actors in policy development and enforcement who decide on the governance parameters, other the close collaboration with other actors involved into this process at every stage could help policymakers to better refer to the needs of agile governance. That a system could encourage innovators to engage proactively with policymakers to co-design the governance ecosystem for their inventions.[589]

7.1.3 *Innovation deals and digital innovation hubs*

Innovation deals are the tools within existing legislation for assessing regulatory barriers to the development and deployment of new technologies.[590] They are

---

587 Amato (n 75) 84.
588 Commission, COM(2018)237 final (n 2) 14–17.
589 World Economic Forum, 'White Paper: Agile Governance. Reimagining Policy Making in the Fourth Industrial Revolution' http://www3.weforum.org/docs/WEF_Agile_Governance_Reimagining_Policy-making_4IR_report.pdf accessed 22 July 2020.
590 See, https://ec.europa.eu/info/research-and-innovation/law-and-regulations/identifying-barriers-innovation_en accessed 22 July 2020.

multipartite voluntary agreements between the EU institutions, innovators and member states authorities. Their objective is to gain a thorough understanding of how EU regulations work in practice. If they are found to be an obstacle to innovations, they would be flagged and marked as needing further action.

Innovation deals as a quasi-regulatory measure would best fit into the idea of creating an integrated EU market for AI-enhanced products, services and applications.[591] The specific areas as for example, data protection and privacy, consumer protection and competition law by design.[592] Important considerations for the uptake of AI in areas with a high societal and policy stake are related to fairness, transparency and accountability of algorithmic decision-making model and impact of AI on human behaviour and societal reception.[593] Also, intellectual property issues should also be explored to ensure that the regulatory framework rightly addresses problems specific to AI.[594] One of the expected final results is promoting its sustainable and efficient development.[595]

Such funding as the scheme available within the InvestEU Programme to support re-setting enterprises towards AI-enabled solutions should be available for all companies in all sectors and should focus on fostering incorporation of Trustworthy AI technologies. All the EU programmes and initiatives, together with the network of Digital Innovation Hubs, are supposed to help to create the measures for start-ups and SMEs to easy funding and needed commercialising advice. Part of that should be supported in SMEs and start-ups to define their AI transition needs, build plans upon them, propose accessible financial schemes to facilitate their transformation, help to upskill the employees. This should include all sorts of business advice including investments and intellectual property rights.[596]

The network of Digital Innovation Hubs is to be used in the context of making available a legal and other needed support to implement trustworthy AI systems being in line with the Ethics Guidelines. It especially refers to providing technical know-how to SMEs that do not have sufficient funds and experience in this area.

---

591 The Commission is constantly exploring areas of concern in algorithmic decision making, mostly in the online platform tools, in order to enhance trust through different approaches to transparency, fairness and accountability. See, Commission, COM (2018) 795 final annex (n 68).
592 See, GDPR (n 125).
593 See, the Joint Research Centre HUMANIT, https://ec.europa.eu/jrc/communities/community/humain accessed 22 July 2020.
594 Blodget-Ford (n 353) 320.
595 Commission, COM(2018) 795 final (n 3) 18.
596 See, https://ec.europa.eu/info/law/law-making-process/planning-and-proposing-law/better-regulation-why-and-how_en accessed 22 July 2020.

7.2 Leading industries self-regulation practices

7.2.1 Automotive

The automotive industry, with increasing automation and connectivity is one of the greatest beneficiaries of Artificial Intelligence solutions. The scope and extent of the use of these technologies imply the level of automation of the vehicle. Currently, several automotive industry organisations,[597] provide the schemes describing different levels of automated driving, which depend on the level of autonomy of the driver versus the vehicle's autonomy. According to the Society of Automotive Engineers, there are 6 levels of automation. Zero level—the driver only—where the driver's eyes and hands are on and where the driver is continuously exercising control over the vehicle. Level one is considered as assisted driving where the system accompanies steering or brake/acceleration control. In level two, there is partial driving automation, in which the driver can take temporarily hands-off, while has to monitor the system at all times. The system has steering and brake/acceleration control over the vehicle in a specific use case. Vehicles of levels 1 and 2 are already widely present on the market. Level 3 – conditional driving automation – allows the driver not to monitor the system at all times; however, it is expected that the system may request the driver to resume control within the appropriate time margin. Level 4 – high automation allows for the system to cope with all situations automatically and the driver is not required during defined use. Level 5 equals to full automation, where no driver is required, and the system can cope with all situations during the entire journey.[598] Regardless of the level of automated driving, the progress in the automotive industry, powered by AI, is undeniable. The benefits are various—from road safety,[599] through expanding new types of mobility services, reducing emissions and improving the urban planning.[600] Also, like in no other case, there is a vivid debate taking place around serious ethical issues relating in particular to levels 4 and 5. It can be illustrated by the famous 'trolley problem'—trying to describe ethical dilemmas of decision making in the situation when possible

---

597 Ex, German Association of the Automotive Industry (VDA), the Society of Automotive Engineers (SAE) or the National Highway Traffic Safety Administration (NHTSA).

598 See, https://www.sae.org/news/press-room/2018/12/sae-international-releases-updated-visual-chart-for-its-%E2%80%9Clevels-of-driving-automation%E2%80%9D-standard-for-self-driving-vehicles accessed 22 July 2020. Daniel Watzenig, Martin Horn, 'Introduction to Automated Driving' in Daniel Watzenig, Martin Horn (eds.), *Automated Driving. Safer and More Efficient Future Driving* (Springer 2017) 4–6.

599 Commission, 'Report on Saving Lives: Boosting Car Safety in the EU', (Communication) COM(2016) 787.

600 Commission, 'On the Road to Automated Mobility: An EU Strategy for Mobility of the Future' (Communication) COM(2018)283 final. See also, Jan Gogoll, Julian F. Müller, 'Autonomous Cars: In Favour of a Mandatory Ethics Setting' (2017) 23 Science and Engineering Ethics 682–685.

outcomes of decisions are always ethically and morally doubtful.[601] In case of automated driving this ethical dilemma is translated into the design of the software, which should be trained in an appropriate way to take a decision in case of a potentially fatal collision which seems to be unavoidable. However serious this problem can be, there is a growing number of scholars works, expressing concerns that the usefulness of trolley cases in the reflection on ethics of autonomous vehicles is limited.[602] There is a variety of other traffic situations which may seem mundane yet need the ethical reflection as well. These include approaching a pedestrian crossing with limited visibility, navigating with busy intersections, or simply left turning with ongoing traffic.[603] The ethical questions here are related to the fact that humans' certain decisions take intuitively, while machines don't. While human drivers may differ in their driving style, which may depend on their experience, age, gender, cultural and geographical origin, an autonomous vehicle needs to be specific and uniform in its operation.

Without going into detailed scholar analysis of ethical aspects of autonomous vehicles, we should turn to the policy-making and regulatory response to it. Among the European Union member states, German example is of particular importance. Germany, being the leader of the automotive industry, made an effort to establish the Ethics Commission on automated and connected driving, which was composed of legal, ethical, engineering scholars, representatives of automotive companies, consumer associations, the German automobile club ADAC, catholic bishop, former Public Prosecutor and former judge of German Federal Constitutional Court.[604] In June 2017 the commission drafted a report containing the code of ethics for automated and connected vehicular traffic.[605] The code covers 20 ethical guidelines touching upon major problems, mainly relating to levels 4 and 5, which the automotive industry is faced with nowadays. The code stresses the principal goal of the automated transport system, which is an increase in road safety and joins it with the principle of human autonomy and human centricity. The rule should be that the driver can retain accountability over the vehicle, voluntarily overrule the system and drive by himself (ethical guidelines 1,4, 16–17). Further, it develops on the necessity to protect individuals, whose benefits shall take precedence over utilitarian considerations. The code agrees with a positive balance of risk in terms of reduction of the level

---

601 Johannes Himmelreich, 'Never Mind the Trolley: The Ethics of Autonomous Vehicles in Mundane Situations' (2018) 21 Ethical Theory and Moral Practice 671.
602 See, Himmelreich (601) 672–673; Noah J. Goodall, 'Away from Trolley Problems and Toward Risk Management' (2016) 30 Applied Artificial Intelligence 810–821; Sven Nyholm, Jilles Smids, 'The Ethics of Accident-Algorithms for Self-Driving Cars: An Applied Trolley Problem?' (2016) 19 Ethical Theory and Moral Practice 1276–1277.
603 Himmelreich (601) 678.
604 Christoph Luetge, 'The German Ethics Code for Automated and Connected Driving' (2017) 30 Philosophy and Technology 548.
605 See, https://www.bmvi.de/SharedDocs/EN/publications/report-ethics-commission. pdf?__blob=publicationFile accessed 22 July 2020.

of harm caused by automated systems versus human driving (ethical guideline 2). From the operational and regulatory point of view, the code stresses the responsibility of public sector to introduce licencing and monitoring of processes guaranteeing the safety of automated vehicles and not leaving it to the manufacturers themselves (ethical guideline 3). Analysed ethical code, devotes a lot of attention to the unavoidable accidents and dilemma situations (ethical guidelines 5–9). In general, the prevention comes as a major rule — vehicles should be designed in a way that critical situation does not arise and that vehicles drive in a defensive and anticipatory manner. Also, fully automated driving systems should not be obligatory. In the case of hazardous situations, the protection against damage of human life enjoys the priority over damage to animals or property. In truly dilemmatic situations, which involve the decision of sacrificing one human life for another, there should not be any standardisation in programming such ethically questionable problems. Against this background, there is a prohibition on any distinction made, which is based on personal features of either drivers or possible victims. However, general programming to reduce the number of personal injuries may be justifiable.[606] Probably the most important in terms of their practical relevance are the ethical rules concerning accountability (ethical guidelines 10–11). Ethical guidelines shift the accountability from the car's owner[607] to the manufacturers and operators of the vehicles and their technological systems.

Guidelines also touch the problems of transparency and public information, which should be ensured by the suitable independent body (regulator); security (in particular cyber-security) and safety and data protection (ethical guidelines 12–15). There are as well ethic rules on machine learning methods applied in autonomous cars, limiting their use to the situations when they meet the safety requirements regarding functions relevant to vehicle control. In an emergency situation, the vehicle should on its own enter the state of the safe condition (ethical guidelines 18–19). Finally, the need for proper education and training on the side of the user of the automated vehicle is stressed (ethical guideline 20).

The discussed guidelines, even if they are non-binding and shall be treated as soft law, indicate the direction in which future legislation and regulation on autonomous driving should be designed.

7.2.2 *Aviation*

Application of Artificial Intelligence in the aviation industry is multifaceted. Firstly, it may impact aircraft design and operation, bringing technologies which will make fully autonomous flights possible one day. Also, new solutions changing relation between pilot and systems may come to play, reducing the use of human resources. AI technologies can also be used for aircraft predictive

---

606 Luetge (604) 550–553.
607 See, Geneva Convention on Road Traffic (1949) and Vienna Convention on Road
     Traffic (1968).

maintenance, allowing to anticipate failures and provide preventive measures. Big data processing may improve air traffic management, safety risk management, cybersecurity, sharing of passenger information. With carbon emissions, being so much in a spotlight, AI applications may work for the optimisation of trajectories or assessment of the fuel consumption.[608]

In terms of the regulatory approach in the EU, the aviation industry is already extensively regulated at the supranational level through three levels of rules, combining binding measures and non-binding standards (soft law). Regulatory measures of binding character cover the basic regulation 2018/1139 adopted by the European Parliament and Council[609] and its implementing rules (delegated or implementing regulations adopted by the Commission[610]). On the top of it the European Union Aviation Safety Agency, being a proper regulator of aviation industry adopts non-binding standards, which take the form of Certification Specifications (CS), Acceptable Means of Compliance (AMC) and Guidance Material (GM). AMCs intend to illustrate means to assure compliance with the binding rules of basic regulation and its implementing rules. Even if they do not create additional obligations, their goal is to provide legal certainty and uniform implementation of binding 'hard' law. According to EASA's policy, AI-related regulation should stem from soft law measures, which based on the AI Roadmap adopted by EASA should be delivered in three major phases starting from 2021 until 2035. In the first phase, there should be guidance development concerning human assistance augmentation and human-machine collaboration. From 2024 the phase two will commence, aiming at consolidating framework where guidance for more autonomous machine shall be drafted. Finally, from 2029 phase three will start with the goal to push further innovations in AI for the aviation industry, allowing for fully autonomous commercial air transport operations.[611]

Currently, the drone industry is one of the fastest-growing branches of aviation.[612] Artificial Intelligence solutions bring new opportunities for drones, mainly in the field of data analytics and navigation. There is already widespread use of AI-powered software which assist police, firefighters and other emergency services in collecting data that can be used to fight with public security threats.[613]

---

608 EASA, 'Artificial Intelligence Roadmap. A Human-centric Approach to AI in Aviation' (2020 easa.europa.eu/ai) 7–11. See also, Ruwantissa Abeyratne, *Legal Priorities in Air Transport* (2019 Springer) 214–221.

609 Regulation (EU) 2018/1139 of the European Parliament and of the Council of 4 July 2018 on common rules in the field of civil aviation and establishing a European Union Aviation Safety Agency (2018) OJ L 212/1.

610 See, https://www.easa.europa.eu/regulations accessed 22 July 2020.

611 EASA, 'Artificial Intelligence Roadmap' (n 608) 13.

612 Pam Storr, Christine Storr, 'The Rise and Regulation of Drones: Are We Embracing Minority Report or WALL-E?' in Marcelo Corrales, Mark Fenwick, Nikolaus Forgó (eds.), *Robotics AI and the Future of Law*, (Springer 2018) 105–108.

613 Sam Daley, 'Fighting Fires and Saving Elephants: How 12 Companies Are Using the AI Drone to Solve Big Problems', (10 March 2019) https://builtin.com/artificial-intelligence/drones-ai-companies accessed 22 July 2020.

At the EU level, even if drones' operations are regulated in a uniform way, currently applicable delegated regulation 2019/945[614] and implementing regulation 2019/947[615] does not provide any explicit guidance on the algorithmic aspects of the operation of unmanned aircraft. However, a general reference to data protection and privacy under general rules of GDPR and obligation of the registration of operators of unmanned aircraft if they operate an unmanned aircraft which is equipped with a sensor able to capture personal data brings some limitations which are in line with general ethical rules on AI.

7.2.3 Financial services

Two major drivers fuel the increased importance of AI in the financial sector: the amount of data available to financial institutions which need AI in order to manage and make use of it and the very capacity of AI-related technologies to build competitive advantages of companies in the increased levels of efficiency, cost reduction and enhanced quality of services.[616] Financial sector is already widely using AI technologies, mainly in five areas: compliance, fraud and anti-money laundering detection, loans and credit assessment, cybersecurity and trading and investment decisions.[617] Financial sector is also the one in which multilevel and multijurisdictional regulation is already at place. Soft law and hard law are particularly intertwined one with another and laws of national, international and supranational character need to be taken into consideration by financial institutions operating on global markets. Artificial intelligence solutions are particularly impactful on FinTech (financial technology) sector, but also, they are revolutionising regulatory compliance,[618] bringing up the RegTech as the area of convergence of regulation and technology.[619] RegTech uses new technological developments, including AI, to assure new forms of market monitoring

---

614 Commission Delegated Regulation (EU) 2019/945 of 12 March 2019 on unmanned aircraft systems and on third-country operators of unmanned aircraft systems (2019) OJ L 152/1.

615 Commission Implementing Regulation (EU) 2019/947 of 24 May 2019 on the rules and procedures for the operation of unmanned aircraft [2019] OJ L 152/45. See, Anna Konert, Tadeusz Dunin, 'A Harmonized European Drone Market? – New EU Rules on Unmanned Aircraft Systems (2020) 5 Advances in Science, Technology and Engineering Systems Journal 93–99.

616 Pamela L. Marcogliese, Colin D. Lloyd, Sandra M. Rocks, 'Machine Learning and Artificial Intelligence in Financial Services' (2018) Harvard Law School Forum on Corporate Governance https://corpgov.law.harvard.edu/2018/09/24/machine-learning-and-artificial-intelligence-in-financial-services/ accessed 22 July 2020.

617 Jon Truby, Rafael Brown, Andrew Dahdal, 'Banking on AI: Mandating a Proactive Approach to AI Regulation in the Financial Sector' (2020) 14 Law and Financial Markets Review 111–112.

618 More on compliance norms, see Tomasz Braun, *Compliance Norms in Financial Institutions. Measures, Case Studies and Best Practices* (Palgrave Macmillan 2019) 29–49.

619 Ibid; Douglas W. Arner, Janos Barberis, Ross P. Buckley, 'FinTech, RegTech and the Reconceptualization of Financial Regulation' (2016) Northwestern Journal of

or reporting processes which were not possible before. Leading examples include AML and Know-your-client compliance requirements or prudential regulatory reporting.[620]

Regardless of the purpose for which AI technologies within the financial sector are being used, there are some common challenges that need to be addressed by the regulators and relevant actors (banks, fintech companies, financial institutions). In 2017 Basel Committee on Banking Supervision published a consultative document containing sound practices relating to implications of fintech development.[621] Apart from naming particular types of risks related to the fintech development in general, but also resulting in using enabling technologies like AI and machine learning (ex. strategic risk, high operational risk in systemic and idiosyncratic dimension, compliance requirements risks regarding AML and data privacy, outsourcing risks, cyber-risk, liquidity risk), the Basel Committee addressed the recommendation to banks to ensure effective IT and sound risk management processes that address the emerging technological risks and implement effective control mechanisms necessary to support key innovations.[622]

In general, regulation on AI aspects of financial institutions in the EU should be aligned with the Ethics Guidelines for Trustworthy AI and future general EU regulation on ethical aspects of AI.[623] The crucial points to be developed in more detailed measures, should focus on bias and discrimination in financial decision making, model risk management based on data sets and liability and cybersecurity, data privacy and transparency of data sources.[624]

7.2.4 Medicine

Healthcare and medicine sector gain huge benefits from AI solutions. They allow for the patient data information, medical records, diagnostic results, and clinical studies to be collected, processed and applied in a way that improves public health system, diagnostics and disease prevention. Also, having in mind Europe's demographic situation and ageing society, AI technologies can be deployed in the field of support of elderly care and constant monitoring of patients' conditions. There are new branches of health services emerging, with e-health,[625]

International Law & Business, Forthcoming 13–17 https://ssrn.com/abstract=2847806 accessed 22 July 2020.

620 Douglas W. Arner et al. (n 619) 24.

621 Basel Committee on Banking Supervision, 'Sound Practices: Implications of Fintech Developments for Banks and Bank Supervisors' (Consultative Document) (2017) https://www.bis.org/bcbs/publ/d415.pdf accessed 16 July 2020.

622 Ibid 28–30.

623 See, Pasquale (n 45) 127.

624 Truby et al. (n 617) 115.

625 See WHO on e-health https://www.who.int/ehealth/en/ accessed 22 July 2020.

encompassing the use of information and communication technologies for health, in particular, mobile health applications (m-health).[626]

In Europe regulatory approach towards trustworthy AI in Medicine and Healthcare should encompass involvement in research, financed from the EU funds (mainly Horizon 2020 and beyond), coordination and implementation of general ethical rules towards AI, proper legislative measures adopted in response to changing technological environment and finally education of the EU citizens in the field of new risks, benefits and ethical issues that AI has on medicine and health sector.[627]

In the field of research, the Commission is intending to support, via Horizon 2020 the project aiming at the development of a common database of health images, which will be dedicated to fighting cancer, improving its diagnosis and treatment.[628] Another research priority will be initiated on linking genomics repositories and building rare disease registries. In both cases, AI is believed to be treated as a tool enabling better diagnostics, supporting clinical research and decision making.[629]

Ethical issues of particular importance in the Medicine and Healthcare sector include the data quality and security, since it may impact the quality of diagnostic decisions. Furthermore, the data which is at the heart of AI systems applied in medicine is considered to be of sensitive character concerning most private and intimate aspects of the patient's life. Also, the explainability and interpretability of decisions taken by the AI-based software bring particular concerns. There are serious ethical questions here—do we need to accept results provided by the AI system without understandable explanations, since it is understood that such systems in certain tasks give better results than humans[630]? Another group of questions emerge with the issue of liability. As Gómez-González indicate, there are no update regulatory standards for most types of AI applications.[631] With greater use of these technologies, problems of assigning liability shall be determined. The liability schemes may differ depending on the type of AI application used — robotic or software and the type of action or service provided with the help of such an application.[632] In

---

626 Chris Holder, Maria Iglesias (eds.), Jean-Marc Van Gyseghem, Jean-Paul Triaille, *Legal and Regulatory Implications of Artificial Intelligence. The Case of Autonomous Vehicles, m-Health and Data Mining* (Publication Office of the EU Luxembourg 2019) 19.

627 Emilio Gómez-González, Emilia Gómez, *Artificial Intelligence in Medicine and Healthcare: Applications, Availability and Societal Impact* (Publication Office of the EU Luxembourg 2020) 45–46.

628 Commission, COM(2018) 795 final (n 3) 7.

629 Commission, COM(2018) 795 final annex (n 68) 15.

630 Gómez-González (n 627) 17.

631 Ibid.

632 More on the liability issues in surgical robotics and medical devices, Chris Holder, Vikram Khurana, Fay Harrison, Louisa Jacobs, 'Robotics and Law: Key Legal and Regulatory Implications of the Robotics Age (Part I of II)'(2016) 32 Computer Law & Security Review 389–390; Chris Holder Vikram Khurana, Joanna Hook, Gregory Bacon, Rachel Day, 'Robotics and Law: Key Legal and Regulatory Implications of the Robotics Age (Part II of II)' (2016) 32 Computer Law & Security Review 568–569; Shane O'Sullivan et al.

case of m-health solutions, there are situations when producers, physicians or even patients may be held liable. However, these are the problems usually regulated at the levels of national laws and some application may contain a contractual provision on liability.[633]

One of the most regulated areas of medical and healthcare system in the EU concerns medical devices. Currently, there is a uniform regulation (EU) 2017/745[634] on this issue. Medical device, according to art. 2 (1) of that regulation means 'any instrument, apparatus, appliance, software, implant, reagent, material or other article intended by the manufacturer to be used, alone or in combination, for human beings for one or more of the following specific medical purposes:

— diagnosis, prevention, monitoring, prediction, prognosis, treatment or alleviation of disease,
— diagnosis, monitoring, treatment, alleviation of, or compensation for, an injury or disability,
— investigation, replacement or modification of the anatomy or of a physiological or pathological process or state,
— providing information by means of in vitro examination of specimens derived from the human body, including organ, blood and tissue donations,

and which does not achieve its principal intended action by pharmacological, immunological or metabolic means, in or on the human body, but which may be assisted in its function by such means'. This broad definition covers major applications of AI used in e-health, m-health or surgical robotics. When AI application is covered by the abovementioned definition, the company behind it (manufacturer or importer), shall comply *inter alia* with CE marking, appropriate labelling, clinical evaluation or requirements of the detailed quality management system.[635] The main characteristics of the currently applicable regulation on medical devices is to extend its scope to a wider range of products (mostly using new technologies like AI), extend liability in relation to defective products and strengthening of the requirement of clinical data and traceability of

---

'Legal, Regulatory, and Ethical Frameworks for Development of Standards in Artificial Intelligence (AI) and Autonomous Robotic Surgery' (2018) 15 The International Journal of Medical Robotics and Computer Assisted Surgery 5–7.

633 Van Gyseghem et al. (n 626) 23–24.

634 Regulation (EU) 2017/745 of the European Parliament and of the Council of 5 April 2017 on medical devices, amending Directive 2001/83/EC, Regulation (EC) No 178/2002 and Regulation (EC) No 1223/2009 and repealing Council Directives 90/385/EEC and 93/42/EEC [2017] OJ L 117/1. Regulation 2017/745 was amended by Regulation (EU) 2020/561 of the European Parliament and of the Council of 23 April 2020 as regards the dates of application of certain its provision (2020) OJ L 130/18. The amendment was dictated by the COVID-19 outbreak and the willingness to extend the date for the adoption of necessary common specification until 26 May 2021.

635 Art. 10–13 of the regulation 2017/745.

the devices.[636] It is worth mentioning that apart from hard regulation, the Commission adopts so-called MEDDEVs, which are non-binding guidelines on legislation related to medical devices. Adoption of MEDDEVs is an example of co-regulation because they are drafted by authorities responsible with safeguarding public health in conjunction with relevant stakeholders like industry associations, health professional associations, notified bodies and European standardisation organisations.[637]

7.2.5 Military and defence

The application of AI in the military and defence sector brings the biggest ethical concerns in regard to lethal autonomous weapons systems (LAWS). This problem is going beyond national or even the EU policy and is debatable at the United Nations level since it is touching upon the most fundamental aspects of international humanitarian law and human rights law.

Lethal autonomous weapon systems are defined as systems which upon their activation have the capacity to track, identify and attack targets with violent force without meaningful human control.[638] The autonomy of weapons systems may be viewed through different perspectives — by taking into account some cognitive characteristics of the systems, but also looking at it through the lens of the existing human supervisory control and human-machine interactions. In terms of ethical framework adopted at the EU level, the latter aspect is closely connected to the requirement of human oversight, taking forms of human 'in the loop', 'on the loop' or 'out of the loop'.[639]

The crucial element of the definition of LAWS is 'meaningful human control' which must entail some form of control and surveillance on the delivery of force against human targets.[640] As Roff and Moyes indicate any system in which machine applying force operates without any human control should be contradictory to this condition. Also, against this idea would be the situation in which such control is reduced to simple button pressing, without cognitive clarity or awareness on the side human operator.[641]

636 Filippo Pesapane, Caterina Volonté, Marina Codari, Francesco Sardanelli, 'Artificial Intelligence as a medical device in radiology: ethical and regulatory issues in Europe and the United States' (2018) 9 Insights into Imagining 748.

637 See, https://ec.europa.eu/health/sites/health/files/md_sector/docs/md_guidance_meddevs.pdf accessed 22 July 2020.

638 Ingvild Bode, Hendrik Huelss, 'Autonomous Weapons Systems and Changing Norms in International Relations', (2018) 44 Review of International Studies 397; see also, European Parliament, 'Resolution of 12 September 2018 on Autonomous Weapon Systems' (n 197).

639 Bode and Huelss (n 638) 397.

640 Noto La Diega (n 235) 3.

641 Heather M. Roff, Richard Moyes, 'Meaningful Human Control, Artificial Intelligence and Autonomous Weapons' (2016) Briefing Paper Prepared for the Informal Meeting of Experts on Lethal Autonomous Weapons Systems, UN Convention on Certain

The LAWS have the potential of fundamentally changing armed conflicts and the most controversial issue of their use is connected with the possibility of making and performing autonomous decisions on ending human lives. These concerns seem impossible to comply with legal and ethical rules.[642] According to the study run by the Human Rights Watch and Harvard Law School's International Human Rights Clinic, LAWS would not be consistent with international humanitarian law and would increase the number of civilian casualties during armed conflicts.[643] This is the main reason for the debate taking place right now within the international community. It is believed that such weapons are currently developed, tested and deployed by the US, Israel, China, South Korea and Russia and the United Kingdom,[644] yet as it is stated in the European Parliament's resolution on LAWS 'an unknown number of countries, publicly funded industries and private industries are reportedly researching and developing lethal autonomous weapon systems, ranging all the way from missiles capable of selective targeting to learning machines with cognitive skills to decide whom, when and where to fight'.[645] Against this background, we should recall that since 2013, under the UN Convention on Certain Conventional Weapons (CCW), members of the international community are discussing the LAWS issues. In 2016 the Group of Governmental Experts of the parties of the CCW was established. This Group has chiefly a discussion mandate and EU, through its High Representative of the Union for Foreign Affairs and Security Policy, uses this forum to express the EU position on LAWS and build on consultations with the UN in this field. Unfortunately, there is no progress at the UN level on binding common approach towards regulating LAWS. The debate is supposed to be continued for the next two years.[646] In the meantime, European Parliament in 2018 passed the resolution explicitly calling for adoption at the international level a legally binding instrument prohibiting LAWS, in particular lacking human control in critical functions such as target selection and engagement.[647] The European strict approach is focused on offensive LAWS. Weapon systems which

Conventional Weapons, 1–2 http://www.article36.org/wp-content/uploads/2016/04/MHC-AI-and-AWS-FINAL.pdf accessed 22 July 2020.

642 Noto La Diega (n 235) 4–6.

643 'Losing Humanity. The Case against Killer Robots' (Report 2012) https://www.hrw.org/sites/default/files/reports/arms1112_ForUpload.pdf accessed 22 July 2020.

644 Mary Wareham, 'Banning Killer Robots in 2017' https://www.hrw.org/news/2017/01/15/banning-killer-robots-2017 accessed 22 July 2020.

645 European Parliament, 'Resolution of 12 September 2018 on Autonomous Weapon Systems' (n 197).

646 Alexandra Brzozowski, 'No Progress in UN Talks on Regulating Lethal Autonomous Weapons' (22.11.2019) https://www.euractiv.com/section/global-europe/news/no-progress-in-un-talks-on-regulating-lethal-autonomous-weapons/ accessed 22 July 2020.

647 European Parliament, 'Resolution of 12 September 2018 on Autonomous Weapon Systems' (n 197).

are designed to defend own platforms, forces and populations against hostile highly dynamic threats shall not be covered by the LAWS definition.[648]

7.2.6 Public sector – justice and administration

Justice and public administration are probably the most fundamental sectors where AI tools' impact shall be particularly scrutinised due to their capacity to shape the proper functioning of democratic systems. The benefits of AI technologies used in democratic systems touch upon the effectiveness of decision-making, both timewise and resources-wise. AI solutions can provide an opportunity to speed up and improve the efficiency and effectiveness of public service delivery.[649] On one hand, they can increase the level of legal certainty by assuring the better quality and consistency of services delivered. They can also improve the application of policy measures which can target selected goals, enhance the effectiveness of public procurement, strengthen security, identity management, improve social services.[650] In the justice system, technological development has the potential of improving access to justice and reduce the time and costs involved in dispute resolution.[651] For legal services, the emergence of blockchain technology enabling smart contracts, may render them more affordable, fast and secure, by reducing the execution and enforcement costs of contracting processes.[652] For citizens and legal entities, AI-based decisions can simplify the relationship between authorities and beneficiaries through the integration of wider public interest or regulatory considerations. AI can bring a new dimension to citizen-government interaction through conversational systems, multilingual services and automated translation. Also, as was indicated earlier in algorithmic technologies may have an important impact on the democratic participatory mechanisms, by empowering citizens with new forms and platforms of deliberation. AI is also becoming present in traditional constitutional processes — electoral campaigns or e-voting.

With all the benefits, come risk and challenges. All the ethical and legal requirements that have been discussed above are to be followed for building modern, reliable judicial and public governance sectors. Yet, this filed is particularly sensitive in terms of the technological trust, since AI solutions that are used serve as carriers and enablers of trust towards public institutions. This touches upon the most fundamental aspect of European

---

648 Ibid.
649 Coglianese Lehr (n 48) 1160–1161.
650 Commission, COM(2018) 795 final (annex) (n 68) 20–21.
651 Sir Henry Brooke, 'Algorithms, Artificial Intelligence and the Law' (12 November 2019) Lecture for BAILII Freshfields Bruckhaus Deringer, London 3–4.
652 Stuart D. Levi, Alex B. Lipton, 'An Introduction to Smart Contracts and Their Potential and Inherent Limitations' (2018) Harvard Law School Forum on Corporate Governance 3 https://corpgov.law.harvard.edu/2018/05/26/an-introduction-to-smart-contracts-and-their-potential-and-inherent-limitations/ accessed 22 July 2020.

societies—democracy. The crucial axiological, constitutional and political foundation of the European Union. If Europe truly wants to set standards in the approach towards AI, it should start all the policy and law making processes in the field of AI, and in particular in its aspects relating to the justice system and public governance, by assuring the rule of law, democracy and human rights 'by design'.[653]

Once we take a look at different policy initiatives, which are not necessarily translated into binding legislative measures but have the regulatory impact on the functioning of the public sector at the EU and Member States level, we should conclude that Commission is encouraging new forms of testing arrangements and regulatory sandboxes which allow discussing areas of public procurement AI solutions or cybersecurity issues. Commission together with member states is intending to engage in peer-learning and the EU-wide exchange of best practices, experiences and data. This should allow for disseminating among member states the information on applications applied by the member states and assess their effectiveness and impact on the quality and reliability of the public services sector in the EU. One of the issues that need to be assured and strongly discussed is that once AI-powered systems take a public decision, it should be motivated (explainability comes to play) and should be subject to judicial review by administrative courts. Users should be ensured that once AI system infringes their rights under applicable law, they are entitled to the effective redress. Also, in the public sphere, addressees or beneficiaries of decisions powered by AI should be enabled to switch to the human interlocutor, whenever they consider it necessary. Such solutions, necessitate, from the very beginning of the design phase, appropriate mechanisms to assure such alternative solutions and procedures which would facilitate the adequate level of human oversight. This is crucial for auditability of the systems and transparency requirement.[654]

Europe, having a strong public sector, should set the proper standards for the use of trustworthy AI in this area. In general, EU policy direction in the field of public administration and justice is connected with the idea of e-government. This notion covers the application of advanced digital technologies (including AI) and internet platforms to deliver, exchange and advance government's services for citizens and business entities aiming at improving the quality of those services while reducing their costs.[655] Apart from this major goal, e-government allows for better government transparency and trust, providing citizens with easy access to public information. Brings more effective dimension of citizen participation and have a positive environmental impact by eliminating large amounts of paper documents used.[656]

653 Nemmitz (n 3) 3.
654 HLEG AI, 'Policy and Investment Recommendations for Trustworthy AI' (n 5) 41.
655 Omar Saeed Al-Mushayt, 'Automating E-Government Services With Artificial Intelligence' (2019) 7 IEEE Access, 146822.
656 Ibid.

The EU's commitment towards building the modern e-government was confirmed by the Ministerial Declaration on e-Government adopted in Tallinn on 6 October 2017.[657] Ministers responsible for e-Government policy from 32 countries of the European Union (EU) and the European Free Trade Area (EFTA) signed under the vision laid out in the EU e-Government Action Plan 2016–2020.[658] According to this vision public administrations and public institutions in the 'EU should be open, efficient and inclusive, providing borderless, interoperable, personalised, user-friendly, end-to-end digital public services to all citizens and businesses'.[659] In line with the major policy directions of e-government, Member States, with the support of the Commission are encouraged to finance the initiatives which would deploy AI-enabled services to understand better the added value and potential impact of AI-enabled public services and policy making. AI-based solutions will also benefit the justice and law enforcement sectors. Another promising public application sector is the monitoring and enforcement of single market rules for goods, services and people. All the innovations within e-government should maintain the high quality of human relationships with public administration and should safeguard the human-centric approach.[660]

657 See, https://ec.europa.eu/digital-single-market/en/news/ministerial-declaration-egovernment-tallinn-declaration accessed 22 July 2020.
658 Commission, 'EU e-Government Action Plan 2016–2020. Accelerating the Digital Transformation of Government' (Communication) COM(2016) 179 final.
659 Ibid 2.
660 Commission COM(2018) 795 final (annex) (n 68) 20–21.

8 Conclusions

Worldwide discussions on AI ethics had intensified after Japan's G7 Presidency when it was put high on the agenda in 2016. Taking into account the global technological interconnections and AI development in terms of data exchange and algorithmic development the EU should continue its efforts to bring to the international stage a consensus on a human-centric AI.[661]

With the current exponential growth of algorithmic technologies presence in all spheres of live being discussed all around the world, its international outreach is crucially important. The development and deployment of innovative technologies will benefit from international cooperation, in particular, among those countries where investments strengthen research and innovation. Constant internationalisation of technologies makes the challenges related to the cross border as well. Part of these challenges relates to various sorts of standards that need to be set. The attempt to develop international standards would facilitate new technologies deployment and acceptance. This particularly refers to AI. The EU is intending to promote the AI ethics guidelines internationally and launch a wide dialogue and cooperation with all interested governments and other stakeholders open to sharing the same values.

To succeed in this, the EU should align its outreach efforts related to the changing technological landscape and pool all efforts for the responsible development of AI and other digital applications worldwide. It needs to rethink if there is a chance to agree upon and promote a joined position on this topic. To strengthen its voice, the EU, together with member states and stakeholders like tech companies, academia, influencers, industries and consumer representatives, should build alliances for responsible technology. The UE should strive to organise an international dialogue and forging a global consensus on the ethical implications of AI. It can use a range of available instruments to engage with international partners on regulatory and ethical matters. There are even more ambitious proposals to organise an intergovernmental process similar to the panel on Climate Change. In the particular dimension of the international security of

---

661 Commission, COM (2019) 168 final (n 6) 8.

regarding AI policies, it could be built around the High Representative in the Global Tech Panel as well as within the United Nations and other multilateral fora.

The EU should contribute its expertise and targeted financial schemes to build AI more firmly into its broader development policy. There is very little matching so impactfully as a tool for contributions to global challenges as AI. More broadly, digital technologies can underpin affordable solutions, including for people in precarious circumstances without compromising necessary respect to ethical and privacy issues. For example, the EU could contribute to support deploying AI more firmly in development policy that could focus within the Southern Mediterranean and Africa.[662]

The EU could lead in developing worldwide AI guidelines and related assessment frameworks by strengthening multilevel cooperation of various stakeholders by exploring the extent to which convergence can be achieved. Together with other countries, the EU could promote drafting ethics guidelines and building a group of like-minded countries in view of preparing a broader discussion.[663]

It could also explore how companies and organisations from all over the world through testing and validation are able to contribute to formulating of the AI ethical guidelines. The EU also must continue playing its role as a driver of international discussions and initiatives that engage other stakeholders in dialogues with non-EU countries to build a consensus on human-centric and trustworthy AI.[664]

This could represent a chance to mitigate the pressing challenges reflected globally and listed within the UN Sustainable Development Goals, that the societies are heading like ageing populations, social inequalities and pollution.[665] The list of identifiable issues that could be helped by the digital technologies is long but an active deployment of it, and AI, in particular, could help to tackle at least some of these challenges.[666] For instance, the climate change which should be a key priority for authorities across the world could be helped by the deployment of digital instruments that have a potential to reduce anthropogenic environmental impact and enable the efficient use of natural resources and energy.[667] Trustworthy AI that could collect, process, analyse, detect and suggest energy needs more accurately could contribute to its efficient use and consumption.[668]

---

662 Commission, COM(2018) 795 final, (n 3) 20-21.
663 Regulation (EU) No 234/2014 of the European Parliament and of the Council of 11 March 2014 establishing a Partnership Instrument for cooperation with third countries [2014] OJ L 77/77.
664 Commission, COM(2019)168 final (n 6) 8-9.
665 See https://sustainabledevelopment.un.org/?menu=1300 accessed 22 July 2020.
666 HLEGoAI, 'Ethics Guidelines for Trustorthy AI',(n 134) 32.
667 See, the Commission BRIDGE initiative, supporting EU projects aiming at digitally driven energy transition, https://www.h2020-bridge.eu/ accessed 22 July 2020.
668 See for instance the Encompass project http://www.encompass-project.eu accessed 22 July 2020.

At the same time, the EU should create an efficient investment environment in the context of global competition. The new EU programmes set solid frameworks towards enhanced investment in AI. However, it is necessary to do more in building even more favourable environment. It needs a strong engagement of the private multi-stakeholder sectoral alliances that foster trust across policymakers, regulators, industries, academia and the society. Only that could secure the needed investments in the field of trustworthy AI.

To achieve these goals, the EU necessities an ambitious holistic strategy with a long-term vision that can capture the opportunities and addresses the emerging challenges by creating a friendly regulatory and governance framework that would allow continuous monitoring and adapting impactful corrective actions. In the context of the worldwide economic competition, it is indispensable to build the capabilities to fast and consistently apply and learn all needed measures. Multiple reports, policy documents and strong involvement of academia so far have all contributed to establishing the foundation for this durable strategy. Building on this, at present, further cross-sectoral recommendations are necessary to identify which actions should be undertaken for various strategic sectors, covering all the areas, expected impacts and the suitable enablers to implement them.

The major AI-enabled opportunity is ahead of the world. It is the right time to demonstrate the readiness to respond to this opportunity. This, however, requires action now. This sense of urgency should be recognised by policymakers at all levels to gain momentum in applying Trustworthy AI for the benefit of individuals and societies.[669]

---

669 HLEG AI, 'Policy and Investment Recommendations' (n 5) 49.

Bibliography

Literature

1 Abbott Ryan, 'The Reasonable Computer: Disrupting the Paradigm of Tort Liability' (2018) *86 George Washington Law Review* 1–45.
2 Abbott Ryan, Sarch Alex F., 'Punishing Artificial Intelligence: Legal Fiction or Science Fiction' (2019) *53 UC Davis Law Review* 323–384.
3 Abeyratne Ruwantissa, *Legal Priorities in Air Transport* (Springer 2019).
4 Adner Ron, 'Match Your Innovation Strategy to Your Innovation Ecosystem' (2006) *Harvard Business Review* https://hbr.org/2006/04/match-your-innovation-strategy-to-your-innovation-ecosystem accessed 22 July 2020.
5 Allen Robin, Masters Dee, 'Artificial Intelligence: The Right to Protection From Discrimination Caused by Algorithms, Machine Learning and Automated Decision-Making' (2019) ERA Forum https://doi.org/10.1007/s12027-019-00582-w accessed 22 July 2020.
6 Amato Cristina, 'Product Liability and Product Security: Present and Future' in Sebastian Lohsse, Reiner Schulze, Dirk Staudenmayer (eds.), *Liability for Artificial Intelligence and the Internet of Things. Muenster Colloquia on EU Law and the Digital Economy IV* (Hart Publishing, Nomos 2019).
7 Arner Douglas W., Barberis Janos, Buckley Ross P., 'FinTech, RegTech and the Reconceptualization of Financial Regulation' (2016) *Northwestern Journal of International Law & Business*, Forthcoming, https://ssrn.com/abstract= 2847806 accessed 22 July 2020.
8 Barfield Woodrow, Pagallo Ugo (eds.), *Research Handbook on the Law of Artificial Intelligence* (Edward Elgar 2018).
9 Barocas Solon, Hardt Moritz, Narayanan Arvind, 'Fairness and Machine Learning. Limitations and Opportunities' https://fairmlbook.org/ accessed 22 July 2020.
10 Barocas Solon, Selbst Andrew D., 'Big Data's Disparate Impact' (2016) *104 California Law Review* 671–732.
11 Beever Jonathan, McDaniel Rudy, Stamlick Nancy A., *Understanding Digital Ethics. Cases and Contexts* (Routledge 2020).
12 Bernitz Ulf et al. (eds.), *General Principles of EU law and the EU Digital Order* (Kluwer Law International 2020).
13 Bevir Mark, Phillips Ryan (eds.), *Decentring European Governance* (Routledge 2019).
14 Black Julia, 'Learning from Regulatory Disasters', (2014) *24 LSE Law, Society and Economy Working Papers* 3 http://dx.doi.org/10.2139/ssrn. 2519934 accessed 22 July 2020.

15 Black Julia, 'Decentring Regulation: Understanding the Role of Regulations and Self-Regulation in a Post-Regulatory World' (2001) *54 Current Legal Problems* 103–146.

16 Black Julia, Murray Andrew D., 'Regulating AI and Machine Learning: Setting the Regulatory Agenda' (2019) *10 European Journal of Law and Technology* 1–21 http://eprints.lse.ac.uk/102953/ accessed 22 July 2020.

17 Blodget-Ford S. J., 'Future Privacy: A Real Right to Privacy for Artificial Intelligence' in Woodrow Barfield, Ugo Pagallo (eds.), *Research Handbook on the Law of Artificial Intelligence* (Edward Elgar 2018).

18 Boddington Paula, *Towards a Code of Ethics for Artificial Intelligence, Artificial Intelligence: Foundations, Theory, and Algorithms* (Springer Int. Publishing 2017).

19 Bode Ingvild, Huelss Hendrik, 'Autonomous Weapons Systems and Changing Norms in International Relations', (2018) *44 Review of International Studies* 397.

20 Bojarski Łukasz, Schindlauer Dieter, Wladasch Katerin (eds.), *The Charter of Fundamental Rights as a Living Instrument. Manual* (CFREU 2014) 9–10 https://bim.lbg.ac.at/sites/files/bim/attachments/cfreu_manual_0.pdf accessed 22 July 2020.

21 Borghetti Jean-Sebastien, 'How can Artificial Intelligence be Defective?' in Sebastian Lohsse, Reiner Schulze, Dirk Staudenmayer (eds.), *Liability for Artificial Intelligence and the Internet of Things. Muenster Colloquia on EU Law and the Digital Economy IV* (Hart Publishing, Nomos 2019).

22 Braun Tomasz, *Compliance Norms in Financial Institutions. Measures, Case Studies and Best Practices* (Palgrave Macmillan 2019).

23 Brkan Maja, 'Do Algorithms Rule the World? Algorithmic Decision-Making and Data Protection in the Framework of the GDPR and Beyond' (2019) *27 International Journal of Law and Information Technology* 91–121.

24 Brooke Sir Henry, '*Algorithms, Artificial Intelligence and the Law*' (12 November 2019) Lecture for BAILII Freshfields Bruckhaus Deringer, London.

25 Brownsword Roger, *Law, Technology and Society. Re-imagining the Regulatory Environment* (Routledge 2019).

26 Bryson Alex, Barth Erling, Dale-Olsen Harald, 'The Effects of Organizational Change on Worker Well-Being and the Moderating Role of Trade Unions'(2013) *66 ILR Review* 989–1011.

27 J. Bryson Joanna, E. Diamantis Mihailis, D. Grant Thomas, 'Of, for, and by the People: The Legal Lacuna of Synthetic Persons' (2017) *25 Artificial Intelligence Law* 273–291.

28 Bua Adrian, R. Escoba Oliver, 'Participatory-Deliberative Processes and Public Agendas: Lessons for Policy and Practice' (2018) *1 Policy Design and Practice* 2 126–140.

29 Burri Thomas, 'Free Movement of Algorithms: Artificially Intelligent Persons Conquer the European Union's Internal Market' in Woodrow Barfield, Ugo Pagallo (eds.), *Research Handbook on the Law of Artificial Intelligence* (Edward Elgar 2018).

30 Busby Helen, K. Hervey Tamara, Mohr Alison, 'Ethical EU Law? The Influence of the European Group on Ethics in Science and New Technologies' (2008) *33 European Law Review* 803–842.

31 Bussani Mauro, Palmer Vernon Valentine, 'The Liability Regimes of Europe – Their Façades and Interiors' in Mauro Bussani, Vernon Vaalentine Palmer (eds.), *Pure Economic Loss in Europe* (Cambridge University Press 2011 reprint).

32 Bussani Mauro, Palmer Vernon Valentine (eds.), *Pure Economic Loss in Europe* (Cambridge University Press 2011 reprint).

33 Casanovas Pompeu et al. (eds.), *AI Approaches to the Complexity of Legal Systems* (Springer 2014).

34 Castets-Renard Celine, 'The Intersection Between AI and IP: Conflict or Complementarity' (2020) *51 ICC-International Review of Intellectual Property and Competition Law* 141–143.

35 Cath Corinne et al., 'Artificial Intelligence and the 'Good Society': The US, EU, and UK Approach, Science and Engineering Ethics' (2017) *24 Science and Engineering Ethics* 507–528.

36 Cath Corinne, 'Governing Artificial Intelligence: Ethical, Legal and Technical Opportunities and Challenges' (2018) *376 Philosophical Transactions A, The Royal Society* 1–8.

37 Cihon Peter, 'Standards for AI Governance: International Standards to Enable Global Coordination in AI Research and Development' (2019) https://www.fhi. ox.ac.uk/wp-content/uploads/Standards_-FHI-Technical-Report.pdf accessed 22 July 2020.

38 Coglianese Cary, Lehr David, 'Regulating by Robot: Administrative Decision Making in the Machine-Learning Era' (2017) *105 Georgetown Law Journal* 1147–1223.

39 Comande Giovanni, 'Multilayered (Accountable) Liability for Artificial Intelligence' in Sebastian Lohsse, Reiner Schulze, Dirk Staudenmayer (eds.), *Liability for Artificial Intelligence and the Internet of Things. Muenster Colloquia on EU Law and the Digital Economy IV* (Hart Publishing, Nomos 2019).

40 Covoukian Ann, 'Privacy by Design. The 7 Foundational Principles. Implementation and Mapping of Fair Information Practices' https://iapp.org/media/pdf/resource_ center/pbd_implement_7found_principles.pdf accessed 22 July 2020.

41 A. Cubert Jeremy, G.A. Bone Richard, 'The Law of Intellectual Property Created by Artificial Intelligence' in Woodrow Barfield, Ugo Pagallo (eds.), *Research Handbook on the Law of Artificial Intelligence* (Edward Elgar 2018).

42 Danaher John, 'Algocracy as Hypernudging: A New Way to Understand the Threat of Algocracy' (2017) https://ieet.org/index.php/IEET2/more/ Danaher20170117?fbclid=IwAR3gm6lIWN8Twb8bE6lTIdtintwhYSWF2FTDk RGzMs1xa8XTD4bGgoQJiXw accessed 22 July 2020.

43 Danaher John, 'The Threat of Algocracy: Reality, Resistance and Accommodation' (2016) *29 Philosophy and Technology* 245–268.

44 Valerio de Stefano, 'Negotiating the Algorithm: Automation, Artificial Intelligence and Labour Protection' (2018) *International Labour Office*, Employment Working Paper No. 246, 5.

45 Dignum Virginia et al., 'Ethics by Design: Necessity or Curse?' (2018) AIES Proceedings of the 2018 AAAI/AM Conference o AI, Ethics, and Society 60–66.

46 Dopierała Renata, 'Prywatność w perspektywie zmiany społecznej' (Nomos 2013).

47 Doran Derek, Schulz Sarah, R Besold Tarek, 'What Does Explainable AI Really Mean? A New Conceptualization Perspectives' (2017) arXiv:1710.00791 accessed 22 July 2020.

48 Elstub Stephen, Escobar Oliver, 'A Typology of Democratic Innovations', Paper for the Political Studies Association's Annual Conference, 10th –12th April 2017, Glasgow, https://www.psa.ac.uk/sites/default/files/conference/papers/

2017/A%20Typology%20of%20Democratic%20Innovations%20-%20Elstub %20and%20Escobar%202017.pdf accessed 22 July 2020.

49 Falcone R., Singh Munindar, Tan Yao Hua (eds.), *Trust in Cyber-societies: Integrating the Human and Artificial Perspectives* (Springer 2001).

50 Felzman Heike et al., 'Transparency You Can Trust: Transparency Requirements for Artificial Intelligence between Legal Norms and Contextual Concerns' (2019) *Big Data & Society*, Jan–June 1–14.

51 Fjelland Ragnar, 'Why General Artificial Intelligence Will Not Be Realized' (2020) *7 Humanities and Social Sciences Communications* 1–9.

52 Floridi Luciano et al., 'AI4 People – An Ethical Framework for a Good Society: Opportunities, Risks, Principles and Recommendations' (2018) *28 Minds and Machines* 689–707.

53 Floridi Luciano, 'Soft Ethics and the Governance of the Digital' (2018) *31 Philosophy & Technology* 1–8.

54 Floridi Luciano, *The 4th Revolution. How Infosphere Is Reshaping Human Reality* (Oxford University Press 2016).

55 Fosch Villaronga Eduard, Kieseberg Peter, Li Tiffany, 'Humans Forget, Machines Remember: Artificial Intelligence and the Right to be Forgotten' (2017) *Computer Security and Law Review* (forthcoming) https://ssrn.com/abstract= 3018186 accessed 22 July 2020.

56 Freitas M. Pedro, Andrale Francisco, Novais Paulo, 'Criminal Liability of Autonomous Agents: From the Unthinkable to the Plausible' in Pompeu Casanovas et al. (eds.), *AI Approaches to the Complexity of Legal Systems* (Springer 2014).

57 Gal Michal S., Elkin-Koren Niva, 'Algorithmic Consumers' (2017) *30 Harvard Journal of Law and Technology* 309–353.

58 Galand-Carval Suzanne, 'Comparative Report on Liability for Damage Caused by Others', in Spier Jaap (ed.), *Unification of Tort Law: Liability for Damage Caused by Others* (Kluwer Law International 2003).

59 Gasson Susan, 'Human-centered vs. User-centered Approaches to Information System Design' (2003) *5 The Journal of Information Technology Theory and Application* 29–46.

60 Geissel Brigitte, 'Introduction: On the Evaluation of Participatory Innovations' in Geissel Brigitte, Joas Marko (eds.), *Participatory Democratic Innovations in Europe: Improving the Quality of Democracy?* (Barbara Budrich Publishers 2013).

61 Geissel Brigitte, Joas Marko (eds.), *Participatory Democratic Innovations in Europe: Improving the Quality of Democracy?* (Barbara Budrich Publishers 2013).

62 Geslevich Packin, Lev-Aretz Yafit Nizan, 'Learning Algorithms and Discrimination' in Woodrow Barfield and Ugo Pagallo (eds.), *Research Handbook on the Law of Artificial Intelligence* (Edward Elgar 2018).

63 Gogoll Jan, F. Müller Julian, 'Autonomous Cars: In Favour of a Mandatory Ethics Setting' (2017) *23 Science and Engineering Ethics* 681–700.

64 Gómez-González Emilio, Gómez Emilia, 'Artificial Intelligence in Medicine and Healthcare: Applications, Availability and Societal Impact' (Publication Office of the EU Luxembourg 2020).

65 Gonschior Agata, 'Ochrona danych osobowych a prawo do prywatności w Unii Europejskiej' in Dagmara Kornobis-Romanowska (ed.), *Aktualne problemy prawa Unii Europejskiej i prawa międzynarodowego – aspekty teoretyczne i praktyczne*

(E-Wydawnictwo. Prawnicza i Ekonomiczna Biblioteka Cyfrowa. Wydział Prawa, Administracji i Ekonomii Uniwersytetu Wrocławskiego 2017).

66 Goodall Noah J., 'Away from Trolley Problems and Toward Risk Management' (2016) *30 Applied Artificial Intelligence* 810–821.

67 Goodman Bryce, Flaxman Seth, 'European Union Regulations on Algorithmic Decision-Making and a Right to Explanation' (2016) arXiv:1606.08813 accessed 22 July 2020.

68 Grimm Dieter, Kemmerer Alexandra, Möllers Christoph (eds.), *Human Dignity in Context. Explorations of a Contested Concept* (Hart Publishing, Nomos 2018).

69 Hacker Philipp, 'Teaching Fairness to Artificial Intelligence: Existing and Novel Strategies against Algorithmic Discrimination under EU Law' (2018) *55 Common Market Law Review* 1143–1185.

70 Hallevy Gabriel, 'The Criminal Liability of Artificial Intelligence Entities' (2010) Ono Academic College, Faculty of Law https://papers.ssrn.com/sol3/papers.cfm?abstract_id=1564096 accessed 22 July 2020.

71 Hancke T., Besant C.B., Ristic M., Husband T.M., 'Human-centred Technology' (1990) *23 IFAC Proceedings Volumes* 59–66.

72 Herber Zech, 'Liability for Autonomous Systems: Tackling Specific Risks of Modern IT' in Sebastian Lohsse, Reiner Schulze, Dirk Staudenmayer (eds.), *Liability for Artificial Intelligence and the Internet of Things. Muenster Colloquia on EU Law and the Digital Economy IV* (Hart Publishing, Nomos 2019).

73 Hildebrandt Mireille, *Smart Technologies and the End(s) of Law* (Edward Elgar 2015).

74 Hilgendorf Eric, 'Problem Areas in the Dignity Debate and the Ensemble Theory of Human Dignity' in Dieter Grimm, Alexandra Kemmerer, Christoph Möllers (eds.), *Human Dignity in Context. Explorations of a Contested Concept* (Hart Publishing, Nomos 2018).

75 Himmelreich Johannes, 'Never Mind the Trolley: The Ethics of Autonomous Vehicles in Mundane Situations' (2018) *21 Ethical Theory and Moral Practice* 669–684.

76 Holder Chris, Khurana Vikram, Harrison Fay, Jacobs Louisa, 'Robotics and Law: Key Legal and Regulatory Implications of the Robotics age (Part I of II)' (2016) *32 Computer Law & Security Review* 383–402.

77 Holder Chris, Khurana Vikram, Hook Joanna, Bacon Gregory, Day Rachel, 'Robotics and Law: Key Legal and Regulatory Implications of the Robotics Age (Part II of II)' (2016) *32 Computer Law & Security Review* 557–576.

78 Holzinger Andreas, et al., 'What Do We Need to Build Explainable AI Systems for the Medical Domain' (2017) 3–6 arXiv: 1712.09923v1 accessed 22 July 2020.

79 Howard Ayanna, Borenstein Jason, 'The Ugly Truth About Ourselves and Our Robot Creations: The Problem of Bias and Social Inequity' (2018) *24 Science and Engineering Ethics* 1521–1536.

80 Jabłonowska Agnieszka, et al., 'Consumer Law and Artificial Intelligence. Challenges to the EU Consumer Law and Policy Stemming from the Business' Use of Artificial Intelligence', Final report of the ARTSY project EUI Working Papers Law 2018/11.

81 Jano Dorian, 'Understanding the 'EU Democratic Deficit': A Two Dimension Concept on a Three Level-of-Analysis' (2008) *14 Politikon IAPSS Journal of Political Science* 61–74.

82 Jirjahn Uwe, Smith Stephen 'What Factors Lead Management to Support or Oppose Employee Participation—With and Without Works Councils? Hypotheses and Evidence from Germany' (2006) *45 Industrial Relations: A Journal of Economy and Society* 650–680.

83 Johnston David (ed.), *The Cambridge Companion to Roman Law* (Cambridge University Press 2015).

84 Karner Ernst, 'Liability for Robotics: Current Rules, Challenges, and the Need for Innovative Concepts' in Sebastian Lohsse, Reiner SchulzeDirk Staudenmayer (eds.), *Liability for Artificial Intelligence and the Internet of Things. Muenster Colloquia on EU Law and the Digital Economy IV* (Hart Publishing, Nomos 2019).

85 Karner Ernst, Oliphant Ken, Steininger Barbara C. (eds.), *European Tort Law: Basic Texts* (Jan Sramek Verlag 2018).

86 Keats Citron Danielle, Pasquale Frank, 'The Scored Society: Due Process for Automated Predictions' (2014) *89 Washington Law Review 1-33*.

87 Kelsen Hans, *General Theory of Law and State* (A. Wedberg tr., Harvard University Press, 1945).

88 Konert Anna, Dunin Tadeusz, 'A Harmonized European Drone Market? – New EU Rules on Unmanned Aircraft Systems' (2020) *5 Advances in Science, Technology and Engineering Systems Journal* 93–99.

89 Kornobis-Romanowska Dagmara (ed.), *Aktualne problemy prawa Unii Europejskiej i prawa międzynarodowego – aspekty teoretyczne i praktyczne* (E-Wydawnictwo. Prawnicza i Ekonomiczna Biblioteka Cyfrowa. Wydział Prawa, Administracji i Ekonomii Uniwersytetu Wrocławskiego 2017).

90 Koziol Helmut, 'Comparative Conclusions' in Helmut Koziol (ed.), *Basic Questions of Tort Law from a Comparative Perspective* (Jan Sramek Verlag 2015).

91 Krick Eva, Gornitzka Åse, 'The Governance of Expertise Production in the EU Commission's 'High Level Groups'. Tracing Expertisation Tendencies in the Expert Group System' in Mark Bevir, Ryan Phillips (eds.), *Decentring European Governance* (Routledge 2019).

92 Kuner Christopher et al., 'Machine Learning with Personal Data: Is Data Protection Law Smart Enough to Meet the Challenge' (2017) *7 International Data Privacy Law* 1–2.

93 Levi Stuart D., Lipton Alex B., 'An Introduction to Smart Contracts and Their Potential and Inherent Limitations' (2018) *Harvard Law School Forum on Corporate Governance* https://corpgov.law.harvard.edu/2018/05/26/an-introduction-to-smart-contracts-and-their-potential-and-inherent-limitations/ accessed 22 July 2020.

94 Lohsse Sebastian, Schulze Reiner, Staudenmayer Dirk (eds.), *Liability for Artificial Intelligence and the Internet of Things. Muenster Colloquia on EU Law and the Digital Economy IV* (Hart Publishing, Nomos 2019).

95 Luetge Christoph, 'The German Ethics Code for Automated and Connected Driving' (2017) *30 Philosophy and Technology* 547–558.

96 Łuków Paweł, 'A Difficult Legacy: Human Dignity as the Founding Value of Human Rights' (2018) *19 Human Rights Review* 313–329.

97 Magnus Urlich, 'Why Is US Tort Law so Different?' (2010) *1 Journal of European Tort Law* 102–124.

98 Makridakis Spyros, 'The Forthcoming Artificial Intelligence Revolution' (2017) 1 Neapolis University of Paphos (NUP), Working Papers Series https://www.researchgate.net/publication/312471523_The_Forthcoming_Artificial_Intelligence_AI_Revolution_Its_Impact_on_Society_and_Firms accessed 20 July 2020.

99 Marchant Gary E., 'The Growing Gap Between Emerging Technologies and the Law' in Gary E. Marchant, Braden R. Allenby, Joseph R. Herkert (eds.), *The Growing Gap Between Emerging Technologies and Legal-Ethical Oversight. The Pacing Problem* (Springer 2011).

100 Marchant Gary E., Allenby Braden R., Herkert Joseph R. (eds.), *The Growing Gap Between Emerging Technologies and Legal-Ethical Oversight. The Pacing Problem* (Springer 2011).

101 Marcogliese Pamela L., Lloyd Colin D., Rocks Sandra M., 'Machine Learning and Artificial Intelligence in Financial Services' (2018) Harvard Law School Forum on Corporate Governance, https://corpgov.law.harvard.edu/2018/09/24/machine-learning-and-artificial-intelligence-in-financial-services/ accessed 22 July 2020.

102 Martinez Rex, 'Artificial Intelligence: Distinguishing Between Types & Definitions' (2019) *19 Nevada Law Journal* 1015–1042.

103 McCrudden Christopher, 'Human Dignity and Judicial Interpretation of Human Rights' (2008) *19 European Journal of International Law* 655–724.

104 Mcknight D. Harrison,Chervany Norman L., 'Trust and Distrust Definitions: One Bite at a Time' in Rino Falcone, Munindar Singh, Yao Hua Tan (eds.), *Trust in Cyber-societies: Integrating the Human and Artificial Perspectives* (Springer 2001).

105 Metz Julia, 'Expert Groups in the European Union: A Sui Generis Phenomenon?' (2013) *32 Policy and Society* 267–278.

106 Michie Jonathan, Sheehan Maura, 'Labour Market Deregulation, "Flexibility" and Innovation' (2003) *27 Cambridge Journal of Economics* 123–143.

107 Nemitz Paul, 'Constitutional Democracy and Technology in the Age of Artificial Intelligence' (2018) *376 Philosophical Transactions A, The Royal Society* 3 https://ssrn.com/abstract=3234336 accessed 20 July 2020.

108 Noto La Diega Guido, 'The Artificial Conscience of Lethal Autonomous Weapons: Marketing Ruse or Reality' (2018) *1 Law and the Digital Age* 1–17.

109 Nyholm Sven, Smids Jilles, 'The Ethics of Accident-Algorithms for Self-Driving Cars: an Applied Trolley Problem?' (2016) *19 Ethical Theory and Moral Practice* 1275–1289.

110 O'Sullivan Shane et al., 'Legal, Regulatory, and Ethical Frameworks for Development of Standards in Artificial Intelligence (AI) and Autonomous Robotic Surgery (2018) *15 The International Journal of Medical Robotics and Computer Assisted Surgery* 1968–1970.

111 Pagallo Ugo et al., 'AI4 People. Report on Good AI Governance. 14 Priority Actions, a S.M.A.R.T. Model of Governance, and a Regulatory Toolbox' (2019) 11 https://www.eismd.eu/wp-content/uploads/2019/11/AI4Peoples-Report-on-Good-AI-Governance_compressed.pdf accessed 22 July 2020.

112 Pagallo Ugo, '*Apples, Oranges, Robots: Four Misunderstandings in Today's Debate on the Legal Status of AI Systems*' (2018) *376 Philosophical Transactions Royal Society A* 1–16.

113 Pagallo Ugo, Quattrocolo Serena, 'The Impact of AI on Criminal Law, and Its Twofold Procedures' in Woodrow Barfield, Ugo Pagallo (eds.), *Research Handbook on the Law of Artificial Intelligence* (Edward Elgar 2018).

114 Pasquale Frank, *The Black Box Society. The Secret Algorithms That Control Money and Information* (Harvard University Press 2015).

115 Pesapane Filippo, Volonté Caterina, Codari Marina, Sardanelli Francesco, 'Artificial Intelligence as a Medical Device in Radiology: Ethical and Regulatory Issues in Europe and the United States' (2018) *9 Insights into Imagining* 745–753.

116 Prince Anya E.R., Schwarcz Daniel, 'Proxy Discrimination in the Age of Artificial Intelligence and Big Data' (2020) *105 Iowa Law Review* 1257–1318.

117 Riedl Mark O., 'Human-centered Artificial Intelligence and Machine Learning' (2018) *33 Human Behaviour and Emerging Technologies* 1–8.

118 Roff Heather M., Moyes Richard, 'Meaningful Human Control, Artificial Intelligence and Autonomous Weapons' (2016) Briefing paper prepared for the Informal Meeting of Experts on Lethal Autonomous Weapons Systems, UN Convention on Certain Conventional Weapons, http://www.article36.org/wp-content/uploads/2016/04/MHC-AI-and-AWS-FINAL.pdf accessed 22 July 2020.

119 Russel Stuart, Dewey Daniel, Tegmark Max, 'Research Priorities for Robust and Beneficial Artificial Intelligence' (2015) *36 AI Magazine* 105–114.

120 Russel Stuart, Norvig Peter, *Artificial Intelligence. A Modern Approach* (3rd edition, Prentice Hall 2010).

121 Saeed Al-Mushayt Omar, 'Automating E-Government Services with Artificial Intelligence' (2019) *7 IEEE Access*, 146822.

122 Safjan Marek, 'Prawo do ochrony życia prywatnego' in *Szkoła Praw Człowieka* (Helsińska Fundacja Praw Człowieka Warszawa 2006).

123 Savaget Paulo, Chiarini Tulio, Evans Steve, 'Empowering Political Participation Through Artificial Intelligence' (2018) *46 Science and Public Policy* 369–380.

124 Sax Marijn, Helberger Natali, Bol Nadine, 'Health as Means Towards Profitable Ends: mHealth Apps, User Autonomy, and Unfair Commercial Practices' (2018) *41 Journal of Consumer Policy* 103–134.

125 Schuller Allan, 'At the Crossroads of Control: The Intersection of Artificial Intelligence in Autonomous Weapon Systems with International Humanitarian Law' (2017) *8 Harvard National Security Journal* 379–425.

126 Schwartz Paul M., 'Global Data Privacy: The EU Way' (2019) *94 New York University Law Review* 771–818.

127 Sirks A.J.B., 'Delicts' in David Johnston (ed.), *The Cambridge Companion to Roman Law* (Cambridge University Press 2015).

128 Smith Graham, *Democratic Innovations. Designing Institutions for Citizen Participation* (Cambridge University Press 2009).

129 Solaiman S.M., 'Legal Personality of Robots, Corporations, Idols and Chimpanzees: A Quest for Legitimacy' (2017) *25 Artificial Intelligence Law* 155–179.

130 Spier Jaap (ed.), *Unification of Tort Law: Liability for Damage Caused by Others* (Kluwer Law International 2003).

131 Spindler Gerald, 'User Liability and Strict Liability in the Internet of Things and for Robots' in Sebastian Lohsse, Reiner Schulze, Dirk Staudenmayer (eds.),

Liability for Artificial Intelligence and the Internet of Things. Muenster Colloquia on EU Law and the Digital Economy IV (Hart Publishing, Nomos 2019).

132 Storr Pam, Storr Christine, 'The Rise and Regulation of Drones: Are We Embracing Minority Report or WALL-E?' in Marcelo Corrales, Mark Fenwick, Nikolaus Forgó (eds.), *Robotics AI and the Future of Law* (Springer 2018).

133 Surden Harry, 'Ethics f AI in Law: Basic Questions' in Forthcoming chapter in Oxford Handbook of Ethics of AI (2020) 731 https://ssrn.com/abstract= 3441303 accessed 22 July 2020.

134 Teubner Gunther, 'Digital Personhood? The Status of Autonomous Software Agents in Private Law' (2018) *Ancilla Iuris* https://www.anci.ch/articles/ Ancilla2018_Teubner_35.pdf accessed 25 May 2020.

135 Truby Jon, Brown Rafael, Dahdal Andrew, 'Banking on AI: Mandating A Proactive Approach to AI Regulation in the Financial Sector' (2020) *14 Law and Financial Markets Review* 110–120.

136 Turner Jacob, *Robot Rules. Regulating Artificial Intelligence* (Palgrave Macmillan 2019).

137 Valentini Laura, 'Dignity and Human Rights: A Reconceptualisation' (2017) Oxford *37 Journal of Legal Studies* 862–885.

138 van Boom Willem, Koziol Helmut, Witting Christian (eds.), *Pure Economic Loss* (Springer 2004).

139 van den Hoven van Genderen Robert, 'Do We Need Legal Personhood in the Age of Robots and AI' in Marcelo Corrales, Mark Fenwick, Nikolaus Forgó (eds.), *Robotics AI and the Future of Law* (Springer 2018).

140 van den Hoven van Genderen Robert, 'Legal Personhood in the Age of Artificially Intelligent Robots' in Woodrow Barfield and Ugo Pagallo (eds.), *Research Handbook on the Law of Artificial Intelligence* (Edward Elgar 2018).

141 Velasquez Manuel, Claire Andre, Shnaks Thomas, J. Meyer Michael, 'Justice and Fairness' https://www.scu.edu/ethics/ethics-resources/ethical-decision-making/justice-and-fairness/ accessed 22 July 2020.

142 Voigt Paul, Axel von dem Bussche, *The EU General Data Protection Regulation (GDPR). A Practical Guide* (2017 Springer).

143 von Ungern-Sternberg Antje, 'Autonomous Driving: Regulatory Challenges Raised by Artificial Decision-Making and Tragic Choices' in Woodrow Barfield, Ugo Pagallo (eds.), *Research Handbook on the Law of Artificial Intelligence* (Edward Elgar 2018).

144 Wachter Sandra, Mittelstadt Brent, Floridi Luciano, 'Why a Right to Explanation of Automated Decision-Making Does Not Exist in the General Data Protection Regulation' (2017) *7 International Data Privacy Law* 76–99https://ssrn.com/abstract=2903469 accessed 22 July 2020.

145 Watzenig Daniel, Horn Martin (eds.), *Automated Driving. Safer and More Efficient Future Driving* (Springer 2017).

146 Watzenig Daniel, Horn Martin, 'Introduction to Automated Driving' in Daniel Watzenig, Martin Horn (eds.), *Automated Driving. Safer and More Efficient Future Driving* (Springer 2017).

147 Weller Adrian, 'Transparency: Motivations and Challenges' (2019) arXiv:1708.01870v2 accessed 22 July 2020.

148 Wildhaber Isabelle, 'Artificial Intelligence and Robotics, the Workplace, and Workplace-Related Law' in Woodrow Barfield, Ugo Pagallo (eds.), *Research Handbook on the Law of Artificial Intelligence* (Edward Elgar 2018).
149 Winfield Alan F.T., Jirotka Marina, 'Ethical Governance Is Essential to Build Trust in Robotics and Artificial Intelligence Systems' (2018) *36 Philosophical Transactions Royal Society A* 2.
150 Winiger Benedikt, Karner Ernst, Oliphant Ken (eds.), *Digest of European Tort Law III: Essential Cases on Misconduct* (De Gruyter 2018).
151 Woolley J. Patrick, 'Trust and Justice in Big Data Analytics: Bringing the Philosophical Literature on Trust to Bear on the Ethics of Consent', (2019) *32 Philosophy and Technology* 111–134.
152 Xenidis Rafhaële, Senden Linda, 'EU Non-discrimination law in the Era of the Artificial Intelligence: Mapping the Challenges of Algorithmic Discrimination' in Ulf Bernitz et al. (eds.), *General Principles of EU Law and the EU Digital Order* (Kluwer Law International 2020).
153 Xu Catherina, Doshi Tulsee, 'Fairness Indicators: Scalable Infrastructure for Fair ML Systems' (2019) *Google AI Blog* https://ai.googleblog.com/2019/12/fairness-indicators-scalable.html accessed 22 July 2020
154 Yeung Karen, 'Hypernudge: Big Data as a Mode of Regulation by Design' (2016) *1,19 TLI Think! Paper Information, Communication and Society.*
155 Zarsky Tal Z., 'Governmental Data Mining and its Alternatives' (2011) *116 Penn State Law Review* 285–330.

Legislation

International law

1 European Convention for the Protection of Human Rights and Fundamental Freedoms [1950] https://www.echr.coe.int/Documents/Convention_ENG.pdf accessed 22 July 2020.
2 European Patent Convention [1973] https://www.epo.org/law-practice/legal-texts/html/epc/`2016/e/index.html accessed 10 July 2020.
3 UN Convention on the Rights of persons with disabilities [2006] https://www.un.org/development/desa/disabilities/convention-on-the-rights-of-persons-with-disabilities.html accessed 22 July 2020.

EU law

1 Consolidated versions of the Treaties [2012] OJ C326/13.
2 Charter of Fundamental Rights of the EU [2012] OJ C326/391.
3 Council Directive 85/374/EEC of 25 July 1985 on the approximation of the laws, regulations and administrative provisions of the Member States concerning liability for defective products [1985] OJ L210/29.
4 Council Directive 89/391/EEC of 12 June 1989 on the introduction of measures to encourage improvements in the safety and health of workers at work [1989] OJ L183/1.
5 Directive 96/9/EC of the European Parliament and of the Council of 11 March 1996 on the legal protection of databases [1996] OJ L77/20.

6 Directive 98/6/EC of the European Parliament and of the Council of 16 February 1998 on consumer protection in the indication of the prices of products offered to consumers [1998] OJ L 80/27.

7 Directive 2000/31/EC of the European Parliament and of the Council of 8 June 2000 on certain legal aspects of information society services, in particular electronic commerce in the Internal Market [2000] OJ L 178/1.

8 Council Directive 2000/43/EC of 29 June 2000 implementing the principle of equal treatment between persons irrespective of racial or ethnic origin, [2000] OJ L 180/22.

9 Council Directive 2000/78/EC of 27 November 2000 establishing a general framework for equal treatment in employment and occupation [2000] OJ L 303/16.

10 Directive 2001/29/EC of the European Parliament and of the Council of 22 May 2001 on the harmonisation of certain aspects of copyright and related rights in the information society [2001] OJ L 167/10.

11 Directive 2001/95/EC of the European Parliament and of the Council of 3 December 2001 on general product safety [2001] OJ L 11/4.

12 Council Regulation (EC) 6/2002 of 12 December 2001 on Community designs [2001] OJ L 3/1.

13 Council Directive 2004/113/EC of 13 December 2004 implementing the principle of equal treatment between men and women in the access to and supply of goods and services [2004] OJ L 373/37.

14 Directive 2005/29/EC of the European Parliament and of the Council of 11 May 2005 concerning unfair business-to-consumer commercial practices in the internal market [2005] OJ L 149/22.

15 Directive 2006/42/EC of the European Parliament and of the Council of 17 May 2006 on machinery, and amending Directive 95/16/EC (recast) [2006] OJ L157/24.

16 Directive 2006/54/EC of the European Parliament and of the Council of 5 July 2006 on the implementation of the principle of equal opportunities and equal treatment of men and women in matters of employment and occupation (recast) [2006] OJ L 294/23.

17 Directive 2009/24/EC of the European Parliament and of the Council of 23 April 2009 on the legal protection of computer programs [2009], OJ L 111/16.

18 Directive 2011/83/EU of the European Parliament and of the Council of 25 October 2011 on consumer rights [2011] OJ L 304/64.

19 Regulation (EU) 234/2014 of the European Parliament and of the Council of 11 March 2014 establishing a Partnership Instrument for cooperation with third countries [2014] OJ L 77/77.

20 Directive 2014/53/EU of the European Parliament and of the Council of 16 April 2014 on the harmonisation of the laws of the Member States relating to the making available on the market of radio equipment and repealing Directive 1999/5/EC [2014] OJ L 153/62.

21 Directive (EU) 2015/2436 of the European Parliament and of the Council of 16 December 2015 to approximate the laws of the Member States relating to trade marks [2015] OJ L336/1.

22 Regulation (EU) 2016/679 of the European Parliament and of the Council of 27 April 2016 on the protection of natural persons with regard to the processing of personal data and the free movement of such data (GDPR) [2016] OJ L 119/1.

23 Directive (EU) 2016/680 of the European Parliament and of the Council of 27 April 2016 on the protection of natural persons with regard to the processing of personal data by competent authorities for the purposes of the prevention, investigation, detection or prosecution of criminal offences or the execution of criminal penalties, and on the free movement of such data [2016] OJ L 119/89.

24 Commission Decision (EU) 2016/835 of 25 May 2016 on the renewal of the mandate of the European Group on Ethics in Science and New Technologies, OJ L 140/21.

25 Commission Decision of 30 May 2016 establishing horizontal rules on the creation of Commission expert groups [2016] C(2016) 3301 final.

26 Directive (EU) 2016/943 of the European Parliament and of the Council of 8 June 2016 on the protection of undisclosed know-how and business information (trade secrets) against their unlawful acquisition, use and disclosure [2016] OJ L 157/1.

27 Council Recommendation of 19 December 2016 on Upskilling Pathways: New Opportunities for Adults [2016] OJ C 484/1.

28 Regulation (EU) 2017/745 of the European Parliament and of the Council of 5 April 2017 on medical devices, amending Directive 2001/83/EC, Regulation (EC) No 178/2002 and Regulation (EC) No 1223/2009 and repealing Council Directives 90/385/EEC and 93/42/EEC [2017] OJ L 117/1.

29 Regulation (EU) 2017/1001 of the European Parliament and of the Council of 14 June 2017 on the European Union trade mark [2017] OJ L 154/1.

30 Regulation (EU) 2018/302 on geo-blocking of the European Parliament and of the Council of 28 February 2018 on addressing unjustified geo-blocking and other forms of discrimination based on customers' nationality, place of residence or place of establishment within the internal market [2018] OJ L60/1.

31 Commission Recommendation (EU) 2018/790 of 25 April 2018 on access to and preservation of scientific information [2018] OJ L 134/12.

32 Regulation (EU) 2018/1139 of the European Parliament and of the Council of 4 July 2018 on common rules in the field of civil aviation and establishing a European Union Aviation Safety Agency [2018] OJ L 212/1.

33 Regulation (EU) 2018/1807 of the European Parliament and of the Council of 14 November 2018 on a framework for the free flow of non-personal data in the European Union [2018] OJ L 303/59.

34 Commission Delegated Regulation (EU) 2019/945 of 12 March 2019 on unmanned aircraft systems and on third-country operators of unmanned aircraft systems [2019] OJ L 152/1.

35 Regulation (EU) 2019/881 of the European Parliament and of the Council of 17 April 2019 on ENISA (the European Union Agency for Cybersecurity) and on information and communications technology cybersecurity certification and repealing Regulation (EU) No 526/2013 (Cybersecurity Act) [2019] OJ L 151/15.

36 Directive (EU) 2019/790 of the European Parliament and of the Council of 17 April 2019 on copyright and related rights in the Digital Single Market and amending Directives 96/9/EC and 2001/29/EC [2019] OJ L130/92.

37 Directive (EU) 2019/770 of the European Parliament and of the Council of 20 May 2019 on certain aspects concerning contracts for the supply of digital content and digital services [2-19] OJ L 136/1.

38 Directive (EU) 2019/771 of the European Parliament and of the Council of 20 May 2019 on certain aspects concerning contracts for the sale of goods, amending Regulation (EU) 2017/2394 and Directive 2009/22/EC, and repealing Directive 1999/44/EC [[2019] OJ L 136/28.

39 Commission Implementing Regulation (EU) 2019/947 of 24 May 2019 on the rules and procedures for the operation of unmanned aircraft [2019] OJ L 152/45.

40 Directive (EU) 2019/1024 of the European Parliament and of the Council of 20 June 2019 on open data and the re-use of public sector information [2019] OJ L172/56.

41 Regulation (EU) 2019/1150 of the European Parliament and of the Council of 20 June 2019 on promoting fairness and transparency for business users of online intermediation services [2019] OJ L 186/ 57.

42 Directive (EU) 2019/2161 of the European Parliament and of the Council of 27 November 2019 amending Council Directive 93/13/EEC and Directives 98/6/EC, 2005/29/EC and 2011/83/EU of the European Parliament and of the Council as regards the better enforcement and modernisation of Union consumer protection rules [2019] OJ L328/7.

43 Regulation (EU) 2020/561 of the European Parliament and of the Council of 23 April 2020 as regards the dates of application of certain its provision [2020] OJ L 130/18.

Policy documents

European Commission communications, recommendations and working documents

1 Commission, '*Communication on the Precautionary Principle*', COM(2000) 0001 final.

2 Commission, '*European Strategy for a Better Internet for Children*' (Communication) COM(2012)196 final.

3 Commission, '*A Digital Single Market Strategy for Europe*' (Communication) COM(2015)192 final.

4 Commission, '*EU e-Government Action Plan 2016-2020. Accelerating the digital transformation of government*' (Communication) COM(2016) 179 final.

5 Commission, '*A New Skills Agenda for Europe. Working together to strengthen human capital, employability and competitiveness*' COM(2016)381 final.

6 Commission, '*Report on Saving Lives: Boosting Car Safety in the EU*', (Communication) COM(2016) 787.

7 Communication, '*The Mid-Term Review on the implementation of the Digital Single Market Strategy. A Connected Digital Single Market for All*' (Communication) COM(2017) 228 final.

8 Commission, '*Communication on the Digital Education Action Plan*' (Communication) COM(2018) 22 final.

9 Commission, '*Guidance on sharing private sector data in the European data economy*' (Staff Working Document), SWD (2018) 125 final.

10 Commission, '*Towards a common European data space*' (Communication) COM (2018) 232 final.

11 Commission, '*Artificial Intelligence for Europe*' (Communication) COM(2018) 237 final.

12 Commission Staff Working Document on Liability (SWD (2018)137)7, accompanying Commission Communication, COM(2018) 237 final.

13 Commission, 'On the Road to Automated Mobility: An EU Strategy for Mobility of the Future' (Communication) COM(2018) 283 final.

14 Commission, '*Proposal for a regulation of the European Parliament and of the Council establishing the European Cybersecurity Industrial, Technology and Research Competence Centre and the Network of National Coordination Centres*' COM(2018) 630.

15 Commission, '*Coordinated Plan on AI*' (Communication) COM(2018) 795 final.

16 Commission, '*Annex to Coordinated Plan on AI*' COM(2018) 795 final.

17 Commission, '*Reflection Paper. Towards a Sustainable Europe by 2030*' COM (2019) 22.

18 Commission, '*Building Trust in Human-Centric Artificial Intelligence*' (Communication) COM(2019)168 final.

19 Commission, '*Commission Work Programme 2020*' (Communication) COM (2020) 37 final.

20 Commission, '*Report on the safety and liability implications of Artificial Intelligence, the Internet of Things and robotics*' COM(2020) 64 final.

21 Commission, '*White Paper On Artificial Intelligence – A European approach to excellence and trust*' COM(2020) 65 final.

22 Commission, '*A European strategy for data*' (Communication) COM(2020) 66 final.

Expert Groups deliverables

1 European Group on Ethics in Science and New Technologies, '*Future of Work, Future of Society*' (Publications Office of the EU Luxembourg 2018).

2 European Group on Ethics in Science and New Technologies '*Statement on AI, Robotics and 'Autonomous' Systems*' (Brussels 2018).

3 High Level Group on Industrial Technologies, Report on '*Re-Defining Industry. Defining Innovation*' (Publication Office of the EU Luxembourg 2018).

4 Expert Group on Liability and New Technologies, '*Liability for Artificial Intelligence and other emerging digital technologies*' (Report from New Technologies Formation) (Publication Office of the EU Luxembourg 2019).

5 High-Level Expert Group on the Impact of the Digital Transformation on EU Labour Markets, '*Report on The Impact of the Digital Transformation on EU Labour Markets*', (Publications Office of the EU Luxembourg 2019).

6 High Level Expert Group on AI, '*Policy and Investment Recommendations for Trustworthy AI*' (Brussels 2019).

7 High Level Expert Group on AI, '*A Definition of AI: Main Capabilities and Disciplines*' (Brussels 2019).
8 High Level Expert Group on AI, '*The Ethics Guidelines for Trustworthy Artificial Intelligence*' (Brussels 2019).

Other EU institutions' documents

1 European Economic and Social Committee, '*Opinion on AI*' INT/806-EESC-2016-05369-00-00-AC-TRA.
2 European Parliament, '*Resolution of 16.02.2017 with recommendations to the Commission on Civil Law Rules on Robotics*' 2015/2103(INL).
3 European Council meeting (19 October 2017) – Conclusions, EUCO 14/17 http://data.consilium.europa.eu/doc/document/ST-14-2017-INIT/en/pdf accessed 20 July 2020.
4 European Union Agency for Fundamental Rights (FRA),'AI, Big Data and fundamental rights' (2018) https://fra.europa.eu/en/project/2018/artificial-intelligence-big-data-and-fundamental-rights accessed 22 July 2020.
5 European Parliament, '*Resolution of 12 September 2018 on autonomous weapon systems*' (2018/2752(RSP), OJ C433/86.
6 European Parliament, '*Draft report with recommendations to the Commission on a framework of ethical aspects of AI, robotics and related technologies*', 2020/2012(INL).
7 European Parliament, 'Intellectual property rights for the development of artificial intelligence technologies' 2020/2015(INI).
8 European Parliament, '*Draft Report with recommendations to the Commission on a Civil liability regime for artificial intelligence*' 2020/2014(INL).
9 European Union Aviation Safety Agency (EASA), '*Artificial Intelligence Roadmap. A Human-centric approach to AI in Aviation*' (2020 easa.europa.eu/ai).

Other secondary sources

1 Basel Committee on Banking Supervision, 'Sound Practices: Implications of fintech developments for banks and bank supervisors' (Consultative Document) (2017) https://www.bis.org/bcbs/publ/d415.pdf (accessed 16.07.2020).
2 Borgesius Frederik Zuiderveen, '*Discrimination, artificial intelligence, and algorithmic decision-making*' (*Council of Europe* 2018) 1–51.
3 Bourguignon Didier, '*The precautionary principle. Definitions, applications and governance*' (European Parliament 2016).
4 Broekaert Kris, Espinel Victoria A., *How can policy keep pace with the Fourth Industrial Revolution*, https://www.weforum.org/agenda/2018/02/can-policy-keep-pace-with-fourth-industrial-revolution/ accessed 22 July 2020.
5 Bughin Jacques, et al., '*Notes from the AI Frontier: Modelling the Impact of AI on the World Economy*' (McKinsey Global Institute 2018).
6 Carretero Stephanie, Vuorikari Riina, Punie Yves, '*The Digital Competence Framework for Citizens. With eight proficiency levels and examples of use*' (Publications Office of the EU Luxembourg 2017).
7 Code of Practice on Disinformation https://ec.europa.eu/digital-single-market/en/news/code-practice-disinformation accessed 22 July 2020.

8 Consultative Committee of the Convention for the Protection of Individuals with Regard to Automatic Processing of Personal Data [Convention 108]. Guidelines on Artificial Intelligence and Data Protection, T-PD(2019)01 (Council of Europe 2019).

9 Consumer vulnerability across key markets in the EU. Final report (2016) https://ec.europa.eu/info/sites/info/files/consumers-approved-report_en.pdf. accessed 22 July 2020.

10 Council of Europe Study '*Algorithms and Human Rights. Study on the human rights dimensions of automated data processing techniques and possible regulatory implications*' DGI[2017]12 (Council of Europe 2017).

11 Craglia Max (ed) et al., '*Artificial Intelligence: a European Perspective*' (Publications Office of the EU Luxembourg 2018).

12 Deloitte Insights, 'How artificial intelligence could transform government' (2017) https://www2.deloitte.com/insights/us/en/focus/artificial-intelligence-in-government.html accessed 20 July 2020.

13 Duch-Brown Nestor, Martens Bertin, Mueller-Langer Frank, 'The economics of ownership, access and trade in digital data. Joint Research Centre Digital Economy Working Paper 2017-01' (European Union 2017) https://ec.europa.eu/jrc/en/publication/eur-scientific-and-technical-research-reports/economics-ownership-access-and-trade-digital-data accessed 22 July 2020.

14 Eggers William D., Turley Mike, Kishnani Pankaj, 'The future of regulation', https://www2.deloitte.com/us/en/insights/industry/public-sector/future-of-regulation/regulating-emerging-technology.html#endnote-sup-49 accessed 22 July 2020.

15 E-relevance of Culture in the Age of AI, Expert Seminar on Culture, Creativity and Artificial Intelligence, 12-13 October 2018, Rijeka, Croatia https://www.coe.int/en/web/culture-and-heritage/-/e-relevance-of-culture-in-the-age-of-ai accessed 22 July 2020.

16 European Commission for the Efficiency of Justice (CEPEJ), '*European ethical Charter on the use of AI in judicial systems and their environment* '(Council of Europe 2019).

17 European Parliamentary Research Service, Scientific Foresight Unit (STOA), '*The ethics of artificial intelligence: Issues and initiatives*', PE 634.452 March 2020.

18 European Political Strategy Center, 'EU Industrial Policy After Siemens-Alstom, Finding a New Balance Between Openness and Protection' (Brussels 2019) https://ec.europa.eu/epsc/sites/epsc/files/epsc_industrial-policy.pdf accessed 22 July 2020.

19 EY, 'Artificial Intelligence in Europe, Outlook for 2019 and Beyond' (EY 2018) https://info.microsoft.com/WE-DIGTRNS-CNTNT-FY19-09Sep-27-DENMARKArtificialIntelligence-MGC0003160_02ThankYou-StandardHero.html accessed 24 July 2020.

20 Guidelines to respect, protect and fulfil the rights of the child in the digital environment, Recommendation CM/Rec(2018)7 of the Committee of Ministers (Council of Europe 2018).

21 Holder Chris, Iglesias Maria (eds.), Jean-Marc Van Gyseghem, Jean-Paul Triaille, '*Legal and regulatory implications of Artificial Intelligence. The case of autonomous vehicles, m-health and data mining*' (Publication Office of the EU Luxembourg 2019) *19*.

22 Human rights and business, Recommendation CM/Rec(2016)3 of the Committee of Ministers to member states (Council of Europe 2016).

23 Iglesias Maria, Shamuilia Sharon, Anderberg Amanda, '*Intellectual Property and Artificial Intelligence. A literature review*', EUR 30017 EN (Publications Office of the EU Luxembourg 2019).

24 Lorenzo Rocío et al., 'The Mix That Matters. Innovation Through Diversity' (BCG 2017) https://www.bcg.com/publications/2017/people-organization-leadership-talent-innovation-through-diversity-mix-that-matters.aspx accessed 22 July 2020.

25 Losing Humanity. 'The Case against Killer Robots' (Report 2012), https://www.hrw.org/sites/default/files/reports/arms1112_ForUpload.pdf accessed 22 July 2020.

26 Mantelero Alessandro, 'Consultative Committee of the Convention for the Protection of Individuals with Regard to Automatic Processing of Personal Data [Convention 108]. Report on AI. AI and Data Protection: Challenges and Possible Remedies (Council of Europe 2019).

27 McKinsey, 'Digital Europe: Realizing the continent's potential' (2016) https://www.mckinsey.com/business-functions/mckinsey-digital/our-insights/digital-europe-realizing-the-continents-potential# accessed 20 July 2020.

28 McKinsey, Business functions and operations. Secrets of successful change implementation https://www.mckinsey.com/business-functions/operations/our-insights/secrets-of-successful-change-implementation accessed 22 July 2020.

29 Nedelkoska L., Quintini G., 'Automation, Skills Use and Training' (2018) 22 OECD Social, Employment and Migration Working Papers (OECD Publishing) https://doi.org/10.1787/2e2f4eea-en accessed 24 July 2020.

30 PwC's Global Artificial Intelligence Study: Exploiting the AI Revolution. (2017). https://www.pwc.com/gx/en/issues/data-and-analytics/publications/artificial-intelligence-study.html accessed 22 July 2020.

31 Rapporteur Report, '20th Anniversary of the Oviedo Convention', Strasbourg 2017 https://rm.coe.int/oviedo-conference-rapporteur-report-e/168078295c accessed 22 July 2020.

32 Recommendation by the Council of Europe Commissioner for Human Rights '*Unboxing Artificial Intelligence: 10 steps to protect Human Rights*' (Council of Europe 2019).

33 Recommendation CM/Rec(2017)5 of the Committee of Ministers to member States on standards for e-voting, (Council of Europe 2017).

34 Recommendation CM/Rec(2020)1 of the Committee of Ministers to member states on the human rights impacts of algorithmic society (Council of Europe 2020).

35 Report of the Special Rapporteur, 'Promotion and protection of the right to freedom of opinion and expression', A/73/348, see https://freedex.org/wp-content/blogs.dir/2015/files/2018/10/AI-and-FOE-GA.pdf accessed 22 July 2020.

36 Special Eurobarometer 382, '*Public Attitudes Towards Robots*' (2012).

37 Tarín Quirós Carlota et al., 'Women in the digital age' A study report prepared for the European Commission (2018) https://ec.europa.eu/digital-single-market/en/news/increase-gender-gap-digital-sector-study-women-digital-age accessed 22 July 2020.

38 UN Guiding Principles on Business and Human Rights. Implementing the UN 'Protect, Respect and Remedy' Framework (2011) https://www.ohchr.org/documents/publications/guidingprinciplesbusinesshr_en.pdf accessed 22 July 2020.

39 UNESCO Report, 'I'd blush if I could – Closing Gender Divides in Digital Skills through Education' (2019) https://2b37021f-0f4a-464083520a3c1b7c2aab.filesusr.com/ugd/04bfff_06ba0716e0604f51a40b4474d4829ba8.pdf accessed 22 July 2020.

40 World Economic Forum, 'The future of Jobs' (2018) http://reports.weforum.org/future-of-jobs-2018/preface/ accessed 22 July 2020.

41 World Economic Forum, 'White Paper: Agile Governance. Reimagining Policy Making in the Fourth Industrial Revolution' http://www3.weforum.org/docs/WEF_Agile_Governance_Reimagining_Policy-making_4IR_report.pdf accessed 22 July 2020.

42 Yeung Karen (rapporteur),' *A Study of the implications of advanced digital technologies (including AI systems) for the concept of responsibility within a human rights framework*', DGI(2019) 5, (Council of Europe 2019).

Internet sources

1 AI and gender equality https://www.coe.int/en/web/artificial-intelligence/-/artificial-intelligence-and-gender-equality accessed 22 July 2020.

2 AI4EU https://www.ai4eu.eu/ai4eu-platform accessed 22 July 2020

3 Algorithmic awareness building https://ec.europa.eu/digital-single-market/en/algorithmic-awareness-building accessed 22 July 2020.

4 Angwin Julia, Parris Jr Terry, 'Facebook Lets Advertisers Exclude Users by Race'(2016) ProPublica, https://www.propublica.org/article/facebook-lets-advertisers-exclude-users-by-race accessed 22 July 2020.

5 Asilomar AI principles https://futureoflife.org/ai-principles/ accessed 22 July 2020.

6 Brzozowski Alexandra, 'No progress in UN talks on regulating lethal autonomous weapons' (22.11.2019) https://www.euractiv.com/section/global-europe/news/no-progress-in-un-talks-on-regulating-lethal-autonomous-weapons/ accessed 22 July 2020.

7 BWVI Ethics Code https://www.bmvi.de/SharedDocs/EN/publications/report-ethics-commission.pdf?__blob=publicationFile accessed 22 July 2020.

8 Chinese State Council Notice concerning Issuance of the Planning Outline for the Construction of a Social Credit System (2014–2020), https://chinacopyrightandmedia.wordpress.com/2014/06/14/planning-outline-for-the-construction-of-a-social-credit-system-2014-2020/ accessed 22 July 2020.

9 Commission's 'Responsible Research and Innovation' workstream: https://ec.europa.eu/programmes/horizon2020/en/h2020-section/responsible-research-innovation accessed 22 July 2020.

10 Covd-19 tracing apps (press release European Parliament) https://www.europarl.europa.eu/news/en/headlines/society/20200429STO78174/covid-19-tracing-apps-ensuring-privacy-and-data-protection accessed 22 July 2020.

11 Cybercrime, Octopus 2018 https://www.coe.int/en/web/cybercrime/resources-octopus-2018 accessed 22 July 2020.

12 Daley Sam, 'Fighting fires and saving elephants: how 12 companies are using the AI drone to solve big problems', (10 March 2019) https://builtin.com/artificial-intelligence/drones-ai-companies accessed 22 July 2020.

13 Digital market, digital scoreboard https://ec.europa.eu/digital-single-market/digital-scoreboard accessed 22 July 2020.

14 Digital Opportunity Traineeships https://ec.europa.eu/digital-single-market/en/digital-opportunity-traineeships-boosting-digital-skills-job accessed 22 July 2020.

15 Digital Skills Jobs Coalition https://ec.europa.eu/digital-single-market/en/digital-skills-jobs-coalition accessed 22 July 2020.

16 ECDL http://www.ecdl.org accessed 22 July 2020.

17 Entering the new paradigm of AI and Series Executive Summary, (2019) December, https://rm.coe.int/eurimages-executive-summary-051219/1680995332 accessed 22 July 2020.

18 E-privacy regulation proposal https://ec.europa.eu/digital-single-market/en/proposal-eprivacy-regulation accessed 22 July 2020.

19 EU agencies, ECSEL https://europa.eu/european-union/about-eu/agencies/ecsel_en accessed 22 July 2020.

20 EU observatory on online platform economy https://ec.europa.eu/digital-single-market/en/eu-observatory-online-platform-economy accessed 20 July 2020.

21 EU social Policy http://ec.europa.eu/social/main.jsp?catId=1415&langId=en accessed 22 July 2020.

22 EU Strategy priorities 2019-2024 https://ec.europa.eu/info/strategy/priorities-2019-2024/europe-fit-digital-age/shaping-europe-digital-future_en accessed 22 July 2020.

23 Euractive on Code of practice on disinformation https://www.euractiv.com/section/digital/news/eu-code-of-practice-on-disinformation-insufficient-and-unsuitable-member-states-say/ accessed 22 July 2020.

24 Euractive on Commission's White Paper on AI https://www.euractiv.com/section/digital/news/leak-commission-considers-facial-recognition-ban-in-ai-white-paper accessed 22 July 2020.

25 Euro HPC Joint undertaking https://ec.europa.eu/digital-single-market/en/blogposts/eurohpc-joint-undertaking-looking-ahead-2019-2020-and-beyond accessed 22 July 2020.

26 European Institute of Innovation Technology https://eit.europa.eu/our-activities/education/doctoral-programmes/eit-and-digital-education-action-plan accessed 22 July 2020.

27 European Investment Bank https://www.eib.org/en/efsi/what-is-efsi/index.htm accessed 22 July 2020.

28 Eurostat statistics on small and medium-sized enterprises' total turnover in the EU https://ec.europa.eu/eurostat/web/structural-business-statistics/structural-business-statistics/sme accessed 22 July 2020.

29 EU's Space Programme Copernicus, Data and Information Access Services: http://copernicus.eu/news/upcoming-copernicus-data-and-information-access-services-dias accessed 22 July 2020.

30 Financial Times https://www.ft.com/content/ff798944-4cc6-11ea-95a0-43d18ec715f5 accessed 22 July 2020.

31 Global Framework reference, Digital Literacy Skills http://uis.unesco.org/sites/default/files/documents/ip51-global-framework-reference-digital-literacy-skills-2018-en.pdf accessed 22 July 2020.

32 'How to Train an AI with GDPR Limitations', September 13, 2019 https://www.intellias.com/how-to-train-an-ai-with-gdpr-limitations/ accessed 22 July 2020.

33 ICT online vacancies http://www.pocbigdata.eu/monitorICTonlinevacancies/general_info/ accessed 22 July 2020.

34 IEEE, 'Ethically Aligned Design: A Vision for Prioritizing Human Well-being with Autonomous and Intelligent Systems' (2017) https://ethicsinaction.ieee.org/ accessed 22 July 2020.

35 International Corporate Governance Network, 'Artificial Intelligence and Board Effectiveness' (February 2020) https://www.icgn.org/artificial-intelligence-and-board-effectiveness accessed 22 July 2020.

36 Knowledge 4 Policy https://ec.europa.eu/knowledge4policy/ai-watch_en accessed 20 July 2020.

37 Montréal Declaration for Responsible AI draft principles https://www.montrealdeclaration-responsibleai.com/ accessed 22 July 2020.

38 New Digital Education Action Plan https://ec.europa.eu/education/news/public-consultation-new-digital-education-action-plan_en accessed 22 July 2020.

39 News on Declaration on AI https://ec.europa.eu/digital-single-market/en/news/eu-member-states-sign-cooperate-artificial-intelligence accessed 20 July 2020.

40 Oxford Learner's Dictionary, 'Explanation definition' https://www.oxfordlearnersdictionaries.com/definition/english/explanation accessed 22 July 202.

41 Partnership on AI https://www.partnershiponai.org/partners/ accessed 22 July 2020.

42 Research EIC https://ec.europa.eu/research/eic/index.cfm?pg=funding accessed 22 July 2020.

43 Robotics Open Letter http://www.robotics-openletter.eu/ accessed 22 July 2020.

44 Berger Roland, 'Artificial Intelligence – A strategy for European start-ups' (2018) https://www.rolandberger.com/fr/Publications/AI-startups-as-innovation-drivers.html accessed 22 July 2020.

45 SAE https://www.sae.org/news/press-room/2018/12/sae-international-releases-updated-visual-chart-for-its-%E2%80%9Clevels-of-driving-automation%E2%80%9D-standard-for-self-driving-vehicles accessed 22 July 2020.

46 Sustainable development (EU) https://ec.europa.eu/environment/sustainable-development/SDGs/index_en.htm accessed 22 July 2020.

47 Sustainable Development Goals https://www.un.org/sustainable development/sustainable-development-goals/ accessed 22 July 2020.

48 The Economist, 'The world's most valuable resource is no longer oil, but data' (2017), https://www.economist.com/leaders/2017/05/06/the-worlds-most-valuable-resource-is-no-longer-oil-but-data accessed 22 July 2020.

49 The Joint Research Centre HUMAINT project aims to understand the impact of AI on human behaviour, with a focus on cognitive and socio-emotional capabilities and decision making https://ec.europa.eu/jrc/communities/community/humain accessed 22 July 2020.

50 Tractica, Artificial Intelligence Market Forecasts https://www.tractica.com/research/artificial-intelligence-market-forecasts accessed 22 July 2020.

51 UNI Global Union Top 10 Principles for Ethical AI http://www. thefutureworldofwork.org/opinions/10-principles-for-ethical-ai/ accessed 22 July 2020.
52 Wareham Mary, 'Banning Killer Robots in 2017' https://www.hrw.org/news/ 2017/01/15/banning-killer-robots-2017 accessed 22 July 2020.
53 White paper '21 jobs of the future. A Guide to getting and staying employed' https:// www.cognizant.com/whitepapers/21-jobs-of-the-future-a-guide-to-getting-and-staying-employed-over-the-next-10-years-codex3049 accessed 22 July 2020.
54 WHO on e-health https://www.who.int/ehealth/en/ accessed 22 July 2020.
55 WIPO, 'Index of AI initiatives in IP offices' https://www.wipo.int/about-ip/ en/artificial_intelligence/search.jsp. accessed 22 July 2020.

IEEE and ISO standards on AI

1 ISO Standards https://www.iso.org/isoiec-jtc-1.html accessed 22 July 2020.
2 IEEE Standards https://standards.ieee.org/content/ieee-standards/en/about/ index.html accessed 22 July 2020.
3 AI - Concepts and terminology (SC42 CD 22989) ISO 'Deliverables' (2019) www.iso.org/deliverables-all.html accessed 22 July 2020.
4 Framework for AI Systems Using Machine Learning (SC42 WD 23053) https:// www.iso.org/standard/74296.html accessed 22 July 2020.
5 Draft Model Process for Addressing Ethical Concerns During System Design (IEEE P7000) https://standards.ieee.org/project/7000.html accessed 22 July 2020.
6 Transparency of Autonomous Systems (defining levels of transparency for measurement) (IEEE P7001) https://standards.ieee.org/project/7001.html accessed 22 July 2020.
7 Data Privacy Process (IEEE P7002) https://standards.ieee.org/project/7002. html accessed 22 July 2020.
8 Algorithmic Bias Considerations (IEEE P7003) https://standards.ieee.org/ project/7003.html accessed 22 July 2020.
9 Standard for child and student data governance (IEEEP7004) https://standards. ieee.org/project/7004.html accessed 22 July 2020.
10 Standard for Transparent employer data governance (IEEE P7005) https:// standards.ieee.org/project/7005.html accessed 22 July 2020.
11 Personal Data AI agent (IEEE P7006) https://standards.eee.org/project/7006. html accessed 22 July 2020.
12 Ontologies standard for Ethically Driven Robotics and Automation Systems (IEEE P7007) https://site.ieee.org/sagroups-7007/ accessed 22 July 2020.
13 Standard for Ethically Driven AI Nudging for Robotic, Intelligent and Autonomous Systems (IEEE P7008) https://standards.ieee.org/project/7008. html accessed 22 July 2020.
14 Standard for Fail-safe design of Autonomous and Semi-Autonomous Sstems (IEEE P7009) https://standards.ieee.org/project/7009.html accessed 22 July 2020.
15 Wellbeing metrics for Autonomous and Intelligent Systems AI (IEEE P7010) https://sagroups.ieee.org/7010/ accessed 22 July 2020.

16 Standard for the Process of Identifying and Rating the Trustworthiness of News Sources (IEEE P7011) https://sagroups.ieee.org/7011/ accessed 22 July 2020.
17 Standard for Machine Readable Personal Privacy Terms (IEEE P7012) https://standards.ieee.org/project/7012.html accessed 22 July 2020.
18 Benchmarking Accuracy of Facial Recognition systems (IEEE P7013) https://spectrum.ieee.org/the-institute/ieee-products-services/standards-working-group-takes-on-facial-recognition accessed 22 July 2020.
19 Standard for Ethical considerations in Emulated Empathy in Autonomous and Intelligent Systems (IEEE P7014) https://standards.ieee.org/project/7014.html accessed 22 July 2020.

Index

Printed in Great Britain
by Amazon